THE

J. I. PACKER

CLASSIC COLLECTION

THE
J. I. PACKER

CLASSIC COLLECTION

Daily Readings for Your Spiritual Journey

J. I. Packer

Compiled by Thomas Womack

NAVPRESS

Discipleship Inside Out™

NAVPRESS

Discipleship Inside Out™

NavPress is the publishing ministry of The Navigators, an international Christian organization and leader in personal spiritual development. NavPress is committed to helping people grow spiritually and enjoy lives of meaning and hope through personal and group resources that are biblically rooted, culturally relevant, and highly practical.

For a free catalog go to www.NavPress.com or call 1.800.366.7788 in the United States or 1.800.839.4769 in Canada.

We can begin each day with the deeply encouraging realization, I'm accepted by God, not on the basis of my personal performance, but on the basis of the infinitely perfect righteousness of Jesus Christ.

—JOHN OWEN

FOREWORD
by Mark Dever

Just when you think a book's life is over, God calls it forward to perform yet another service.

In the 1940s, a retired minister's library is disposed of in Oxford, England. Among the volumes is a nineteenth-century reprint of a seventeenth-century work on sin, written by the great Puritan John Owen. It finds its way into the hands of a young undergraduate student named Jim Packer. Among Jim's friends is his fellow undergraduate Elizabeth Lloyd-Jones. Elizabeth introduces Jim to her father, D. Martyn Lloyd-Jones, minister at Westminster Chapel, London. God used this series of providential coincidences to bring Bible truth to Christians today, many years later, through the pen of J. I. Packer.

By God's grace, some of the main influences shaping Christians today have been the books of J. I. Packer. Though Professor Packer and I are from different denominations, I appreciate how, again and again in his writings, one finds what the Puritans would call "plain" or "mere" Christianity, the kind of Christian life and doctrine that John Bunyan wrote about in *Pilgrim's Progress*. Again and again in Packer's writings, the sharp brain of a theologian and the warm heart of a Puritan preacher produce writings that inform and edify Christians.

Back in 1973, there appeared a book that had an unusually large immediate effect, and an even larger long-term effect. Some older readers may remember how the 1970s and 1980s saw a number of books titled [gerund] God—like Chuck Colson's *Loving God*, John Piper's *Desiring God*, Jerry Bridges' *Trusting God*. Where did that trend come from?

It came from J. I. Packer's book Knowing God. Published in 1973, it has continued to sell, year after year, to seminarians, small-group leaders, Christian study groups. It has been read by hundreds of thousands of Christians. Packer has written many other things that have made him the current grandfather of evangelical Christianity. There is no denying that from his introduction to Owen's *The* Death of Death in the Death of Christ to Packer's own book Evangelism and the Sovereignty of God to his many published articles on theology and history, Packer has been one of the best and clearest and most popular theological tutors of those Christians who've grown up in the evangelicalism of the 1980s and 1990s.

In this volume, many of Packer's classic writings are called to new service. Here selected passages are laid out in an easy-to-use daily arrangement. These readings are meant to help us in our study of God's Word, and in our devotion to God himself.

"Packer's my name and Packer's my game." I've heard Packer say something like that a number of times. He means that he tries to pack sentences and paragraphs full of meaning. And he does! And yet those packed paragraphs are like Jim is himself in person—precise, clear, and kind. In these pages you'll find that same kind of precision, clarity, and kindness. Here you'll find truth for your mind, warmth for your heart, light for your eyes, wisdom for your life, and meat for your soul.

As you read this book, pray that God would use it to guide you to his Word and, through his Word, to himself.

Mark Dever
Capitol Hill Baptist Church
Washington, D.C.

THE WITNESS WITHIN

You have been anointed by the Holy One,
and you all have knowledge.

1 JOHN 2:20

Why do Christians believe the Bible is the Word of God, in which God reveals to us the reality of redemption through Jesus Christ the Savior? The answer is that God himself has confirmed this through what is called the inward witness of the Holy Spirit.

The Spirit's witness to Scripture is like his witness to Jesus, which we find spoken of in John 15:26 and 1 John 5:7-8. It is a matter not of imparting new information but of enlightening previously darkened minds to discern divinity through sensing its unique impact — the impact in the one case of the Jesus of the gospel, and in the other case of the words of Holy Scripture. The Spirit shines in our hearts to give us the light of the knowledge of the glory of God not only in the face of Jesus Christ (2 Corinthians 4:6) but also in the teaching of Holy Scripture. The result of this witness is a state of mind in which both the Savior and the Scriptures have evidenced themselves to us as divine — Jesus, a divine person; Scripture, a divine product — in a way as direct, immediate, and arresting as that in which tastes and colors evidence themselves by forcing themselves on our senses. In consequence, we no longer find it possible to doubt the divinity of either Christ or the Bible.

Thus God authenticates Holy Scripture to us as his Word — not by some mystical experience or secret information privately whispered into some inner ear, not by human argument alone (strong as this may be), nor by the church's testimony alone (impressive as this is when one looks back over two thousand years). God does it, rather, by means of the searching light and transforming power whereby Scripture evidences itself to be divine.

Concise Theology

REBUILT ROAD, REOPENED WELLS

Build up, build up the highway;
clear it of stones.

ISAIAH 62:10

There was a time when all Christians laid great emphasis on the reality of God's call to holiness. Evangelical Protestants, in particular, offered endless variations on the themes of what God's holiness requires of us, what our holiness involves for us, by what means and through what disciplines the Holy Spirit sanctifies us, and the ways in which holiness increases our assurance and joy and usefulness to God.

But how different it is today! To listen to our sermons and to read the books we write for each other and then to watch the zany, worldly, quarrelsome way we behave as Christian people, you would never imagine that once the highway of holiness was clearly marked out for Bible believers. Now we have to rebuild and reopen the road, starting really from scratch.

In the Old Testament we read how "Isaac reopened the wells that had been dug in the time of his father Abraham, which the Philistines had stopped up" (Genesis 26:18, NIV). He knew he would find water in them, once he had cleared them of the earth and debris that malevolent Philistines had piled on top of them.

Isaac's action reflects two simple spiritual principles that apply here in a very direct way:

1. The recovering of old truth, truth that has been a means of blessing in the past, can under God become the means of blessing again in the present, while the quest for newer alternatives may well prove barren.

2. No one should be daunted from attempting such recovery by any prejudice, ill will, or unsympathetic attitudes that may have built up against the old truth during the time of its eclipse.

Drawing on wisdom from yesterday can help us see how the relevant biblical instruction applies to us today.

Rediscovering Holiness

FACING REALITY IN OUR PRAYING

Be fervent in spirit, serve the Lord. Rejoice in hope,
be patient in tribulation, be constant in prayer.
ROMANS 12:11-12

Most Christians pray differently during different life stages. As young Christians, enthusiastic about our newfound faith, we burble before the Lord about our lives in the way in which young children burble to their parents. Later we become less certain that such burbling alone is the essence of prayer. We reach out for a more mature and reverent prayer style, and we become less and less happy about the way we actually pray. We feel we are trudging along in a marsh, getting muddy and messed-up while going nowhere. We make requests to God, then wonder whether they made any difference. *Is God answering my prayers? If not, why not? If he is, how is he doing it? Because what's happening isn't quite what I asked for. Did I ask wrongly?*

There are, of course, many who say, "I can teach you a technique that works." They tell us about such things as listening prayer, centering prayer, labyrinth prayer, prayer in tongues, the prayer of silence, mental prayer, the prayer of union, and how to get through the dark night of the soul. These phases all have meaning, and they do in fact encourage fresh effort in praying. People sit gratefully through talks on these various techniques of prayer, and experiment with them, but they are soon found casting around for further help because their prayer difficulties have not yet been solved. Changed technique, alone, is not the remedy for their problems.

Let us be realistic about where we are and where we are not in this matter of praying. Deep down all of us have found that prayer isn't as easy as some people make it sound, or as easy as we ourselves had hoped it would be once our technique was straightened out.

Praying

GOD'S GUARDIAN GRACE

The LORD is my shepherd. . . .
He leads me. . . . He leads me.
PSALM 23:1-3

The doctrine of guidance appears as one of the principles of what Isaac Watts termed God's guardian grace, and what I refer to as God's covenant care.

"He leads me." *Lead* is the verb that in Psalm 23 carries the promise that our God will bestow the discernment of decision and direction we need in order to keep moving with him along the path of life. Our certainty, as believers, of God's guardian grace and covenant care should always undergird our quest for guidance.

The ethic of guidance appears in the parameters that qualify the promise. God leads "in paths of righteousness" (verse 3), nowhere else. God's guidance never violates the principles of uprightness and integrity, nor will he ever prompt us to irresponsible decisions and actions. He guides us, rather, to obey his Word and to choose between options by the exercise of the Christlike, God-honoring, farseeing wisdom that is modeled for us in the Bible, the wisdom that always aims at what will please God best.

The spirituality of guidance appears as a purpose and policy, not simply of keeping in touch with our Shepherd incidentally as we review the range of possible decisions, but of pursuing our personal relationship with him just as closely as we can when we have decisions to make. The Shepherd "leads me in paths of righteousness *for his name's sake"* (verse 3, emphasis added) — that is, to show his faithfulness and to be honored for it by our thanks and praise. Praising and thanking God in advance because he has promised so to lead us is often a means of coming to a clear discernment of what is the scope of his leading into present decision and action.

Guard Us, Guide Us

LOVE NEEDS LAW

If you love me,
you will keep my commandments.

JOHN 14:15

The Ten Commandments' stock is low today. Why? Partly because they are law, naming particular things that should and should not be done. People dislike law (that is one sign of our sinfulness), and the idea is widespread that Christians should not be led by law, only by love.

But the love-or-law antithesis is false. Law needs love as its drive, and love needs law as its eyes, for love is blind. To want to love someone Christianly does not of itself tell you how to do it. Only as we observe the limits set by God's law can we really do people good.

If anyone was qualified to detect shortcomings in the Ten Commandments and lead us beyond them to something better, it was Jesus. But what did he do? He affirmed them as having authority forever (Matthew 5:18-20) and as central to true religion (19:17-19). He expounded them, and he made a point of insisting that he kept them (Luke 6:6-10). When John says, "This is the love of God, that we keep his commandments" (1 John 5:3), his words remind us that Jesus defined love and discipleship to himself in terms of keeping his own commands (John 14:15,21-24; Matthew 28:19-20). Commandment-keeping is the only true way to love the Father and the Son.

And it is the only true way to love one's neighbor, too. When Paul says that "the one who loves another has fulfilled the law" (Romans 13:8), he explains himself by showing that love to neighbor embraces the specific prohibitions of adultery, murder, stealing, and envy. He does not say that love to neighbor cancels those prohibitions.

The Christian's most loving service to his neighbor is to uphold the authority of God's law as man's one true guide to true life.

Keeping the Ten Commandments

LOVE CHRIST, LOVE HIS CHURCH

> *To him be glory in the church and in Christ Jesus*
> *throughout all generations, forever and ever.*
>
> EPHESIANS 3:21

He was an odd little man, lean, intense, and jerky, with a face that seemed to light up as he spoke. I was there out of loyalty to the college chapel, not expecting to be impressed; but he captured my attention by telling us how in his teens he had experienced a personal conversion to Jesus Christ, like that which I had just undergone myself. "And then," he said, "I got excited about the church. You could say, I fell in love with it."

Never had I heard anyone talk quite like that before, and his words stuck in my memory. Fifty years later, I can still hear him saying them. He then hammered home the point that all who love Jesus Christ the Lord ought to care deeply about the church, just because the church is the object of Jesus' own love. Church-centeredness is thus one way in which Christ-centeredness ought to find expression.

Listen to Paul instructing the Ephesians:

> Christ loved the church and gave himself up for her, that he might sanctify her, having cleansed her by the washing of water with the word, so that he might present the church to himself in splendor, without spot or wrinkle or any such thing, that she might be holy and without blemish. (Ephesians 5:25-27)

The church that Christ loves and sustains is the key feature of God's plan for both time and eternity, and care for the church's welfare, which is what love for the church means, is an aspect of Christlikeness that Christians must ever seek to cultivate. We are right to take the church on our hearts; we should be wrong not to. For our Lord Jesus says to us all, "Love me, love my church."

A Passion for Faithfulness

GUIDANCE TESTED

They received the word with all eagerness,
examining the Scriptures daily to see if these things were so.

ACTS 17:11

God on occasion in Bible times communicated with some people by supernaturally telling them what to do, and he has not said he will never do so again. Some at least of the glowing stories that are told about guidance of this kind can hardly be doubted. Some see reason to deny that God ever did, or will communicate this way now that the canon of Scripture is complete, but that view seems to us to go beyond what is written and to fly in the face of credible testimony. It is not for us to place restrictions on God that he has not placed on himself!

Certainly, no messages from God of this kind could be regarded as canonical in the sense of carrying authority for universal faith and life in the way that Scripture does. This, however, is not to deny that "private revelations," as the Puritans used to call them, ever take place nowadays. On that question we keep an open mind. Though we know that self-deception here is very easy, we would not short-circuit claims to have received words from God; we would instead test them, as objectively and open-mindedly as we can, in light of the teaching of Scripture itself.

Scripture teaches that principle of testing in such passages as Deuteronomy 18:22 where God's people are told to listen to supposed prophets with discernment: "When a prophet speaks in the name of the LORD, if the word does not come to pass or come true, that is a word that the LORD has not spoken; the prophet has spoken it presumptuously. You need not be afraid of him." Similarly Paul instructs the church at Thessalonica in 1 Thessalonians 5:20-21, "Do not despise prophecies, but test everything; hold fast what is good."

Guard Us, Guide Us

A LONG LESSON IN FALSE HOPES

> *God our Father . . . loved us and gave us*
> *eternal comfort and good hope through grace.*
>
> 2 THESSALONIANS 2:16

The twentieth century opened in optimism. The ruling assumption in the West was that we are all basically good and wise, and advancing Christian civilization would soon make the kingdom of God, understood as universal neighbor love, a global reality. A periodical called *The Christian Century* was founded to channel these hopes and chronicle their fulfillment; it still exists, but its title now seems woefully inept. The century witnessed global barbarism in two World Wars and in the careers of power-crazy, money-mad tribalists and the genocidal doings of dictators; we cringed to see profiteering of the world's big businesses as they polluted and raped the environment; and we mourned the Western drift from Christian and moral moorings into relativism, pluralism, secularism, and hedonism. There were escalations of the armaments race and the ability to devastate the world with nuclear weapons.

These developments ensured that many thoughtful people entered the twenty-first century with fear rather than in hope, wondering how far the educated, affluent, and technologically equipped decadence of the West will go and what sort of a world awaits our grandchildren. It can be fairly said that Marxist utopianism, with its collectivist frame, has failed and is not likely to be tried anywhere again.

As the third millennium unfolds, any who expect that politicians' and generals' playing of the power game and business leaders' playing of the profit game will generate global peace and prosperity have buried their heads very deep in the sands. No realistic hope of better things to come can be drawn from the ways of the modern world.

What follows? Is there nothing good to hope for at all? There is, but we must seek this good hope outside the socio-politico-economic process. And this, by the grace of God, we may do.

Never Beyond Hope

THE CHURCH AS CHRIST'S BODY

We are to grow up in every way
into him who is the head, into Christ.

EPHESIANS 4:15

The New Testament idea of the church is that it is the company of those who share in the redemptive renewal of a sin-spoiled creation, which began when Christ rose from the dead. As the individual believer is a new creation in Christ, raised with him out of death into life, possessed of and led by the life-giving Holy Spirit, so also the church as a whole. Its life springs from its union with Christ, crucified and risen. Paul, in Ephesians, pictures the church successively as Christ's *building,* now growing "into a holy temple in the Lord" (2:21); his *body,* now growing toward a state of full edification (4:1-16); and his *bride* (5:25), now being sanctified and cleansed in readiness for "the marriage supper of the Lamb" (Revelation 19:9).

Some modern writers treat Paul's body metaphor as indicating that the church is "really" (in a sense in which it is not "really" anything else) an extension of the manhood and incarnate life of Christ. But according to Paul, the church's union with Christ is symbolically exhibited in baptism; and what baptism symbolizes is not incorporation into Christ's manhood simply, but sharing with him in his death to sin, with all its saving fruits, and in the power and life of his resurrection. When Paul says that the Spirit *baptizes* men into one body, he means that the Spirit makes us members of the body by bringing us into that union with Christ which baptism signifies (1 Corinthians 12:13). Scripture would lead us to call the church an extension of the resurrection rather than of the incarnation! In any case, Paul uses the body metaphor only to illustrate the authority of the Head, and his ministry to his members, and the various ministries that they must fulfill to each other.

Serving the People of God

POWER IN ACTION

> *The wind blows where it wishes, and you hear its sound,*
> *but you do not know where it comes from or where it goes.*
> *So it is with everyone who is born of the Spirit.*
>
> JOHN 3:8

Spirit, like all biblical terms that refer to God, is a picture word with a vivid, precise, and colorful meaning. It pictures breath breathed or panted out, as when you blow out the candles on your birthday cake or blow up balloons or puff and blow as you run. *Spirit* in this sense was what the big bad wolf threatened the little pigs with when he warned, "I'll huff, and I'll puff, and I'll blow your house down!" The picture is of air made to move vigorously, even violently, and the thought the picture expresses is of energy let loose, executive force invading, power in exercise, life demonstrated by activity.

Both the Hebrew and Greek words rendered *spirit* in our Bibles (*ruach* and *pneuma*) carry this basic thought, and both have the same range of association. They are used of (1) the divine Spirit, personal and purposeful, invisible and irresistible; (2) the individual human consciousness (in which sense *spirit* becomes synonymous with *soul*); and (3) the wind that when aroused whirls leaves, uproots trees, and blows buildings over. I wish our language had a word that would carry all these associations. *Puff* and *blow* are two English words that refer to both the outbreathing of air from human lungs and the stirring of the wind, but English has no term that also covers the intellectual, volitional, and emotional individuality of God and of his rational creatures. Spirit in English, by contrast, denotes conscious personhood in action and reaction, but cannot be used of either breath or wind. This is doubtless one reason it does not suggest power in action in the way that *ruach* and *pneuma* did to people in Bible times.

Power in action is in fact the basic biblical thought whenever God's Spirit is mentioned.

Keep in Step with the Spirit

BUILDING LIVES

On this rock I will build my church,
and the gates of hell shall not prevail against it.
MATTHEW 16:18

When we speak of building a church, our minds are usually on the bricks and mortar out of which the new structure will be constructed. But when Jesus spoke of building his church, he was not thinking in those terms. He was thinking, rather, of the complex process whereby the truth about himself is received, the recipients respond to it (or, better, respond to him in terms of it), and the responders are conformed increasingly to him as they share in the things that the church does in obedience to Jesus' word, under his leadership, and in dependence on his power. As the church consists of individuals who by coming to faith and associating as believers have become the Lord's people (his vine, his flock, his temple, his nation), so Christ's building of the church is a matter of his so changing people on the inside — in their hearts — that repentance, faith, and obedience become more and more the pattern of their lives. Thus increasingly they exhibit the humility, purity, love, and zeal for God that we see in Jesus, and fulfill Jesus' call to worship, work, and witness in his name.

And this they do, not as isolated individuals (lone-rangerism!), but as fellow siblings in God's family, helping and encouraging each other in the openness and mutual care that are the hallmarks of "brotherly love" (Hebrews 13:1). Hereby they enter increasingly into the life that constitutes authentic Christianity, the life of fellowship with their heavenly Father, their risen Savior, and each other; and in so doing they are "being built up as a spiritual house, to be a holy priesthood, to offer spiritual sacrifices acceptable to God through Jesus Christ" (1 Peter 2:5).

A Passion for Faithfulness

ONLY BY EXPERIENCE

Pursue righteousness, godliness, faith, love,
steadfastness, gentleness.

1 TIMOTHY 6:11

Holiness, like prayer (which is indeed part of it), is something that, though Christians have an instinct for it through their new birth, they have to learn in and through experience. As Jesus "learned obedience from what he suffered" (Hebrews 5:8, NIV) — learned what obedience requires, costs, and involves through the experience of actually doing his Father's will up to and in his passion — so Christians must, and do, learn prayer from their struggles to pray, and learn holiness from their battles for purity of heart and righteousness of life.

Talented youngsters who go to tennis school in order to learn the game soon discover that the heart of the process is not talking about tactics but actually practicing serves and strokes, thus forming new habits and reflexes, so as to iron out weaknesses of style. The routine, which is grueling, is one of doing prescribed things over and over again on the court, against a real opponent, in order to get them really right.

Prayer and holiness are learned in a similar way as commitments are made, habits are formed, and battles are fought against a real opponent (Satan, in this case), who with great cunning plays constantly on our weak spots. (That these are often what the world sees as our strong points is an index of Satan's resourcefulness: presumptuous self-reliance and proud overreaching on our part serve his turn just as well as do paralyzing timidity, habits of harshness and anger, lack of discipline whether inward or outward, evasion of responsibility, lack of reverence for God, and willful indulgence in what one knows to be wrong.) Satan is as good at judo throws as he is at frontal assaults, and we have to be on guard against him all the time.

Rediscovering Holiness

WAIT EAGERLY

I will hope continually
and will praise you yet more and more.

PSALM 71:14

What the Bible tells us about hope, in a nutshell, is this:

Humans were originally created in fellowship with God so that we might exalt and enjoy him forever, first for a probationary period in this world and then in a place of "pleasures forevermore" (Psalm 16:11) that is off the map of this space-time universe. When sin infected our race, disrupting this fellowship, robbing us all of the hope of heaven and bringing us all under the threat of hell, our Creator acted to form a forgiven and reborn interracial human race, namely, the church, a community that should enjoy humankind's original destiny and more through sovereign divine grace and personal faith in our Lord Jesus Christ.

So believers in every age should live in the knowledge that they are God's adopted children and heirs of what is spoken of as his glory, his city, and his kingdom. They should know that Jesus Christ, who out of love gave his life for the church inclusively (Ephesians 5:25) and for each future believer personally (Galatians 2:20), is now with them individually by his Spirit (Matthew 28:20), to care for them daily as a shepherd for his sheep (John 10:2-4,11-25) and to strengthen them constantly according to their need (Philippians 4:13; 2 Timothy 4:17), and that he will finally take them from this world to see and share the heavenly bliss that is already his (John 14:1-3; 17:24; Romans 8:17). With Paul, therefore, they should "eagerly wait for the hope of righteousness" (Galatians 5:5) — that is, the full fruit of being fully accepted by God, or as the New Living Translation puts it, "eagerly wait to receive by faith the righteousness God has promised to us." The Christian identity is that not only of a believer, but of a hoper too.

Never Beyond Hope

OUR TASK FOR UNITY

> *Eager to maintain the unity of the Spirit*
> *in the bond of peace.*
>
> EPHESIANS 4:3

The Reformers drew a necessary distinction between the church visible and invisible — between the one church of Christ on earth as God sees it and as man sees it; in other words, as it is and as it seems to be. The identity between the two is at best partial, indirect, and constantly varying in degree.

The church as God sees it is necessarily invisible to men, since Christ and the Holy Spirit and faith, the realities which make the church, are themselves invisible. The church becomes visible as its members meet together in Christ's name to worship and hear God's Word. But the church visible is a mixed body. Some who belong, though orthodox, are not true believers — not, that is, true members of the church as God knows it — and need to be converted. The Reformers' distinction thus safeguards the vital truth that visible church membership saves no man apart from faith in Christ.

Another matter on which this distinction throws light is the question of church unity. If a visible organization, as such, were or could be the one church of God, then any organizational separation would be a breach of unity, and the only way to reunite a divided Christendom would be to work for a single international super-church. Also, on this hypothesis, it would be open to argue that some institutional feature is of the essence of the church and is therefore a *sine qua non* of reunion. But, in fact, the church invisible, the true church, is one already. Its unity is given to it in Christ. The proper ecumenical task is not to create church unity by denominational coalescence, but to recognize the unity that already exists and to give it worthy expression on the local level.

Serving the People of God

OUR PROMISE-KEEPER

I have spoken, and I will bring it to pass;
I have purposed, and I will do it.
ISAIAH 46:11

Before the words *promise keepers* were ever used for a contemporary men's movement, becoming a promise-keeper was a character quality that God established as his own. So the basis of all our asking in prayer, as of all of our trusting in God, is and must be knowing his promises, claiming them, relying on them, and holding fast to them whatever happens, in the confidence that they will always be kept. Second Peter 1:4 speaks of the "precious and very great promises" that God has given us. Paul says, "All the promises of God find their Yes" in Christ (2 Corinthians 1:20). And, as we will see in due course, receiving God's promises and trusting those promises is an integral building block, a truly foundational activity in a Christian life.

At the end of his life, Joshua, reviewing the exodus from Egypt and the conquest of Canaan, affirmed to Israel's leaders: "Not one word has failed of all the good things that the LORD your God promised concerning you. All have come to pass for you; not one of them has failed" (Joshua 23:14; see also 21:45). The New Testament views Abraham as the classic model of saving faith, and Paul declares that trusting God's promise with praise was the essence of Abraham's prayer as he waited for the predicted son and heir. "No distrust made him waver concerning the promise of God, but he grew strong in his faith as he gave glory to God, fully convinced that God was able to do what he had promised. That is why his faith was 'counted to him as righteousness'" (Romans 4:20-22). Promise-trusting faith is indeed at the center of the biblical prayer pattern.

Praying

NOT JUST AN INFLUENCE

And I will ask the Father, and he will give you
another Helper, to be with you forever.
JOHN 14:16

In the New Testament, the Holy Spirit is set forth as the third divine person, linked with yet distinct from the Father and the Son, just as the Father and the Son are distinct from each other. He is "the Paraclete" (John 14:16,26; 15:26; 16:7) — a rich word for which there is no adequate English translation, since it means by turns Comforter (in the sense of Strengthener), Counselor, Helper, Supporter, Adviser, Advocate, Ally, Senior Friend — and only a person could fulfill such roles. More precisely, he is "another" Paraclete (14:16), second in line (we may say) to the Lord Jesus, continuing Jesus' own ministry — and only a person, one like Jesus, could do that. John underlines the note by repeatedly using a masculine pronoun (*ekeinos,* "he") to render Jesus' references to the Spirit, when Greek grammar called for a neuter one (*ekeino,* "it") to agree with the neuter noun "Spirit" (*pneuma*): John wants his readers to be in no doubt that the Spirit is he, not it. This masculine pronoun, which appears in 14:26; 15:26; 16:8,13-14, is the more striking because in 14:17, where the Spirit is first introduced, John had used the grammatically correct neuter pronouns (*ho* and *auto*), thus ensuring that his subsequent shift to the masculine would be perceived not as incompetent Greek, but as magisterial theology.

Again, the Holy Spirit is said to hear, speak, witness, convince, glorify Christ, lead, guide, teach, command, forbid, desire, give speech, give help, and intercede for Christians with inarticulate groans, himself crying to God in their prayers. Also, he can be lied to and grieved. Only of a person could such things be said. The conclusion is that the Spirit is not just an influence; he, like the Father and the Son, is an individual person.

Keep in Step with the Spirit

GOD'S WORD IS LIKE A SHEPHERD DOG

He leads me in paths of righteousness
for his name's sake.

PSALM 23:3

Lead is itself an umbrella word covering many modes of direction: thus, the dictionary suggests that lead means to guide by the hand or by showing the way; to have preeminence and control, as in an orchestra, an army, a team, or a project; to draw, entice, allure, influence, and prevail on the other persons to act in a certain way; and more. So we have to ask, What sort of leading is in view in Psalm 23?

In the picture the psalm draws, the shepherd's leading includes all the procedures whereby he induces the sheep to go where he wants them to. Walking ahead of them, he sets them an example and stirs them to follow it — that is, to follow him. Walking behind them as a modern shepherd would do, with trained dogs padding alongside to head off any sheep that start to stray, would be our picture of the same process; but trained dogs were not, it would seem, any part of the ancient shepherd's equipment. What corresponds to this in the life of Christian discipleship? The answer is, God's own instruction from and through his written Word. Direct guidance as to things we should and should not do is found in the Ten Commandments and the case law based on them, in the oracle-sermons of the prophets recalling Israel to God's standards, in the wisdom books of Proverbs and Ecclesiastes, in the teaching of Jesus, and in the many treatments of Christian behavior in the Epistles. And through the Word, via honest commitment to live by the Word and humble experience of the Word's transforming power, God gives wisdom to discern his will in all situations that call for reflective thought.

Guard Us, Guide Us

SHRINKING GOD

> *Behold, the LORD our God*
> *has shown us his glory and greatness.*
> DEUTERONOMY 5:24

I must learn from God's plan of salvation to be awestruck at the greatness of my Maker.

Often in recent decades I have found myself publicly lamenting the way in which our Western culture has indulged unwarrantably great thoughts of humanity and scandalously small thoughts of God. Our time will surely go down in history as the age of the God-shrinkers. The result is that belief in God's sovereignty and omniscience, the majesty of his moral law and the terror of his judgments, the retributive consequences of the life we live here and the endlessness of the eternity in which we will experience them, along with belief in the intrinsic triunity of God and the divinity and personal return of Jesus Christ, is nowadays so eroded as to be hardly discernible. For many in our day, God is no more than a smudge.

The plan of salvation, which tells me how my Creator has become my Redeemer, sets before me in fullest glory the transcendent majesty that today's churches have so largely forgotten. It shows me a God infinitely great in wisdom and power — who knew from all eternity what fallen humanity's plight would be — and who before creating the cosmos had already schemed out in detail how he would save not only me, but each single one of the many billions whom he was resolved to bring to glory. The plan tells me of a vast program for world history, a program involving millennia of providential preparation for the first coming of a Savior, and millennia more of worldwide evangelism, pastoral care, Christianizing of culture, demonstration of God's kingdom, spiritual warfare against its enemies, and building up of the church before the Savior returns.

Rediscovering Holiness

GOD'S CREDIT ON THE LINE

*He has granted to us his precious
and very great promises, so that through them
you may become partakers of the divine nature.*

2 PETER 1:4

Our gracious God has laid his credit on the line in what he has told us
through Christ, through the apostles, and through the entire Bible about
the life to come, and in the promises about the future that he has given to
all believers. Those promises have heaven in view constantly. It would be
sinfully silly and insulting to God to refuse to believe this teaching and
these promises when we receive other things taught by Christ, the
apostles, and the Bible as being divine truth. Can we ever justify not
taking God's word about things? Can we here and now justify withhold-
ing belief from God's own premises about the future? No, of course we
can't. The arrogance of not believing what God had clearly declared was
the sin of Eden; such disbelief was unwarrantable then and would be
equally unwarrantable now.

An observed effect of depression is loss of power to believe that any
good awaits you, and one of the causes of depression is feeling you are a
misfit or an outsider or a failure. Spiritual depression occurs when such
feelings eat away your confidence in the vast, unmeasured, boundless, free
love of your God. I suspect that you know something of these feelings;
many Western Christians, perhaps even most, go through life in a state of
undiagnosed spiritual depression because these feelings regularly get on
top of them. But the final answer to all feelings of inferiority is to remind
yourself that your God loves, redeems, pardons, restores, protects, keeps,
and uses misfits, outsiders, and failures no less than he does beautiful
people of the kind that keep crossing your path and of whom you have
been wishing you were one.

Never Beyond Hope

A LIVELY CHURCH

You are not lacking in any spiritual gift,
as you wait for the revealing of our Lord Jesus Christ.

1 CORINTHIANS 1:7

Public worship at Corinth was the very opposite of a drab routine. Every service was an event, for every worshipper came ready and anxious to share something that God had given him. Paul gave regulations for handling this state of affairs in a way that was orderly and edifying, once it had arisen as the spontaneous creation of the Holy Spirit in that church. And when the Corinthians met for worship, the presence and power of God in their midst was an experienced reality.

This is the basic dimension of spiritual revival. Within the Corinthian fellowship there was a sense of the presence of God that struck awe into people's hearts, just as had happened at Jerusalem in the early days. The knowledge of God, the sense of God's presence among these people, was too much for casual, irresponsible contact. That is how it always is in revival times, and that is how it was at Corinth.

Granted, the Corinthian disorders were grievous. But the Corinthian church was being carried along by a great surge of divine life. Disorder, as such, is demonic; I do not question that. Disorder is not in the least to be desired. But it remains a question whether Holy Ghost life, with all its exuberance and risk of disorder, is not preferable to spiritual deadness, neat and tidy though that deadness might be.

Three centuries ago, John Owen wrote, "I had rather have the order, rule, spirit, and practice of those churches which were planted by the apostles, with all their troubles and disadvantages, than the carnal peace of others in their open degeneracy from all these things." Frankly, I would rather have it too. I hope you feel the same. Give me life with all its disorder rather than death with its tidy inertia.

Serving the People of God

OUR PATERNAL GOD

> *You, O LORD, are our Father,*
> *our Redeemer from of old is your name.*
> ISAIAH 63:16

In his perfection, God behaves toward those who are his in a fatherly way that, as such, is flawless. The biblical ideal of fatherhood blends authority, fidelity, affection, care, discipline, long-suffering, and protection in a course of sustained love that aims always at the children's advance into strength, wisdom, and maturity. God in his triunity relates to all his people according to this fatherly ideal, and more specifically, within that triunity, the first person of the holy Three does so. He, the eternal Father of Jesus the eternal Son, in whom we have been brought into our new life, adopts us sinners to be his sons and heirs with Jesus, who thus becomes our elder brother. Now by means of the ministry to us of the Son and the Spirit, our heavenly Father is leading us home to full Christlikeness and eternal glory.

In the Sermon on the Mount, Jesus says much about how the Father relates to us. "Your *Father* who sees in secret will reward you" (Matthew 6:4,6,18, emphasis added). "Your *Father* knows what you need before you ask him" (6:8, emphasis added). "How much more will your *Father* who is in heaven give good things to those who ask him!" (7:11, emphasis added). In light of all that the New Testament tells us about God's love for his children, we can pray with perfect confidence to the Father as one who will never fail us. Human fathers may let us down, but not God. We can know with certainty that our praying will be heard and responded to in the way that not only is wisest in terms of God's own total purposes but also is best in the long run for us as individuals. It is a truly wonderful thing to be in God's paternal hands.

Praying

NO HOLINESS WITHOUT PRAISE

You are holy,
enthroned on the praises of Israel.

PSALM 22:3

God's plan of salvation covers not only (1) the three-hour agony of Jesus on the cross, vicariously enduring Godforsakenness so that sinners like me would never have to endure it; but also (2) the permanently transforming bodily resurrection of Jesus and the permanently transforming heart-regeneration of everyone who is saved — two demonstrations of power that are, be it said, wholly inexplicable in terms of the created forces that operate in the world. Finally, the plan reaches into the future, promising everyone a new, undying body. In addition, it promises saved sinners like me a new heaven and earth, a vast perfected society, and the visible presence of Jesus, to enjoy through that new body forever.

Such are the wonders of the plan of salvation. God's call to holiness begins by telling me to dwell on these great and awesome realities until I find myself truly awestruck at the greatness of my God, who is making it all happen. In this way I will learn to give him glory (in the sense of praise) for the greatness of his glory (in the sense of self-display) as the one whose revealed wisdom and power, in redemption as in creation, dazzle, surpass, and overwhelm my understanding. The Triune God of the plan is great — transcendent and immutable in his omnipotence, omniscience, and omnipresence. He is eternal in his truthfulness and faithfulness, wisdom and justice, severity and goodness — and he must be praised and adored as such. Praise of this kind is the doxological foundation of human holiness, which always starts here. Just as there could be for Jesus no crown without the cross, so there can be for us no holiness without the praise.

Rediscovering Holiness

ALWAYS GOD

*From everlasting to everlasting
you are God.*

PSALM 90:2

Children sometimes ask, "Who made God?" The clearest answer is that God never needed to be made, because he was always there. He exists in a different way from us: we, his creatures, exist in a dependent, derived, finite, fragile way, but our Maker exists in an eternal, self-sustaining, necessary way — necessary, that is, in the sense that God does not have it in him to go out of existence, just as we do not have it in us to live forever. We necessarily age and die, because it is our present nature to do that; God necessarily continues forever unchanged, because it is his eternal nature to do that.

God's self-existence is a basic truth. At the outset of his presentation of the unknown God to the Athenian idolaters, Paul explained that this God, the world's Creator, "does not live in temples made by man, nor is he served by human hands, as though he needed anything, since he himself gives to all mankind life and breath and everything" (Acts 17:24-25). Sacrifices offered to idols, in today's tribal religions as in ancient Athens, are thought of as somehow keeping the god going, but the Creator needs no such support system. The word aseity, meaning that he has life in himself and draws his unending energy from himself (*a se* in Latin means "from himself"), was coined by theologians to express this truth, which the Bible makes clear.

In our life of faith, we easily impoverish ourselves by embracing an idea of God that is too limited and small. The doctrine of God's aseity stands as a bulwark against this. It is vital for spiritual health to believe that God is great, and grasping the truth of his aseity is the first step on the road to doing this.

Concise Theology

THE CLARITY OF GOD'S SOVEREIGNTY

The Most High God
rules the kingdom of mankind.
DANIEL 5:21

If you are a Christian, I know that you believe the general truth that God is sovereign in his world. How do I know that?

Because I know that if you are a Christian, you pray; and the recognition of God's sovereignty is the basis of your prayers. In prayer, you ask for things and give thanks for things. Why? Because you recognize that God is the author and source of all the good that you have had already, and all the good that you hope for in the future. This is the fundamental philosophy of Christian prayer. The prayer of a Christian is not an attempt to force God's hand, but a humble acknowledgment of helplessness and dependence. When we are on our knees, we know that it is not we who control the world; it is not in our power, therefore, to supply our needs by our own independent efforts; every good thing that we desire for ourselves and for others must be sought from God, and will come, if it comes at all, as a gift from his hands.

If this is true even of our daily bread (and the Lord's Prayer teaches us that it is), much more is it true of spiritual benefits. This is all luminously clear to us when we are actually praying, whatever we may be betrayed into saying in argument afterward. In effect, therefore, what we do every time we pray is to confess our own impotence and God's sovereignty. The very fact that a Christian prays is thus proof positive that he believes in the lordship of his God.

Evangelism and the Sovereignty of God

LEARNING FROM THE TEN COMMANDMENTS

> *I find my delight in your commandments,*
> *which I love.*
> PSALM 119:47

What does God want to teach us today from the Ten Commandments?

First, the Commandments show *what sort of people God wants us to be.* From the list of prohibitions, telling us what actions God hates, we learn the behavior he wishes and loves to see. What does God in the law say "No!" to? Unfaithfulness and irreverence to himself, and dishonor and damage to our neighbor. So what does God want us to be? Persons free of these evils; persons who actively love the God who made them and their neighbors, whom he also made, every day of their lives.

Second, the Commandments show *what sort of lifestyle is truly natural for us.* Rightly have theologians understood the Commandments as declaring "natural" law, the law of our nature — the only form of conduct that fully satisfies human nature. Deviations from it, even where unconscious, are inescapably unfulfilling.

Third, the Commandments show *what sort of people we are in God's eyes* — namely, lawbreakers under sentence, whose only hope lies in God's forgiving mercy. When we measure our lives by God's law, we find that self-justification and self-satisfaction are alike impossible, and we are plunged into self-despair. Thus the law, by exposing us to ourselves as spiritually sick and lost, enables us to appreciate the gospel remedy.

> Let us love, and sing, and wonder;
> Let us praise the Savior's name!
> He has hushed the law's loud thunder,
> He has quenched Mount Sinai's flame;
> He has washed us with his blood,
> He presents our souls to God![1]

Hallelujah!

Keeping the Ten Commandments

MAN OF ZEAL

*Zeal for your house
has consumed me.*

PSALM 69:9

Nehemiah is a model of personal zeal for the honor and glory of God. As he says in one of his prayers, he is among those "who delight to fear your name" (Nehemiah 1:11), and the strength of his passion to magnify the Lord is great. Such zeal, though matched by Jesus and the psalmists and Paul (to look no further), is rarer today than it should be; most of us are more like the lukewarm Laodiceans, drifting along very cheerfully in becalmed churches, feeling confident everything is all right, and thereby disgusting our Lord Jesus, who sees that, spiritually speaking, nothing is right (see Revelation 3:14-22). The rough language of our Lord's threat to spit out the Laodicean church — to repudiate and reject it — shows that zeal for God's house still constrains him in his glory, just as it did on earth when he cleansed the temple (John 2:17).

Back in the days when God used his own people as his executioners, not only in holy war with pagans but also in the disciplining of the church, Phinehas the priest had speared an Israelite and his Midianite whore together, and God through Moses had commended him for a zeal that matched God's own: "He was as zealous as I am for my honor among them.... Therefore tell him I am making my covenant of peace with him ... because he was zealous for the honor of his God" (Numbers 25:11-13, NIV). As God himself is zealous, so must his servants be.

Are you clear what zeal is? It is not fanaticism; it is not wildness; it is not irresponsible enthusiasm; it is not any form of push egoism. It is, rather, a humble, reverent, businesslike, single-minded commitment to the hallowing of God's name and the doing of his will.

A Passion for Faithfulness

ON "PUTTING OUT A FLEECE"

And the LORD turned to him and said, "Go in this might of yours
and save Israel from the hand of Midian; do not I send you?"

JUDGES 6:14

Gideon's situation and ours hardly match. The essence of "putting out a fleece" for guidance (as Gideon did; see Judges 6:36-40) about a private and personal decision is to devise a test to which God is asked to submit in a specified way, so that he dances to a tune that this or that believer composed for him. This comes close to the Devil's second temptation in the desert, which Jesus dismissed by saying: "It is written, 'You shall not put the Lord your God to the test'" (Matthew 4:7). Gideon's words introducing his second request, "Let not your anger burn against me" (Judges 6:39), sound as if Gideon knew there was something presumptuous about what he was doing. Young and untried as he was, however, he desperately needed personal encouragement and something encouraging to tell his troops, and it would be a frigid and feeble comment if we were simply to say that God's promise to him (Judges 6:16), coupled with the early sign (fire from the rock, verse 21), should have been enough. "Lord, I believe; help my unbelief" was what Gideon was expressing, and the searcher of hearts knew that.

God met Gideon where he was, in what we would call a blue funk, and by answering his request kept him going as Israel's generalissimo. What we see here is God's gracious, shepherdlike compassion for the self-confessed weakling, making him strong for the huge-looking task ahead. It would be wrong to see in Gideon's plea for reassurance evidence of an irreverent and presumptuous heart, but it would be a different story if you or we "put out a fleece" for guidance in buying a car or choosing a school. Gideon's was clearly a special case.

Guard Us, Guide Us

GREAT GRATITUDE FOR GREAT MERCY

I will praise the name of God with a song;
I will magnify him with thanksgiving.

PSALM 69:30

It is safe to say that no religion anywhere has ever laid such stress on the need for thanksgiving, nor called on its adherents so incessantly and insistently to give God thanks, as does the religion of the Bible in both its Old and New Testament forms. The reason is not hard to see. The divine gifts and blessings that Scripture sees as given in the good experiences of natural life and the amazing mercy of supernatural salvation are far richer and more abundant, and involve far more of divine generosity, than are dreamed of by any other faith.

Our acts of thanksgiving, to be acceptable, must be genuine expressions of gratitude in the heart for all God's giving—gratitude for what the *Anglican Prayer Book* verbalizes as "our creation, preservation, and all the blessings of this life; but above all for thine inestimable love in the redemption of the world by our Lord Jesus Christ, for the means of grace and for the hope of glory." Of this "inestimable love," the plan of salvation is the chart.

Love (*agape*), in the Christian sense of that word, has been defined as a purpose of making the loved one great. We learn this definition from the revelation of God's love in Christ, the love that saves. As love to sinners deserving hell, it was mercy. As a purpose of raising them from spiritual destitution to the dignity of forgiveness and restoration, acceptance, and adoption into God's family, it was costly—not to us, but to God himself, as Scripture makes very clear.

The measure of all love is its giving. The measure of the love of God is the cross of Christ, where the Father gave the Son to die so that the spiritually dead might have life.

Rediscovering Holiness

REAL DEPENDENCE, REAL STRENGTH

*O Lord GOD, please remember me
and please strengthen me only this once, O God.*

JUDGES 16:28

God in his mercy may have to deal with us eventually as he dealt with Samson. The strength God had given him seemed gone forever; his usefulness seemed gone as well. In the goodness of God, Samson recovered just enough strength for the final act of his life.

God may have to weaken us and bring us down at the points where we thought we were strong in order that we may become truly strong in real dependence on himself. He's done that before, and he may have to do it again with us. If he does, there will be mercy in it. It will be God working to make some sense out of rambling lives that have reached the point where it seems nothing good can come from them anymore.

Another encouraging thought from Samson's story: God does use us. He uses us right now in spite of our flaws. He is a kindly God and uses flawed people as a part of his regular agenda. No matter how conscious we are of our own limitations, shortcomings, and sins, we may look to God to make use of us again — and in his great mercy he will.

We must seek to get and keep our lives in a shape that will glorify God. That's not easy. It means fighting our sins, disciplining our thoughts, changing our attitudes, and critiquing our desires in a way that Samson did not try to do. But let's trust the Lord who uses flawed human material for his glory, and by faith let's seek strength to serve God in good works and attitudes that at this moment we feel are beyond us. Those who seek find; for Samson's God, who is our God, is a God of great patience and great grace.

Never Beyond Hope

INESCAPABLE DIVISIONS

I appeal to you, brothers . . . that there be no divisions among you,
but that you be united in the same mind and the same judgment.

1 CORINTHIANS 1:10

Sometimes division, though not desirable, is inescapable — the best thing
the situation admits of. Still it is always a sad thing when the situation
arises which makes it the best thing to do.

First, there are divisions about beliefs and doctrine. In the New
Testament you have divisions whereby the authentic church differenti-
ates itself from what is really the non-church (as in 1 John 2:18-19), where
previously the two were confused. This sort of division, which identifies
the body rather than divides it, can clear the air in a helpful way. Second,
there are occasions when the faithful church withdraws from the scandalous church. The historical sixteenth-century Reformation was one such
case. Third, there are divisions when a forthright church (or forthright
group of Christians) withdraws from a fuzzy church, where faithful
believers have tried but failed to maintain a clear witness to God's grace
according to the Scriptures. It may be a matter of withdrawing from a
particular denomination, or withdrawing from a local congregation.
Fourth, there are divisions over church order. Incompatible views about
how the church should order its life have broken surface, and particular
groups have had to go their own separate ways. Fifth, there are divisions
for nontheological reasons, for example, over people's race, class, age, or
style.

We must reject, however, divisions over such nontheological factors
as the personalities of leaders, like the division described in 1 Corinthians
1. We must reject that sort of division, because, Paul says, it is wrong. To
be sure, we have our favorite preachers, but that is no reason for dividing
the local congregation. But do not divide the body over that! It would be
Spirit-quenching, very much the Devil's work, and very dishonoring to
the Savior to be part of a division over preachers.

Serving the People of God

HEART QUALITY MEANS EVERYTHING

Call on the Lord
from a pure heart.

2 TIMOTHY 2:22

The authentic path of prayer requires purity of heart as we pray. This means a great deal more than might at first appear. In contemporary society, when we speak of the heart in the metaphorical sense as an aspect of our selfhood, we are likely to be thinking of either a flood of emotional intensity ("I love you with all my heart") or a flow of robust enthusiasm ("his heart is in what he is doing"), and nothing more. But in the consistent Bible view the heart is nothing less than the taproot of the self, the deep source of our character and purposes, of our attitudes and responses, of our self-image and self-projection, in short, of the total human being that each of us is. God, as revealed in the Bible, looks at us from a unitary perspective, and we are, according to the God's-eye view of us, good or bad according to our heart quality. Says Jesus, "What comes out of the mouth *proceeds from the heart*" (Matthew 15:18, emphasis added). A bad-hearted person is like a bad tree producing bad fruit (12:33-35).

Conversely, in the parable of the sower, the seed sown in the good soil represents "those who, hearing the word, hold it fast *in an honest and good heart*, and bear fruit with patience" (Luke 8:15, emphasis added). We today assess people from the outside in grading them mainly by their skills, and we label them *good* people, despite their moral lapses, as long as they use their skills to do what we recognize as a good job. God, however, assesses everyone from the inside out, measuring us entirely by the state of our hearts. It is with God's method of assessment, which digs so much deeper than ours, that we must all finally come to terms.

Praying

THE FLOODLIGHT SHINING ON THE SAVIOR

When the Spirit of truth comes . . . he will glorify me,
for he will take what is mine and declare it to you.

JOHN 16:13-14

The Holy Spirit's distinctive New Covenant role is to fulfill what we may call a floodlight ministry in relation to the Lord Jesus Christ. So far as this role was concerned, the Spirit "was not yet" (John 7:39, literal Greek) while Jesus was on earth; only when the Father had glorified Jesus (17:1,5) could the Spirit's work of making men aware of Jesus' glory begin.

I remember walking to a church one winter evening to preach on the words "he shall glorify me," seeing the building floodlit as I turned a corner, and realizing this was exactly the illustration my message needed. When floodlighting is well done, the floodlights are so placed that you do not see where the light is coming from; what you are meant to see is just the building on which the floodlights are trained. The intended effect is to make it visible when otherwise it would not be seen for the darkness, and to maximize its dignity by throwing all its details into relief so that you see it properly. This perfectly illustrates the Spirit's New Covenant role. He is, so to speak, the hidden floodlight shining on the Savior.

Or think of it as the Spirit standing behind us, throwing light over our shoulder, on Jesus, who stands facing us. The Spirit's message to us is never "Look at me; listen to me; come to me; get to know me" but always "Look at *him*, and see his glory; listen to *him*, and hear his word; go to *him*, and have life; get to know *him*, and taste his gift of joy and peace."

The Spirit, we might say, is the matchmaker, the celestial marriage broker, whose role it is to bring us and Christ together and ensure that we stay together.

Keep in Step with the Spirit

EVERYWHERE ALMIGHTY

Do I not fill heaven and earth?
declares the LORD.
JEREMIAH 23:24

God is present in all places; we should not think of him, however, as filling spaces, for he has no physical dimensions. It is as pure spirit that he pervades all things, in a relationship of immanence that is more than we body-bound creatures can understand. One thing that is clear, however, is that he is present everywhere in the fullness of all that he is and all the powers that he has, and needy souls praying to him anywhere in the world receive the same fullness of his undivided attention. Because God is omnipresent, he is able to give his entire attention to millions of individuals at the same time.

Belief in God's omnipresence, thus understood, is reflected in Psalm 139:7-10; Jeremiah 23:23-24; and Acts 17:24-28. When Paul speaks of the ascended Christ as filling all things (Ephesians 4:10), Christ's availability everywhere in the fullness of his power is certainly part of the meaning that is being expressed. It is true to say that Father, Son, and Holy Spirit are today omnipresent together, though the personal presence of the glorified Son is spiritual (through the Holy Spirit), not physical (in the body).

Job said, "I know that you can do all things, and that no purpose of yours can be thwarted" (Job 42:2). Thus Job testifies to the almightiness (omnipotence) of God. Omnipotence means in practice the power to do everything that in his rational and moral perfection (i.e., his wisdom and goodness) God wills to do. This does not mean that God can do literally everything; he cannot sin, lie, change his nature, or deny the demands of his holy character — nor can he cease to be God. But all that he wills and promises he can and will do.

Concise Theology

COMMITTED, COMPASSIONATE LEADER

Remember me, O my God, concerning this,
and do not wipe out my good deeds.

NEHEMIAH 13:14

Another strength we find in Nehemiah is pastoral commitment: the commitment of a leader, a natural mover and shaker, to compassionate service for the needy. A leader is a person who can persuade others to embrace and pursue his or her own purpose. One is a leader only if one is actually followed, so to be a leader, one has to be able to motivate others. But then one is in danger of becoming a dictator, using one's persuasive power to manipulate and exploit those whom one leads. Nehemiah, however, was not like that. He was no more a dictator than he was a doormat; he did not ride roughshod over people any more than he allowed people to ride roughshod over him. He expressed love for neighbor by his compassionate care, and consciously shouldered responsibility for others' well-being: he saw the restoring of Jerusalem as a welfare operation, no less than an honoring of God, and he took time out at least once from building the walls to help the poor (Nehemiah 5:1-13), in addition to permanently forgoing his right to claim support from those he governed (verses 14-18).

Nehemiah slips a number of his prayers into his memoirs, and some of these have generated puzzlement. "Remember for my good, O my God, all that I have done for this people" (5:19, following the account of his social service) is a case in point. Is Nehemiah aiming to build up a merit balance in God's ledger? Is he asking to be justified by his works? Not at all. He refers to what he has done simply as a token of his integrity and sincerity in ministry, a proof of his genuineness as a servant of the servants of God — as evidence of his living out pastoral commitment.

A Passion for Faithfulness

THE DANGER OF "HOLY HUNCHES"

Trust in the LORD with all your heart,
and do not lean on your own understanding.

PROVERBS 3:5

At the heart of living is decision-making. We are to make our decisions in our character as the sheep of the Lord Jesus Christ, moving through life under the guidance of our Good Shepherd. First a warning: Bad decision-making can take the form of following impressions — hunches masquerading as messages from God. "I feel" is a red-flag phrase in this matter of guidance; self-proclaimed holy hunches can be a source of real danger. True, our Lord does indeed *sometimes* gently nudge his sheep in one direction or the other — particularly those who know him well and are used to recognizing his voice within. But this is less the norm than many people assume, and it is not the place to start when seeking guidance from God.

Healthy decision-making isn't a matter of thinking what we want to think, and then acting as if it were true. It isn't a matter of following our feelings, although if, by the grace of God, we make wise decisions for the living of our life, good feelings and even joy regularly follow. But the wise Christian seeking God's guidance doesn't start with impressions and subjective fantasies. Wise Christians start with the written Word of God, which they receive as their guidebook, as from the hand of Jesus Christ himself. We make our decisions in the light of what Scripture actually says and then, following on from that, in the light of wisdom that comes to us as we soak ourselves in God's Word. The Word and the wisdom: these are the first two basic resources for good decision-making, the activity that promotes and sustains true spiritual health.

Guard Us, Guide Us

THE DEVOTIONAL BASIS
FOR HOLINESS

*I appeal to you therefore, brothers, by the mercies of God,
to present your bodies as a living sacrifice.*

ROMANS 12:1

Christians, says Paul, are to be moved and stirred to consecrated living by their knowledge of God's love, grace, and mercy — the mercy of sovereign salvation, whereby God pardons, accepts, and exalts the undeserving and wretched, at fearsome cost to himself. *Love* means his going out to bless those he sees as having no claim on him; *grace* means his going out to bless those whom he sees as meriting his rejection; and *mercy* means his going out to bless those whose state he sees to be miserable. *Love* expresses God's self-determining freedom, *grace* his self-generated favor, and *mercy* his compassionate kindness. Paul has dwelt on God's sovereign mercy to sinners in Romans 9:15-18 and 11:30-32; now (in 12:1) he says in effect, "Show yourselves truly grateful for this mercy by the thoroughness of your commitment to God henceforth, for holiness means giving your all to God as God has given, is giving, and will give his all to you."

As praise to God for his transcendent greatness is the doxological basis of holiness, so commitment to spend one's life expressing gratitude for God's grace, every way one can, is its devotional basis. As the Puritans used to say, the heart of holiness is holiness in the heart. The holy sacrifice that gives God pleasure is the Christian whose heart never ceases to be grateful to him for his grace. God is pleased with the Christian whose aim every day is to express that gratitude by living to him, through him, and for him, and who is constantly asking, with the psalmist, "What shall I render to the LORD for all his benefits to me?" (Psalm 116:12).

Rediscovering Holiness

GOD'S GRACE TO A DYSFUNCTIONAL FAMILY

I will bless you . . .
so that you will be a blessing.

GENESIS 12:2

From chapter 12 to chapter 50, Genesis is about a dysfunctional family: Abraham's family, traced through three generations, down to the death of Jacob. What you see in the story is God's grace to this one flawed family, God's grace dealing with the dysfunctional relations of these dysfunctional people. And God's grace triumphs in the end in the lives of Abraham and Isaac and Jacob, and of Joseph and his brothers as well. By seeing God's grace to this family, we can find hope for our own.

One of the things you see most gloriously here is the many-sidedness of the grace God shows — the grace that forgives and the grace that forbears, the grace that helps and the grace that holds, the grace that renews and the grace that restores — as family members fumble and stumble and make mistakes and relationships go wrong. Our God is a God of great grace. If you feel that you are a victim of dysfunctional or broken family relationships, there is much to encourage and help you in this story.

The story of this dysfunctional family began with God's selecting Abraham and saying, "I will make of you a great nation . . . and in you all the families of the earth shall be blessed" (Genesis 12:2-3). We are inheritors of that blessing through Jesus Christ our Savior, and it is in the presence of Christ with the power of Christ at hand to help us that we can study this family's story. If perchance it becomes painful because it reminds you of dysfunction in your own family, remember that our Savior forbears and forgives and restores. And Christians are always and only disciples of Jesus Christ; we live day by day through being forgiven, and we couldn't live a single day without being forgiven.

Never Beyond Hope

THE CHURCH AND THE GOSPEL

To those sanctified in Christ Jesus, called to be saints
together with all those who in every place
call upon the name of our Lord Jesus Christ.

1 CORINTHIANS 1:2

The thing that all the New Testament books are consciously *about* is the work of God in Christ. New Testament teaching is kerygmatic, in the sense of being, first to last, exposition and application of the gospel of redeeming love. The doctrine of the church belongs as part of this exposition.

This reflects ultimately the God-centeredness of the Bible. If we view the Bible from the standpoint of its narrative, as a *drama*, we have to acknowledge the Triune God as author, producer, and chief performer. Or if we see the Bible as a *message*, "God's Word written," we have to recognize God himself as its source, subject, and actual speaker. The Bible is about *God*—the Creator redeeming. And when it shows us the church, the substance of what it is showing us is God's work of redemption—particularly, what older divines called the *applying* of redemption.

To study the Christian life—calling, justification, sanctification conflict, preservation, glorification—is to study the applying of redemption to individuals. To study the church—its nature, notes, life, ministry, sacraments—is to study *the same subject* in its corporate aspect. The doctrine of the church is part of the doctrine of grace. Had Paul been asked the theme of his "church epistles" Colossians and Ephesians—or, for that matter, Romans and Galatians, which have as good a claim to be called "church epistles"—he would certainly have said: the grace of God in Christ.

Church should be defined as the family community of those redeemed, called, and united to God—in other words, the church is *defined in terms of the gospel*, and its nature and life should be analyzed in entire correlation to the work of God in grace as the New Testament sets forth.

Serving the People of God

WILLING ONE THING

Let us draw near with a true heart in full assurance of faith,
with our hearts sprinkled clean from an evil conscience.

HEBREWS 10:22

If in everyday speech we refer to pure hearts, we are likely only to be identifying some people as not inclined, as others are, to sexual shenanigans or to the underhand exploitation of others for personal advancement or to cruel abuse of them for some perverted self-gratification. But Kierkegaard put his finger on the deep truth of the matter when he titled one of his books *Purity of Heart Is to Will One Thing*. Jesus spelled out that truth when he said, "You shall love the Lord your God with all your *heart* and with all your *soul* and with all your *mind*" (Matthew 22:37, emphasis added). Heart, soul, and mind here are words of overlapping meaning, almost synonyms; Jesus is saying that we are to love our God with everything we have got. And he is effectively defining for us the purity of heart of which he had elsewhere said, "Blessed are the pure in heart, for they shall see God" (Matthew 5:8). Purity of heart is indeed a matter of willing one thing, namely to live every day of one's life loving God.

It is a matter of saying and meaning what the psalmist said: "There is nothing on earth that I desire besides you" (Psalm 73:25) — nothing, that is, that I would not consent to lose if adhering to God required it. Thus, it is a matter of wanting and valuing "fellowship . . . with the Father and with his Son Jesus Christ" (1 John 1:3) more than I want or value anything else in this world. And it is a matter of making knowing and loving and pleasing and praising God my life task, and of seeking to lead others into the same God-glorifying life pattern.

This is the motivational attitude that is reflected and expressed in all authentic prayer.

Praying

INSPECTING FOR CONVERSION

> *He saved us . . . according to his own mercy,*
> *by the washing of regeneration and renewal of the Holy Spirit.*
>
> TITUS 3:5

Often our thoughts about the new birth are too subjective, by which I mean not too personal (that could hardly be) but too turned in, with all our focus on the individual who believes rather than on the Christ who saves. This is bad thinking, and it produces bad results.

One of them is that our minds get possessed by a standard expectation of emotional experience in conversion (so much sorrow for sin, so much agony of search, so much excess of joy). We deduce this expectation from conversion stories known to us, perhaps starting with those of Paul, Augustine, Luther, Bunyan, Wesley, and our own, and then we use it as a yardstick for judging whether or not our contemporaries are converted. This is sad and silly. Conversion experiences, even those that are sudden and debatable (and perhaps only a minority of them are), vary too much to fit any standard expectations, and the effect of using this yardstick is that we are often found dismissing as unconverted many who show abundant signs of present convertedness, while continuing to treat as converted folk who look as if the standard experience to which they once testified has now completely worn off. The truth is, as the Puritans and Jonathan Edwards knew, no emotional state or sequence as such, no isolated experience considered on its own, can be an unambiguous index of new birth, and we shall make endless errors if we think and judge otherwise. Only a life of present convertedness can justify confidence that a person was converted at some point in his or her past.

Keep in Step with the Spirit

THE STRENGTH OF SELF-CONTROL

*He reasoned about righteousness and self-control
and the coming judgment.*

ACTS 24:25

An uncontrolled self is a deadly force. It wills to defy or ignore God and tries to take the place of God — as Eve, our foremother, and Adam after her, discovered through encounter with the serpent. Idolizing, exalting, celebrating, and indulging oneself as one's god is the root cause of all the shame, folly, decadence, and moral blindness that mark modern Western culture so ruinously. When Jesus declared that the two greatest commands are that we must love God with all of our heart, soul, strength, and mind, and love our neighbor as much as we love ourselves, both of these commands attacked this human idolatry of self in a way that shows us how we are to transcend and overcome it.

If we direct our whole being toward love of God, and if we give as much value to our neighbor as to ourselves, if not indeed more, the project of gaining control of self is well under way, and the fruit of the Spirit includes the habit of behaving in this fashion. As with gentleness, self-control operates from a position of strength. A strong understanding of oneself, a strong sense of selfhood, even of self-worth (under God's governing), is entirely proper and even necessary for fruitful life in Christ. And a self that knows itself and has embraced self-denial and given itself to God's control can become a powerful force for good. Indeed, this is the kind of gift that God asks of us through the apostle Paul: "I appeal to you therefore, brothers, by the mercies of God, to present your bodies as a living sacrifice, holy and acceptable to God, which is your spiritual worship" (Romans 12:1). This path leads deeper and deeper into the grace of self-control.

Guard Us, Guide Us

CENTRAL IN OUR GAZE

> *At the name of Jesus every knee should bow,*
> *in heaven and on earth and under the earth.*
>
> PHILIPPIANS 2:10

It is often said that God's goal in the plan of salvation is to exalt himself by exalting us whom he saves, and that is true. But the New Testament goes further, insisting that the Father's prime purpose throughout is to exalt the Son, Jesus Christ our Lord. The Son of God was and is the agent of all the Father's works in creation, providence, and grace. He is the mediator of all the goodness and mercy that has ever flowed from God to men and women. The New Testament identifies his life, death, resurrection, and enthronement as the hinge of world history, just as it depicts his throne itself as heaven's centerpiece (Revelation 4–5). As the Father loves the Son and expresses that love by honoring him in the eternal fellowship of the Trinity, so he intends that through the outworking of the plan of salvation, in which Jesus is the focal figure, "all may honor the Son, just as they honor the Father" (John 5:23).

To that end, and in direct acknowledgment of the perfection of the Son's costly obedience in making atonement for human sin, "God has highly exalted him and bestowed on him the name that is above every name" (Philippians 2:9).

I should not so focus on the Son that I forget or ignore the Father and the Spirit. Equally, however, I should not so focus on the Father or the Spirit that I fail to keep central in my gaze the unique glory of Christ, as the Father and the Spirit want me to do (John 5:23; 16:14). Both mistakes have been made in the past, and are still being made in some quarters. I have to try to avoid them, or I shall grieve my God and starve my soul.

Rediscovering Holiness

THE FINAL SURPRISE

For the Lord disciplines the one he loves,
and chastises every son whom he receives.

HEBREWS 12:6

We may think we are well on top of spiritual matters and then experience a traumatic shock that will show us up as spiritually shallow, because the first thoughts that surface after the shock will be neither scriptural nor faithful (faith-full, I mean) nor indeed rational. Instead, we may say to ourselves and perhaps to others too, "God has turned against me; he has broken his word; he has let me down; he has forgotten me; there is no hope for me now." These devastating and despairing and self-pitying notions slander God as well as crush us, and when we find them going through our minds, we shall need someone with spiritual depth and clearheadedness to put us straight.

For though our God remains a God of surprises, and though in the short term some of his surprises hurt us and take our breath away, the final surprise to which all the rest are leading is the happy surprise of more good for ourselves and others, more joy, more wisdom, more contentment, and more exultation in God, resulting from the times of trauma, than ever we thought possible.

The full fruitage of coping through Christ with experiential earthquakes and thunderbolts will be realized only in the life to come, but already those with eyes to see begin to discern it both in themselves and in others. God "disciplines us for our good, that we may share his holiness. For the moment all discipline seems painful rather than pleasant, but later it yields the peaceful fruit of righteousness to those who have been trained by it" (Hebrews 12:10-11).

Never Beyond Hope

COMING TO THE TABLE

> *Let a person examine himself, then,*
> *and so eat of the bread and drink of the cup.*
>
> 1 CORINTHIANS 11:28

I don't think we do enough teaching on the meaning of the Lord's Supper and the way to enter into eucharistic worship. And I would urge that as there must be understanding through teaching and learning, so there must be involvement. I don't think we can ever say too much about the importance of an active exercise of mind and heart at the communion service. I am sure it demands more of our minds and hearts than is demanded of us when we come to a Bible or prayer service.

Holy communion demands of us private preparation of heart before the Lord before we come to the table. We need to prepare ourselves for fellowship with Jesus Christ the Lord, who meets us in this ceremony. We should think of him both as the host at the communion table and as enthroned on the true Mount Zion referred to in Hebrews 12, the city of the living God where the glorified saints and the angels are.

We are also to learn the divinely intended discipline of drawing assurance from the sacrament. We should be saying in our hearts, "As sure as I see and touch and taste this bread and this wine, so sure is it that Jesus Christ is not a fancy but a fact, that he is for real, and that he offers me himself to be my Savior, my Bread of Life, and my Guide to glory. He has left me this rite, this gesture, this token, this ritual action as a guarantee of this grace; he instituted it, and it is a sign of life-giving union with him, and I'm taking part in it, and thus I know that I am his and he is mine forever."

Serving the People of God

PURE-HEARTED IN CHRIST

Who can say, "I have made my heart pure;
I am clean from my sin"?

PROVERBS 20:9

Who of us dare think of ourselves as pure-hearted according to the biblical description? The answer is: every regenerate Christian, every born-again believer, without a single exception. For in the new birth God re-creates our disordered, egocentric, anti-God, anti-moral hearts in such a way that the personal disposition we see perfectly embodied and expressed in the Lord Jesus' earthly life and ministry has now become *our* personal disposition at the deepest level, natural and normal to us in the sense that we know only joy, peace, and contentment as we act out what we now find our heart prompting us to do. And what is that? To behave in a Christlike way, forming habits of loving and serving God and neighbor, and resisting the promptings of sin in our spiritual system as it urges us to leave undone the active loving service that is now natural and normal to us, and to do what is now unnatural and abnormal, namely disobey God and go our way rather than his, just as we did before our hearts were changed.

Many Christians, it seems, do not appreciate what has happened to them in their new birth and are careless about obeying and pleasing God; many more have desperate struggles against long-standing sinful habits that in effect have become addictions to unrighteousness, and they often lose the battles they fight; and there are many who evidently think it does not matter whether or not one strives to perfect holiness of life. But it does! For without a purpose of holiness (purity of heart, that is) there can be no authentic praying.

Praying that is really praying presupposes an all-around commitment to Christian living — "love that issues from a pure heart and a good conscience and a sincere faith" (1 Timothy 1:5).

Praying

OUR NEW MAINSPRING

We all . . . were by nature children of wrath,
like the rest of mankind.

EPHESIANS 2:3

In life and in Scripture, the idea of "nature" means the whole of what we are (see, for example, Romans 2:14; Ephesians 2:3), and the whole of what we are is expressed in the various actions and reactions that make up our life. We were born sinners by nature, dominated and driven from the start — and most of the time unconsciously — by self-seeking, self-serving, self-deifying motives and cravings. Being united to Christ in new birth through the regenerating work of the Spirit has so changed our nature that our heart's deepest desire (the dominant passion that rules and drives us now) is a copy, faint but real, of the desire that drove our Lord Jesus. That was the desire to know, trust, love, obey, serve, delight, honor, glorify, and enjoy his heavenly Father — a multifaceted, many-layered desire for God, and for more of him than has been enjoyed so far.

The focus of this desire in Jesus was upon the Father, whereas in Christians it is upon the Father and the Son together (and the latter especially). But the nature of the desire is the same. The natural way for Christians to live is to let this desire determine and control what they do, so that the fulfilling of the longing to seek, know, and love the Lord becomes the mainspring of their life.

To walk with Christ in the path of holy discipleship is the life for which the hearts of Christians truly long. From this follows the equally momentous truth that obeying the promptings of indwelling sin (the sin that still marauds in the systems of Christians though it no longer masters their hearts) is not what they really want to do at all, for sinning is totally unnatural to them.

Rediscovering Holiness

TRUSTWORTHY, BUT INEXPLICABLE

Who are you, O man, to answer back to God?
Will what is molded say to its molder, "Why have you made me like this?"
Has the potter no right over the clay?

ROMANS 9:20-21

Scripture teaches that God, as King, orders and controls all things, human actions among them, in accordance with his own eternal purpose (see Genesis 50:20; Proverbs 16:9; 21:1; Matthew 10:29; Romans 9:20-21; Ephesians 1:11). Scripture also teaches that, as Judge, he holds every man responsible for the choices he makes and the courses of action he pursues (see Matthew 25; Romans 2:1-16; Revelation 20:11-13). Thus, hearers of the gospel are responsible for their reaction; if they reject the good news, they are guilty of unbelief. "Whoever does not believe is condemned already, because he has not believed" (John 3:18; see also Matthew 11:20-24; Acts 13:38-41; 2 Thessalonians 1:7-10).

Again, Paul, entrusted with the gospel, is responsible for preaching it; if he neglects his commission, he is penalized for unfaithfulness. "Necessity is laid upon me. Woe to me if I do not preach the gospel!" (1 Corinthians 9:16; see also Ezekiel 3:17-21; 33:7-9).

God's sovereignty and man's responsibility are taught to us side by side in the same Bible, sometimes, indeed, in the same text. Both are thus guaranteed to us by the same divine authority; both, therefore, are true. It follows that they must be held together, and not played off against each other. Man is a responsible moral agent, though he is also divinely controlled; man is divinely controlled, though he is also a responsible moral agent. God's sovereignty is a reality, and man's responsibility is a reality too.

The Creator has told us that he is both a sovereign Lord and a righteous Judge, and that should be enough for us. Why do we hesitate to take his word for it? Can we not trust what he says?

Evangelism and the Sovereignty of God

MAN OF ACCOMPLISHMENTS

*This work had been accomplished
with the help of our God.*

NEHEMIAH 6:16

An additional strength that Nehemiah displays is practical wisdom, the ability to make realistic plans and get things done. From this standpoint, Nehemiah's memoirs constitute a crash course in managerial skills. Once he has succeeded in exchanging his comfortable life as a high-level palace lackey (royal cupbearer) for the problematical role of governor of Judah, with malcontents constantly yapping at his heels as he seeks to rebuild and reorganize Jerusalem, we see him rising to the challenge of every situation with truly masterful insight and ingenuity. We watch him securing a safe-conduct and chits for building materials from the king; organizing and overseeing the building of the wall; arranging Jerusalem's defenses while the building went on; defusing discontent and averting a threatened strike within the work force; maintaining morale till the job was done; conducting tricky negotiations with both friend and foe; and finally imposing and reimposing unappreciated rules about race, temple services, and Sabbath observance. Nehemiah's headaches as top man were many, and the sanctified versatility with which he handles all these things is wonderful to watch.

And his achievements were as outstanding as his gifts. He rebuilt the ruined wall of Jerusalem in fifty-two days, when nobody else thought it could be rebuilt at all. He restored regular temple worship, regular instruction from God's law, serious Sabbath keeping, and godly family life. He was the true re-founder of Israel's corporate life after the Exile, following the relative failure to restore it during the previous hundred years. He takes his place, by right, as it seems to me, with the greatest leaders of God's people in the Bible story—with Moses and David and Paul. Nehemiah was a truly marvelous man.

A Passion for Faithfulness

AN ECUMENICAL WEAKNESS

I have made you a tester of metals among my people,
that you may know and test their ways.

JEREMIAH 6:27

A working principle of ecumenical thought is that all doctrinal views held by sizable groups within Christendom are facets and fragments of God's truth, and should therefore be regarded as, in some way, complementary to each other. The way to construct a truly catholic theology is, accordingly, to conglomerate and, as far as possible, to fuse together all these different insights.

We regard this conception as only a half-truth. And a half-truth treated as the whole truth becomes a complete untruth.

We agree that all groups within Christendom have much to learn from each other; we know that we are all prone to misunderstand the views of others in an unfavorable sense; we recognize that there is at least a grain of truth in every heresy, and that views which are partly wrong are also partly right. It is indeed important in theological discussion to bear these things in mind. But it is even more important to remember that the essential step in sound theologizing is to bring all views — one's own as well as those of others — to the touchstone of Scripture. This is a step which much ecumenical theology seems to overlook.

The truth is that it is not enough to labor at assimilating the various views to each other. Such labor may serve to promote better mutual understanding, but we are not entitled to infer from the fact that a group of people are drawing nearer to each other that any of them is drawing nearer to the truth. Our first task must be to test all the words of men by the authoritative Word of God, to receive only what Scripture endorses, and to reject all that is contrary to it. The essence of right theological method is thus reformation rather than conglomeration.

"Fundamentalism" and the Word of God

SITUATIONAL PERCEPTION OF WHAT IS BEST

By testing you may discern what is the will of God,
what is good and acceptable and perfect.

ROMANS 12:2

The will of God is the course of action in each situation that God sees as good, pleasing, and complete; the most truly and fully God-glorifying response to each set of needs and possibilities; the most biblical, faithful, and reverent option open to us each time as servants of God and of his Son Jesus Christ. It is this that God wants and helps us to discern and then carry out. We shall make the discernment, says Paul in Romans 12:2, by testing — that is, envisaging and weighing alternatives, and not letting the merely good become the enemy of the best. This means brainwork, which we should do in God's presence, looking to him for light and help; but our reliance on him will not make it any the less brainwork. Discernment of this sort is often hard and demanding, often involves research and consultation to get our facts and principles straight, which takes time and severely tries our patience. Paul is not speaking of a global supernatural disclosure of God's plan for one's whole life, but of a situational perception of what is best to do here and now for God, for others, and for oneself in terms of God's own law and value system, by which his judgments are formed.

The Greek word rendered "perfect" means not so much flawless as complete and adequate, covering all angles in the way most satisfactory to God. Our power thus to perceive God's will — our insight in testing alternatives, that is — will reflect the degree of thoroughness, love, and depth with which we have inventoried our powers of imagination and thought and lovingly consecrated them to God. Should we be lax in this, our discerning of God's will becomes deficient too.

WHAT YOU REALLY WANT

Repent and turn from all your transgressions,
lest iniquity be your ruin.

EZEKIEL 18:30

If being united with Christ has changed our nature, why do we ever sin — let alone make a habit of it, as notoriously we sometimes do? Partly because we let ourselves be deceived into supposing that giving way to this or that inordinate desire — for food, drink, pleasure, ease, gain, advancement, or whatever — is what we really want to do.

Again and again it appears that Christians are not sufficiently in touch with themselves to realize that, because of the way in which their nature has been changed, their hearts are now set against all known sin. So they hang on to unspiritual and morally murky behavior patterns, and kid themselves that this adds to the joy of their lives. Encouraged by Satan, the grand master of delusion, they feel that to give up these things would be impossibly painful and impoverishing, so though they know they should, they do not. Instead, they settle for being substandard Christians, imagining they will be happier that way. Then they wonder why their whole life seems to them to have become flat and empty.

The truth is that they are behaving in a radically unnatural way, one that offers deep-level violence to their own changed nature. In doing what they think they like, they are actually doing what their renewed heart — if they would only let it speak — would tell them that it dislikes intensely, not only because it brings guilt and shame before God but, more fundamentally, because it is in itself repulsive to the regenerate mentality. The regenerate heart cannot love what it knows God hates. So these Christians are behaving unnaturally, occupied in activities against which their own inner nature revolts. Such behavior is always bad medicine, producing sadness, tension, and discontent, if not worse.

Rediscovering Holiness

HIS MERCY FOR ALL

When God saw what they did, how they turned
from their evil way, God relented of the disaster
that he had said he would do to them, and he did not do it.
JONAH 3:10

The prophet Jonah proclaimed Nineveh's imminent destruction, saying nothing about the possibility of mercy. But God moved in their hearts. "The people of Nineveh believed God. They called for a fast and put on sackcloth" (Jonah 3:5). The king himself called for repentance, saying, "Who knows? God may turn and relent . . . so that we may not perish" (verse 9). And God did relent.

Jonah, wanting Nineveh destroyed, was disgusted, but he should not have been.

Whenever you feel hostile to anybody or any group of people, however badly they may have behaved toward you, stop and remember, and say to yourself: "God made them, as God made me. God loves them, as God loves me. If they turn to Christ, they'll be forgiven, as I am forgiven. It's not my part to cherish hostility toward them when my Savior-God has shown such wonderful redemptive love toward sinful me."

This is an element in the Christian mindset that you learn in experience, to love your enemies as well as your friends and to desire God's best for the one category as well as the other. Loving your neighbor includes enemies as well as friends. It takes all of life for some of us to learn it. Some perhaps never do. Some perhaps are slow to realize their need to learn it. But we all must learn it.

The story of revival in Nineveh rubs our noses in the fact that God is supremely glorified when he shows himself merciful — even to those who have acted as his enemies. The Lord Jesus on his cross was praying, "Father, forgive them, for they know not what they do" (Luke 23:34). To be merciful to enemies and wrongdoers, and to desire and seek their welfare, is in truth central to the real Christian life.

Never Beyond Hope

THE SORTING-OUT PRAYER

Thus says the Lord G<small>OD</small>,
Is it to inquire of me that you come?
E<small>ZEKIEL</small> 20:3

When we talk to parents and friends about our anxieties and problems, looking to them for help, they often have to take over leadership in the conversation in order to give it a meaningful shape that our own higgledy-piggledy minds have denied it. We all know what it is to have been pouring out our troubles in full flood and to be pulled up by "Wait a minute; let's get this straight. Now tell me again about so-and-so. . . . Tell me how you felt about it. . . . Then what's the problem?" Thus they sort us out.

We need to see that the Lord's Prayer is offering us model answers to the series of questions God puts to us to shape our conversation with him. Thus: "Who do you take me for, and what am I to you?" (*Our Father in heaven.*) "That being so, what is it that you really want most?" (*The hallowing of your name; the coming of your kingdom; to see your will known and done.*) "So what are you asking for right now, as a means to that end?" (*Provision, pardon, protection.*) Then the "praise ending" answers the question "How can you be so bold and confident in asking for these things? (*Because we know you can do it, and when you do it, it will bring you glory!*) Spiritually, this set of questions sorts us out in a most salutary way.

Sometimes when we pray, we feel there is nobody there to listen and are tempted to think that our feelings tell us the truth. What finally dispels this temptation, under God, is a fresh realization (Spirit-given, for sure) that God is actually questioning us in the way described, requiring us to tell him honestly how we think of him and what we want from him and why.

Praying the Lord's Prayer

WHAT IS REVIVAL?

Restore us again, O God of our salvation,
and put away your indignation toward us!
PSALM 85:4

Revival is *God renewing the church*. Revival is a work of restoring life (that is what the word *revive* means), and it is the people of God who are the subjects of it. It is a social corporate thing. God revives not just the Christian, but the church, and then the new life overflows from the church for the conversion of outsiders and the renovation of society.

Revival is *God turning away his anger from the church*. For God's people to be impotent against their enemies is a sign that God is judging them for their sins. The cry for revival springs from the sense of judgment; the coming of revival is God's comforting of his people and restoring them after judgment.

Revival is *God manifesting himself to his people* — visiting them, coming to dwell with them, pouring out his Spirit on them, quickening their consciences, showing them their sins, and exalting Christ in their eyes in his saving glory. In times of revival, there is a deep awareness of God's presence and an inescapable sense of being under his eye; spiritual things become overwhelmingly real and the truth of God becomes overwhelmingly powerful, both to wound and to heal. Christians become fearless in witness and tireless in labor for their Savior's glory. The manifesting of God's gracious presence awakens them out of sleep and energizes them to serve their Lord in a quiet, unprecedented way.

Revival, lastly, is *God making known the sovereignty of his grace*. Revival is entirely a work of grace, for it comes to churches that deserve only judgment; and God brings it about in such a way as to show that his grace is entirely sovereign in it, and human plans and schemes have had nothing to do with it.

Serving the People of God

A REASON TO KNEEL

Oh come, let us worship and bow down;
let us kneel before the LORD, our Maker!

PSALM 95:6

Some people suppose that when we pray, we are twisting God's arm, as if we are somehow getting onto the throne of the universe, so that we can say to God, "*My* will be done." They think that because they are praying earnestly, whatever they ask for will happen, and the only obstacle to it happening would be if they were not praying earnestly enough. That, however, is a superstitious and mistaken idea. When Jesus says to his disciples, "Ask whatever you wish, and it will be done for you" (John 15:7), he qualifies his invitation by adding controls: they must be abiding in him and his words in them, and the request must be "in his name," that is, one that he endorses, and "according to his will," that is, fitting in with the cosmic plan for the good of his people and others (John 14:13; 15:16; 1 John 5:14).

When we pray, it is not for us to suppose that we twist God's arm or are in any way managing the situation. We aren't. We should learn to think of our praying as less a means of getting from God what we want than as the means whereby God gives us the good things that he purposes to give but that we are not always in a fit condition to receive. God intends all along to give these good things, but he waits to be asked so that we will properly value the gift when it comes, and our hearts will be turned in gratitude and renewed trust to the one who gave.

It is no accident that Christians down the centuries have typically prayed on their knees. In kneeling, the body reminds the mind that God (not the person praying) is in charge.

Praying

OUR COVENANT BOOK

He remembers his covenant forever,
the word that he commanded, for a thousand generations.

PSALM 105:8

The Word of God is not properly understood till it is viewed within a covenantal frame.

The biblical revelation, which is the written Word of God, centers upon a God-given narrative of how successive and cumulative revelations of God's covenant purpose and provision were given and responded to at key points in history. The backbone of the Bible, to which all the expository, homiletical, moral, liturgical, and devotional material relates, is the unfolding in space and time of God's unchanging intention of having a people on earth to whom he would relate covenantally for his and their joy. The story that forms this backbone of the Bible has to do with man's covenant relationship with God first ruined and then restored.

The unifying strands that bind together the books of the Bible are (1) the one covenant promise, sloganized as "I will be your God, and you shall be my people" (Jeremiah 7:23), which God was fulfilling to his elect all through his successive orderings of covenant faith and life; (2) the one messenger and mediator of the covenant, Jesus Christ the God-man, prophet and king, priest and sacrifice, the Messiah of Old Testament prophecy and New Testament proclamation; (3) the one people of God, the covenant community, the company of the elect, whom God brings to faith and keeps in faith, from Abel, Noah, and Abraham through the remnant of Israel to the worldwide New Testament church of believing Jews and Gentiles; and (4) the one pattern of covenant piety, consisting of faith, repentance, love, joy, praise, hope, hatred of sin, desire for sanctity, a spirit of prayer, and readiness to battle the world, the flesh, and the Devil in order to glorify God. Every book of the Bible in effect asks to be read in terms of these unities.

Celebrating the Saving Work of God

THE LORD JESUS, OR JEEVES?

It has been granted to you that for the sake of Christ you should not only believe in him but also suffer for his sake.

PHILIPPIANS 1:29

When our thoughts about the new birth are too subjective, another bad result is that in our evangelistic presentations Christ appears not as the center of attention and himself the key to life's meaning, but as a figure — sometimes a very smudgy figure — brought in as the answer to some present egocentric questions of our own: How may I find peace of conscience? Peace of heart and mind under pressure? Happiness? Joy? Power for living? The necessity of faithful discipleship to Jesus, and the demands of it, are not stressed (some even think that as a matter of principle they should not be), and so the cost of following Jesus is not counted. In consequence, our evangelism reaps large crops of still unconverted folk who think they can cast Jesus for the role of P. G. Wodehouse's Jeeves, calling him in and making use of him as Savior and Helper, while declining to have him as Lord. These folk become deadwood in our churches, if they do not drift away entirely.

Such evangelism also brings in great numbers who, misled by the glowing one-sidedness of our message, have assumed that Christ can be relied on to shield those who are his from all major trouble. This group experiences traumatic upsets — traumatic because they expected the opposite. The nurture that leaves Christians with false expectations of that kind and with no resources save the stiff upper lip for coping when trouble strikes, is defective to the point of cruelty. Where do these expectations come from? It seems plain that the salesmanlike man-centeredness of so much of our evangelism, cracking up the benefits and minimizing the burdens of the Christian life, is one root cause to which they ought to be traced.

Keep in Step with the Spirit

ALWAYS GOOD

> *Give thanks to the LORD, for he is good,*
> *for his steadfast love endures forever.*
>
> PSALM 136:1

God's sovereign redemptive love is one facet of the quality that Scripture calls God's goodness (Psalm 100:5; Mark 10:18), that is, the glorious kindness and generosity that touches all his creatures and that ought to lead all sinners to repentance. Other aspects of this goodness are the mercy or compassion or pity that shows kindness to persons in distress by rescuing them out of trouble and the long-suffering, forbearance, and slowness to anger that continue to show kindness toward persons who have persisted in sinning. The supreme expression of God's goodness is still, however, the amazing grace and inexpressible love that show kindness by saving sinners who deserve only condemnation: saving them, moreover, at the tremendous cost of Christ's death on Calvary.

God's faithfulness to his purposes, promises, and people is a further aspect of his goodness and praiseworthiness. Humans lie and break their word; God does neither. In the worst of times it can still be said, "His mercies never come to an end . . . great is your faithfulness" (Lamentations 3:22-23). Though God's ways of expressing his faithfulness are sometimes unexpected and bewildering, looking indeed to the casual observer and in the short term more like unfaithfulness, the final testimony of those who walk with God through life's ups and downs is that "not one word has failed of all the good things that the LORD your God promised concerning you. All have come to pass for you; not one of them has failed" (Joshua 23:14). God's fidelity, along with the other aspects of his gracious goodness as set forth in his Word, is always solid ground on which to rest our faith and hope.

Concise Theology

THE SECRET OF SENSING GOD'S CALL

For I am the LORD your God. Consecrate yourselves
therefore, and be holy, for I am holy.

LEVITICUS 11:44

Consecration and repentance are one. Repentance is a change of mind issuing in a change of life. Since practical atheism, which disregards God, is natural to fallen human beings, godliness has to be founded on repentance from the start. Repentance means a right-face turn and a quick march in the direction opposite to that in which we were going before. The original direction was the path of self-service, in the sense of treating yourself as God, the supreme value, and gratifying yourself accordingly. The new direction is a matter of saying good-bye to all that and embracing the service of God instead.

So consecration is repentance renewed and sustained, just as repentance is consecration begun; and here lies the secret of sensitivity to God's call. Paul's familiar summons in Romans 12:1-2 to consecration and transformation leads on to the not-so-familiar point that this is in truth the pathway to discerning God's will, which otherwise you are likely to miss.

> I appeal to you therefore, brothers, by the mercies of God, to present your bodies as a living sacrifice, holy and acceptable to God. . . . Do not be conformed to this world, but be transformed by the renewal of your mind, that by testing you may discern what is the will of God. (Romans 12:1-2)

The fact we must face is that impenitent and unconsecrated Christians will be out of earshot when God calls them to service, just as they are out of line already, without being fully aware of it, in regard to the imperatives of daily Christian living. Apathy and sluggishness with regard to ordinary obedience bring deafness when God calls to special service.

A Passion for Faithfulness

STUDY THE BIBLE BIBLICALLY

Stand by the roads, and look,
and ask for the ancient paths, where the good way is;
and walk in it, and find rest for your souls.
JEREMIAH 6:16

Although accused of being die-hard traditionalists who have set their faces against modern biblical scholarship, evangelicals do not wish to put the clock back to the days before scientific study began. What they desire is that modern Bible study should be genuinely scientific — that is to say, fully biblical in its method; their chief complaint against modern criticism is that it so often fails here.

It is true that evangelicals call for a return to principles of Bible study which have a long history in the Christian church, and for some revision of modern critical methods in the light of them. But that is not because these principles are traditional; it is because they are biblical. There is certainly an arrogant, hide-bound type of traditionalism, unthinking and uncritical, which is carnal and devilish. But there is also a respectful willingness to take help from the church's past in order to understand the Bible in the present, and such traditionalism is spiritual and Christian.

Moreover, it is this attitude alone that makes possible real progress in theology, for theology goes forward only by looking back — back through the church's heritage of teaching to Jesus Christ and his apostles.

Evangelicals seek to be traditionalists of this kind. If they lapse from the second kind of traditionalism to the first, they become bad evangelicals, and their fall discredits not their principles, but themselves. No doubt there are bad evangelicals, and the critics of "fundamentalism" have probably met them. Their false impressions may therefore be due simply to mistaking the nature of the genuine evangelical outlook.

"Fundamentalism" and the Word of God

GUIDED BY GOD'S COMMANDS

Go therefore and make disciples . . . teaching them to observe
all that I have commanded you.

MATTHEW 28:19-20

The Bible displays God as one who commands and humans as required to practice obedience. This presentation starts in Eden, where God, having in effect established his covenant with the first human by the words he had already spoken, commanded the man, saying he must not eat fruit from the tree of the knowledge of good and evil (Genesis 2:16-17). Later, God "appeared to Abram and said to him, 'I am God Almighty; walk before me, and be blameless, that I may make my covenant between me and you . . . to be God to you and to your offspring after you. . . . You shall keep my covenant'" (Genesis 17:1-2,7,9). The Ten Commandments, given as part of the covenant-confirmation at Sinai, were and are basic to biblical religion (Exodus 20:1-17; Deuteronomy 5–6; see also Mark 10:17-19; Romans 13:9). At the close of Ecclesiastes we read, "Fear God and keep his commandments, for this is the whole duty of man" (12:13). Paul adds that "neither circumcision counts for anything nor uncircumcision, but keeping the commandments of God" is what counts (1 Corinthians 7:19). John writes, "For this is the love of God, that we keep his commandments. And his commandments are not burdensome" (1 John 5:3).

Little stress is laid these days, even in the church, let alone in our supposedly Christian culture, on the reality and authority of God's commands. But the fundamental dimension of being Christian people guided by God is that we labor to learn his commandments as he has revealed them and to live by them in faithful obedience just as consistently as we possibly can. When, one day, we have to give an account of ourselves to God, it will be important for us to be able to say with truth that we sought to keep all his commandments throughout our Christian lives.

Guard Us, Guide Us

CURL UP SMALL

> *When pride comes, then comes disgrace,*
> *but with the humble is wisdom.*
>
> PROVERBS 11:2

Of his own ministry, in relation to that of the Lord Jesus, John the Baptist declared, "He must increase, but I must decrease" (John 3:30). Of our lives as believers, something similar has to be said. Pride blows us up like balloons, but grace punctures our conceit and lets the hot, proud air out. The result is that we shrink, and end up seeing ourselves as less — less nice, less able, less wise, less good, less strong, less steady, less committed, less of a piece — than ever we thought we were. We stop kidding ourselves that we are persons of great importance. We settle for being insignificant and dispensable.

Off-loading our fantasies of omnicompetence, we start trying to be trustful, obedient, dependent, patient, and willing in our relationship to God. We give up our dreams of being greatly admired for doing wonderfully well. We begin teaching ourselves unemotionally and matter-of-factly to recognize that we are not likely to ever be much of a success by the world's standards. We bow to events that rub our noses in the reality of our own weaknesses, and we quietly look to God for strength to cope. This is part, at least, of what it means to answer our Lord's call to childlikeness.

The Scottish scholar James Denney once said that it is impossible at the same time to leave the impression both that I am a great preacher and that Jesus Christ is a great Savior. In the same way it is impossible at the same time to give the impression both that I am a great Christian and that Jesus Christ is a great Master. So the Christian will practice curling up small, as it were, so that in and through him or her the Savior may show himself great.

Rediscovering Holiness

THE MARTHA SIDE, THE MARY SIDE

Martha, Martha, you are anxious and troubled about many things,
but one thing is necessary. Mary has chosen the good portion,
which will not be taken away from her.

LUKE 10:41-42

In Luke 10, Jesus is not rebuking Martha for not sitting beside Mary and letting him teach her the way Mary is being taught. Had hostess Martha behaved that way, there never would have been any food on the table for any of them. Jesus approves of Martha being out in the kitchen making a meal, just as he approves of Mary sitting at his feet and learning from him. Situational responsibilities are not to be ignored for the sake of devotional exercises, any more than vice versa.

Some have read Jesus' words as if Mary is being justified for not helping in the kitchen and Martha is being condemned for making the meal. I don't believe that either of those implications is right. As part of God's will and of Christ's wish for her as his disciple, Mary was called from time to time to give Martha proper help in the house — but not at this particular moment. And Martha was called, once her hostess responsibilities were finished, to join Mary as Jesus' pupil, listening to his word and benefiting thereby. But Jesus was obliged to rebuke Martha because by her attitude both to Mary and to him, Martha had let herself down.

We ought to have space in our lives for doing what Mary did: spending time with the Word of God, learning from Jesus by listening to him in worship and adoration — which is the most important activity of our life. But let us also learn that from time to time we are to be doing the practical helpful things that are needed around the house and around the church. Some of us skimp the Martha side of our discipleship, just as some skimp the Mary side. Skimping either way is wrong.

Never Beyond Hope

OUR HIGHEST HOPE ON EARTH

So the word of the Lord continued to increase
and prevail mightily.

ACTS 19:20

When the church experiences revival, *God comes down,* in the sense that he gives a deepened awareness of his inescapable presence as the Holy One, mighty and majestic, dwelling among his people. Revival experience begins with being forced to realize, like Isaiah in the temple, the intimacy of the supernatural and the closeness of the living God.

God's Word comes home, in the sense that the Bible, its message, and its Christ reestablish the formative and corrective control over faith and life that is theirs by right. In revival the divine authority of the Bible is realized afresh.

God's purity comes through, as God uses his Word to quicken consciences. The perverseness, ugliness, and guiltiness of sin are seen and felt with new clarity, and the depth of one's own sinfulness is realized as never before, so that the forgiveness of sins becomes the most precious truth.

God's people come alive. Joyful assurance of salvation, conscious communion with a living Savior, a spirit of prayer and praise, a readiness to share with other believers, and a love that reaches out to all in need are the characteristic marks of revived Christians. Inhibitions dissolve, and a new forthrightness in utterance and initiative in action take their place.

Outsiders come in, drawn by the moral and spiritual magnetism of what goes on in the church.

Scripture shows, and history confirms, that revival is a distinctive and recurring work of God whereby he has again and again revitalized flagging churches and through the consequent evangelistic outflow vastly extended the kingdom of Christ. Revival, therefore, is the highest hope for the church on earth until the Lord comes to take us home.

Serving the People of God

BIBLE-SOAKED

Oh how I love your law!
It is my meditation all the day.

PSALM 119:97

The Eastern way of meditation is to concentrate on objects (for instance, stones) or abstract patterns or notions such as one hand clapping. But the Christian way, or ways rather (there are several), concentrates mind and heart, spiritual eyes and ears, on God as he has shown himself to us in Holy Scripture.

We should first soak ourselves in the Bible, so that our minds are awash with it — or, as C. H. Spurgeon put it, till our blood is "bibline."

Second (and this goes with the first), traverse the Bible in terms of overall images of its nature as God's communication to us, and of our due response as recipients of his messages. Images affect our imagination, and imagination is the midwife, if not the mother, of insight. See the Bible as a *library* of sixty-six books of very different kinds, written over something like a millennium and a half, yet meshing with each other to tell a single story. Explore the Bible as a *landscape* of human life in all its many modes and relationships, both with and without God. Read the Bible as a *letter* from its divine Author to every reader. Value the Bible as your *listening post* in enemy-occupied territory, which is what the world is. Rate all that Scripture says about living in faith and obedience as *law*, in the sense of the Hebrew word torah — the kind of instruction, authoritative, yet affectionate, that children in a good family receive from a parent. Reckon the Bible to be your *light* in a world of darkness surrounding you. And cling to your Bible as a *lifeline*; hold on like grim death to its promises and its assurance that almighty God always knows what he is doing on all occasions.

Praying

HIGHEST, RICHEST RELATIONSHIP

You refuse to come to me
that you may have life.
JOHN 5:40

The New Testament views knowing your Maker as your Father, and yourself as his child and heir, as the highest privilege and richest relationship of which any human being is capable. Not to know God in this way is, by contrast, to be in a state of fallenness and guilt, cut off from God's life, exposed to his judgment, and under demonic control, whence flows only misery. But this is every man's natural condition.

Can it be changed? Jesus said, "I am the way, and the truth, and the life. No one comes to the Father except through me" (John 14:6). It is as if he said, Yes, a filial relationship to God is possible through relating to me and my mediatorial ministry — though not otherwise. For sonship of God, in the sense that guarantees mercy and glory, is not a fact of natural life, but a gift of supernatural grace. "To all who did receive him, who believed in his name, he gave the right to become children of God" (John 1:12). The doctrine of the bestowal of sonship is part of the proper exposition of 1 Peter 3:18: "Christ . . . suffered once for sins, the righteous for the unrighteous, that he might bring us to God." The only begotten Son, who died for us, presents us to his Father as his brothers and sisters; thus we are adopted. But to this privilege unbelievers remain strangers, to their own infinite loss.

One who shrugs off the gospel gains nothing from the mediation of Jesus Christ.

The spiritually unadopted lack a God they can call Father. There is only one way they can find him as Father, and that is by coming to terms with — accepting terms already announced by — God's Son, Jesus Christ, the living Lord.

Celebrating the Saving Work of God

HEAVEN STARTS NOW

The promised Holy Spirit . . . is the guarantee
of our inheritance.
Ephesians 1:13-14

I hold that the Holy Spirit is the "guarantee" or "earnest" (Ephesians 1:14, kjv) of our inheritance in this precise sense: that by enabling us to see the glory of Christ glorified, and to live in fellowship with him as our Mediator and with his Father as our Father, the Spirit introduces us to the inmost essence of the life of heaven. At the heart of our thoughts about heaven is the actual relationship with the Father and the Son that is perfected there. It is of this that the Spirit's present ministry to us is the first installment. By means of the ministry to us of the indwelling Spirit, heaven begins for us here and now, as through Christ and in Christ we share in his resurrection life. "You have died," writes Paul to believers, "and your life is hidden with Christ in God" (Colossians 3:3). This "life" is eternal life, heaven's life, which never starts anywhere else but here.

Along with this, I hold that praying in the Spirit (Ephesians 6:18) includes four elements. First, it is a matter of seeking, claiming, and making use of access to God through Christ (Ephesians 2:18). Then, the Christian adores and thanks God for his acceptance through Christ and for the knowledge that through Christ his prayers are heard. Third, he asks for the Spirit's help to see and do what brings glory to Christ, knowing that both the Spirit and Christ himself intercede for him as he struggles to pray for rightness in his own life (Romans 8:26-27,34). Finally, the Spirit leads the believer to concentrate on God and his glory in Christ with a sustained, single-minded simplicity of attention and intensity of desire that no one ever knows save as it is supernaturally wrought.

Keep in Step with the Spirit

WHERE WE FIND AUTHORITY

All authority in heaven and on earth
has been given to me.
MATTHEW 28:18

Jesus Christ constituted Christianity a religion of biblical authority. He is the church's Lord and Teacher, and he teaches his people by his Spirit through his written Word. As the Westminster Confession puts it,

> The Supreme Judge, by which all controversies of religion are to be determined, and all decrees of councils, opinions of ancient writers, doctrines of men, and private spirits, are to be examined, and in whose sentence we are to rest, can be no other but the Holy Spirit speaking in the Scripture.[2]

Subjection to the authority of Christ involves subjection to the authority of Scripture. Anything short of unconditional submission to Scripture, therefore, is a kind of impenitence; any view that subjects the written Word of God to the opinions and pronouncements of men involves unbelief and disloyalty toward Christ. Types of Christianity which regard as authoritative either tradition or reason are perversions of the faith, for they locate the seat of authority not in the Word of God, but in the words of men.

Evangelicalism, however, seeking as it does to acknowledge in all things the supremacy of Scripture, is in principle Christianity at its purest and truest. We would not, indeed, deny that evangelicals often fall below their principles, just as those in other types of Christianity are themselves sometimes inconsistent and give to Scripture a position of authority which their principles would seem to disallow. Evangelicalism has no monopoly of gifts and graces. But that is not the point here. What we insist on is that the evangelical principle of authority is authentically Christian.

"Fundamentalism" and the Word of God

GUIDED BY GOD'S BOOK

Make me know the way I should go,
for to you I lift up my soul.
PSALM 143:8

When people read the Bible, or at least brood on what they know of its teaching, even when they are beginners who do not as yet know the sacred text well, messages from God come through to set their hearts in a way that is both startling and encouraging. Bible readers sense again and again that God is speaking significantly to them, "for teaching, for reproof, for correction, and for training in righteousness" (2 Timothy 3:16). Arousing the expectation that this will happen and teaching Christians that each time they turn to Scripture they should have in their heart and mind the prayer "Open my eyes, that I may behold wondrous things out of your law" (Psalm 119:18) are key elements in good discipleship training. Certainly, the closer and more thorough one's acquaintance with the Bible as a whole, the more clearly and fully will one discern its wisdom for living the whole of one's life. But God is gracious and good; he meets people where they are, and often showers beginner Christians with insights for their personal guidance as they take their first hesitant steps in forming the habit of daily Bible reading.

Sometimes biblical imperatives and narratives of godly and ungodly conduct speak directly to our own situation and show us directly how we should behave, but more often the decisions we have to make seem circumstantially quite distant from anything we read in the Bible; so how may we find God's guidance in those cases? The clue lies in the fact that Scripture contains God's commands, which establish parameters and set limits for all our behavior. As God's promises give direction to all our hopes, so God's commands direct us in establishing attitudes and policies with regard to every aspect and department of our life activities.

Guard Us, Guide Us

EVERYDAY REPENTANCE

Return to the LORD your God, for he is gracious and merciful,
slow to anger, and abounding in steadfast love.

JOEL 2:13

When Peter writes, "Grow in the grace and knowledge of our Lord and Savior Jesus Christ" (2 Peter 3:18), and when Paul speaks of growing into Christ (Ephesians 4:15) and rejoices that the Thessalonians' faith is growing (2 Thessalonians 1:3), what they have in view is a progress into personal smallness that allows the greatness of Christ's grace to appear. The sign of this sort of progress is that they increasingly feel and say that in themselves they are nothing and God in Christ has become everything for their ongoing life.

Christians are called to a life of habitual repentance, as a discipline integral to healthy holy living. The first of Luther's ninety-five theses, nailed to the Wittenberg church door in 1517, declared, "When our Lord and Master Jesus Christ said, 'Repent' [Matthew 4:17], he willed that the whole life of believers should be one of repentance." Philip Henry, a Puritan who died in 1696, met the suggestion that he made too much of repentance by affirming that he hoped to carry his own repentance up to the gate of heaven itself.

In speaking of habitual repentance, I do not mean to imply that repentance can ever become automatic and mechanical, as our table manners and our driving habits are. It cannot. Every act of repentance is a separate act and a distinct moral effort, perhaps a major and costly one. Repenting is never a pleasure. Always, in more senses than one, it is a pain, and will continue so as long as life lasts. No, when I speak of habitual repentance, I have in mind the forming and retaining of a conscious habit of repenting as often as we need to — though that, of course, means every day of our lives.

Rediscovering Holiness

OVERCOMING OUR UNBELIEF

*Martha, the sister of the dead man, said to him, "Lord, by this time
there will be an odor, for he has been dead four days."*

JOHN 11:39

At Lazarus's tomb, Martha didn't intend to be an obstructionist, but she
was. Her instincts for taking charge and deciding the best thing to do
were driving her. She was not allowing her true faith to teach her submission to Jesus' wisdom and power.

You and I can learn from her. Truth is wisdom. Our Lord, our Savior,
knows what he is doing with our lives. We must not try to control him.
We must overcome our mistrust of him. I say *mistrust* because your heart,
like mine, still has sin and unbelief prowling around inside it, and the
instinct of unbelief will try to lead us to hold out on our Lord. Ever since
the Garden of Eden, unbelief of what God says has opened the door to
further sins of every kind. We've got to learn to recognize unbelief for
the monstrous anti-God gesture it is and to say no to it when we find
ourselves drawn to any form of noncompliance with any divine word. We
cannot doubt that Martha realized afterward how foolish and faithless she
had been to try to stop Jesus from having the stone rolled away.

You and I have also had experiences in which, through timidity and
mistrust, we shrank back from letting our Lord Jesus have his way without qualification in our lives, and we've learned by experience that this
is not the fruitful path to tread. We can be sure that we're going to face
further situations in which we'll be tempted to shrink back in just the
same way. Let the example of Martha teach us the perversity of doing this
when our hand is in Christ's hand, and he, our Savior and Master, is leading us home through this world to glory.

Never Beyond Hope

SOMETHING NEW

Behold, I am doing a new thing;
now it springs forth, do you not perceive it?
ISAIAH 43:19

In all its respects, renewal of the Christian people is a theme for humble, penitent, prayerful, faith-full exploration before the Lord, with a willingness to change and be changed, and if necessary to be the first to be changed, if that is what the truth proves to require. To absorb ideas about renewal ordinarily costs nothing, but to enter into renewal could cost us everything we have, and we shall be very guilty if, having come to understand renewal, we then decline it. John Calvin once declared that it would be better for a preacher to break his neck while mounting the pulpit if he did not himself intend to be the first to follow God. In the same way, it would be better for us not to touch the study of renewal at all if we are not ourselves ready to be the first to be renewed.

The renewal of the church is in essence a spiritual and supernatural matter, a work of the Holy Spirit enriching our fellowship with the Father and the Son. Renewal is precisely God doing a new thing, and though every work of renewal has basic qualities or dimensions in common with every other, we must recognize that the contours of the cultures within which the church has from time to time lost its vitality, and also the contours of that loss in itself, have varied; which means that it is not safe for us to assume that the outward forms and phenomena of revival in this or any future age will always prove to have exact historical precedents. At this point sad mistakes in judgment have been made in the past, and I suspect are being made by some in the present. Let us strive not to be of their number.

Serving the People of God

BOTH DISTANT AND NEAR

The God who made the world and everything in it,
being Lord of heaven and earth. . . .
Yet he is actually not far from each one of us.

ACTS 17:24,27

One function of praise prayer — the prayer of praise — is that our spoken words declare who God is and our relationship to him. Why does God invite our praise? In part it is because as we praise God in prayer, we verbally declare and inwardly realize, every time, that "he is God and we are not." Hearing words of praise to God from our own lips helps us recognize our distance from God. Yet paradoxically these prayers of praise also take us into his presence. As we proclaim both to God and to each other how far he is above us and beyond us in his wisdom, power, and purity, a sense of his closeness to us is repeatedly given.

Psalm 95 illustrates this. It starts by celebrating God as our Creator, "the Rock of our salvation," whose hand holds "the depths of the earth," the "mountain peaks," and "the sea . . . for he made it," and the entire landscape since "his hands formed the dry land" (verses 1,4-5, NIV). What is the appropriate response to such a God? For us to draw near, but not with any sense of pride. We are to "sing for joy to the LORD" (verse 1, NIV), but how? The psalmist calls for a praise shaped by humility, so that we acknowledge even with our bodies our great distance from this almighty Creator God: "Come, let us bow down in worship, let us kneel before the LORD our Maker" (verse 6, NIV). To bow and to kneel are universal, time-honored gestures of acknowledging greatness in some form. Praise prayer acknowledges our dependence on the God who is great in power and wisdom, when we are neither. Our mental attitude, our posture, our very words must ever declare the difference and distance between God and us.

Praying

IN THE SUNSHINE

You were at that time separated from Christ . . .
having no hope and without God in the world.

EPHESIANS 2:12

Hopelessness is hell — literally. As God made us to fulfill a function and attain an end (for "man's chief end is to glorify God, and to enjoy him for ever"[3]), so he made us creatures for whom hope is life, and whose lives become living deaths when we have nothing good to look forward to. As the deep hopelessness of post-Christian Western culture tightens its chilly grip on us, we are made to feel this increasingly, and so can better appreciate the infinite value for life today of that exuberant, unstoppable, intoxicating, energizing hope of joy with Jesus in the Father's presence forever, which is so pervasive a mark of New Testament Christianity.

Whereas those without Christ are without God and without hope, living already in a dusk of the spirit that is destined to grow darker and colder, Christians are in the sunshine, endlessly rejoicing in "Christ Jesus our hope" (1 Timothy 1:1). The inescapable alternatives are *false* hope (Marxism? Spiritism? Happiness through having things? Endless good health? — false hopes, every one), or else *no* hope (total pessimism, inviting suicide), or else *Christian* hope, the electrifying knowledge of "Christ in you, the hope of glory" (Colossians 1:27). It is a pity that so little is heard these days about what has been called "the unknown world with its well-known inhabitant" to which the New Testament teaches Christians to look forward; for, as the hymn says: "The Lamb is all the glory of Emmanuel's land,"[4] and declaring that glory is part of what it means to relate the New Testament witness to the person and place of Jesus Christ.

Celebrating the Saving Work of God

CONFIDENT INTELLECTUALLY

> *Since we have such a hope,*
> *we are very bold.*
>
> 2 CORINTHIANS 3:12

It is the distinctive mark of evangelicalism to keep itself loyal to Christ by constantly measuring, correcting, and developing its faith and life by the standard of the Word of God. Evangelicalism at its best has shown itself to be intellectually virile, church-centered in its outlook, vigorous in social and political enterprise, and a cultural force of great power. The careers and achievements of such men as John Calvin, John Owen, John Wesley, Jonathan Edwards, and Abraham Kuyper reflect something of the breadth of evangelicalism when it is true to itself.

The evangelical is not afraid of facts, for he knows that all facts are God's facts; nor is he afraid of thinking, for he knows that all truth is God's truth, and right reason cannot endanger sound faith. He is called to love God with all his mind; and part of what this means is that, when confronted by those who, on professedly rational grounds, take exception to historic Christianity, he must set himself not merely to deplore or denounce them, but to out-think them. It is not his business to argue men into faith, for that cannot be done; but it is his business to demonstrate the intellectual adequacy of the biblical faith and the comparative inadequacy of its rivals, and to show the invalidity of the criticisms that are brought against it.

This he seeks to do, not from any motive of intellectual self-justification, but for the glory of God and of his gospel. A confident intellectualism expressive of robust faith in God, whose Word is truth, is part of the historic evangelical tradition. If present-day evangelicals fall short of this, they are false to their own principles and heritage.

"Fundamentalism" and the Word of God

APPRAISING YOUR REPENTANCE

To the Gentiles also God has granted
repentance that leads to life.
ACTS 11:18

Repentance signifies going back on what one was doing before and renouncing the misbehavior by which one's life or one's relationship was being harmed. In the Bible, repentance is a theological term, pointing to an abandonment of those courses of action in which one defied God by embracing what he dislikes and forbids.

Repenting in the full sense of the word is possible only for Christians, believers who have been set free from sin's dominion and made alive to God. Repenting in this sense is a fruit of faith, and as such a gift of God. The process, alliteratively, includes the following:

1. Realistic recognition that one has disobeyed and failed God, doing wrong instead of doing right.
2. Regretful remorse at the dishonor one has done to the God one is learning to love and wanting to serve.
3. Reverent requesting of God's pardon, cleansing of conscience, and help to not lapse in the same way again.
4. Resolute renunciation of the sins in question, with deliberate thought as how to keep clear of them and live right for the future.
5. Requisite restitution to any who have suffered material loss through one's wrongdoing.

An alternative alliteration (as if one were not enough!) would be: (1) discerning the perversity, folly, and guilt of what one has done; (2) desiring to find forgiveness, abandon the sin, and live a God-pleasing life from now on; (3) deciding to ask for forgiveness and power to change; (4) dealing with God accordingly; (5) demonstrating, whether by testimony and confession or by changed behavior or by both together, that one has left one's sin behind.

Rediscovering Holiness

A NEW RENAISSANCE

You shall love the Lord your God . . .
with all your mind.
MATTHEW 22:37

Few men have so vigorously expressed the rational superiority of evangelicalism over its modern rivals as J. G. Machen, who died in 1937. Liberalism, he maintained, is really superficial and can be shown to be so; the true remedy against liberalism is for men to think not less (as some fundamentalists seemed to suppose) but more — more deeply, more vigorously, more clearly, and more critically.

Paradoxically, Machen analyzed the basic cause of the current eclipse of evangelicalism as the radically anti-intellectual outlook of the twentieth century. The very quantity of books to read and facts to master with which the twentieth-century man is confronted encourages him to think broadly and superficially about much, but hinders him from thinking deeply and thoroughly about anything.

In 1925 Machen wrote,

> We believe that our cause will come to its rights again only when youth throws off its present intellectual lethargy . . . and recovers some genuine independence of mind. . . . We are seeking in particular to arouse youth from its present uncritical repetition of current phrases into some genuine examination of the basis of life; and we believe that Christianity flourishes not in the darkness, but in the light. A revival of the Christian religion . . . will not be the work of man, but the work of the Spirit of God. But one of the means which the Spirit will use, we believe, is an awakening of the intellect. . . . The new Reformation, in other words, will be accompanied by a new Renaissance; and the last thing in the world that we desire to do is to discourage originality or independence of mind.[5]

"Fundamentalism" and the Word of God

NEVER IN THE GRIP OF BLIND FORCES

The lot is cast into the lap,
but its every decision is from the LORD.

PROVERBS 16:33

Clear thinking about God's involvement in the world process and in the acts of rational creatures requires complementary sets of statements, thus: a person takes action, or an event is triggered by natural causes, or Satan shows his hand — yet God overrules. This is the message of the book of Esther, where God's name appears nowhere. Again: things that are done contravene God's will of command — yet they fulfill his will of events (Ephesians 1:11). Again: humans mean what they do for evil — yet God who overrules uses their actions for good (Genesis 50:20; Acts 2:23). Again: humans, under God's overruling, sin — yet God is not the author of sin (James 1:13-17); rather he is its judge.

The nature of God's "concurrent" or "confluent" involvement in all that occurs in his world as he makes his will of events come to pass — without violating the nature of things, the ongoing causal processes, or human free agency — is a mystery to us, but the consistent biblical teaching about God's involvement is as stated above.

Of all the evils that infect God's world (moral and spiritual perversity, waste of good, and the physical disorders and disruptions of a spoiled cosmos), it can summarily be said: God permits evil; he punishes evil with evil; he brings good out of evil; he uses evil to test and discipline those he loves; and one day he will redeem his people from the power and presence of evil altogether.

The doctrine of providence teaches Christians that they are never in the grip of blind forces (fortune, chance, luck, fate); all that happens to them is divinely planned, and each event comes as a new summons to trust, obey, and rejoice, knowing that all is for one's spiritual and eternal good (Romans 8:28).

Concise Theology

INFORMED LEADER

As soon as I heard these words I sat down and wept and mourned for days,
and I continued fasting and praying before the God of heaven.

NEHEMIAH 1:4

Nehemiah received communication about people's needs, and that was one of the significant items that combined to lead Nehemiah from his routine palace job to the hazards of being Jerusalem's governor, builder, morale-raiser, events organizer, and spiritual leader — a killing role he could hardly have sustained had he not been sustained himself by a strong sense that God had sent him to fulfill it and was standing by him as he discharged it.

Bad news came from Jerusalem: Walls flattened, gates burned, morale at rock bottom (Nehemiah 1:3). Nehemiah had asked anxiously after the state of things in Jerusalem (verse 2) because he cared so much about the glory of God and the good of souls there; now he took note that the Jerusalem Jews were in really desperate need. It was, I think, Oswald Chambers who said that the need is not the call but the occasion for the call, and that is a wise word. There are far more needs in the church and the world than any of us has time or energy to meet, and no one is required to try to relieve them all. Nonetheless, God's call to service will be a call to meet some human need or other, and the sense of what we might and should do to serve God will crystallize in our hearts only out of knowledge of what the needs are. So we should explore the needs that surround us and collect information about them and hold them in our hearts if we want to be led to the particular ministry that God has in mind for us. Cheerful, self-absorbed Christians who fail to do this are not likely to be so led. But Nehemiah's big-hearted burden-bearing for Jerusalem sets us a different example.

A Passion for Faithfulness

A RIGHT REASON TO REACT

I write these things to you about those who are trying to deceive you.
But the anointing that you received from him abides in you,
and . . . his anointing teaches you about everything.

1 JOHN 2:26-27

We must not judge the original fundamentalists (of the early 1900s) too harshly. There is no doubt that their evangelicalism was narrowed and impoverished by their controversial entanglements. However, it was better to fight clumsily than not at all.

The fundamentalist rejection of liberalism expressed not a mere natural human reluctance to abandon an old thing, but a God-given spiritual insight into the character of the new thing. Liberalism maintained that modern literary and historical criticism had exploded the doctrine of an infallible Bible; modern science had made it impossible to believe in the supernatural as Scripture presents it; modern comparative study of religions had shown that Christianity, after all, was not unique; and modern philosophy required the dismissal of such basic biblical concepts as original sin, the wrath of God, and expiatory sacrifice as primitive superstitions. Against each of these positions sensitive Christian consciences protested, as they always will. Each position involves a denial of the apostolic gospel; therefore, Christian consciences sense at once that they are false, even before it is clear what in detail is wrong with them.

John spoke of the Christian's God-given capacity to discern denials of the gospel for what they are when he wrote, "You have been anointed by the Holy One, and you all have knowledge" (1 John 2:20). God's Spirit will not witness to a repudiation of God's Word or a perversion of Christ's gospel. Those evangelicals who reacted against liberalism so violently as to repudiate the use of reason in religion altogether were certainly wrong; the antidote for bad reasoning is not no reasoning, but better reasoning. But in that they did react, they were just as certainly right. A sound spiritual instinct guided them, and we should thank God for the tenacity with which they held their ground.

"Fundamentalism" and the Word of God

TWO SIDES OF FREEDOM

For the law of the Spirit of life has set you free in Christ Jesus
from the law of sin and death.

ROMANS 8:2

Freedom exists when not only have we been freed *from* whatever oppressed us, but we are also now enjoying the state of dignity, happiness, fulfillment, and contentment we were freed *for*. Freedom is thus two-sided. So it is when it appears today as a political ideology; so it was when God freed Israel from Egyptian captivity for *shalom* (peace and prosperity) in the Promised Land.

The same two-sidedness was implicit when the Lord Jesus Christ told those around him, "If you abide in my word, you are truly my disciples, and you will know the truth, and the truth will set you free" (John 8:31-32), just as it is implicit when Paul tells believers, "For freedom Christ has set us free; stand firm therefore" (Galatians 5:1). Jesus explains that the freedom he gives his followers as they engage with his Word is freedom from sin's dominion for life as a child of God, at home with one's Father (John 8:34-36). So freedom is a supreme gift, inasmuch as it covers both our forgiveness and acceptance (justification, adoption, and freedom from final condemnation) and also the anchoring of us in the life of enjoying, serving, and pleasing our heavenly Father. The gift thus changes both our status and our state in relation to God. Constant batterings from circumstances outwardly and fears and temptations inwardly make the life of freedom a constant struggle for us, as anchored boats are tossed and made to strain at their cables by stormy seas. But our anchor holds, our freedom remains, and our deep joy and contentment in the knowledge of being limitlessly loved by the Father, the Son, and the Holy Spirit continue within us as we labor to hold steady. This is a quality of life that only believers know.

Guard Us, Guide Us

NO SMALL SINS

As he who called you is holy,
you also be holy in all your conduct.

1 PETER 1:15

God, as Creator, has a right to prescribe how his rational creatures should behave. He has done this in his moral law, which requires us to be holy as he is holy — in our character and our conduct, in our desires, our decisions, and our delights. We are to invest all our powers in living a life of grateful worship and loyal service — a life of fidelity, uprightness, integrity, and love toward both himself and our fellow humans — a life shaped by the purpose of glorifying him through wise and skillful obedience to his revealed will. We are required in all circumstances to be honest, godly, single-minded, energetic, passionate persons who behave at all times in a Jesus-like way, with hearts aflame, heads cool, and all our wits about us. Total righteousness is called for, expressing total devotion and commitment. Nothing less will do.

The purity and uprightness of God's own character, and his judgments of value, are fixed and immutable. God cannot be other than hostile to individuals and communities that flout his law. He cannot do other than visit them sooner or later in displays of retributive judgment, so that all his rational creatures may see the glory of his moral inflexibility.

Because of God's majesty as sovereign ruler of the universe, sin (lawlessness, missing the moral mark, failing to practice righteousness with all one's heart and soul) is a major matter. Secular Western culture, which has deliberately atrophied the sense of God's majesty, finds this hard to believe, but it is so. Some sins are intrinsically greater and intrinsically worse than others — but there can be no small sins against a great God.

Rediscovering Holiness

THE BREADTH OF GOD'S PEACE

Peace I leave with you;
my peace I give to you.
JOHN 14:27

Peace (Hebrew *shalom;* Greek *eirene*) is one of the great Bible words in both the Old and New Testaments. Its overtones are always of total well-being and happiness, so that peace in English is hardly forceful enough to express it. It means, to start with, peace with God, sin forgiven, guilt gone, your person accepted. It also means peace with yourself; if God has forgiven you the grisly things you've done, you must learn to be at peace with yourself now that you're at peace with God. It means peace with your circumstances too; if the Lord of circumstances is at peace with you, you can henceforth be sure he orders and controls circumstances for your good.

"Peace be with you," the risen Jesus said to the disciples (John 20:19) — essentially meaning, "Peace with God, peace with yourself, peace with your circumstances. I bring you peace." And when he said this, we're told, "he showed them his hands and his side" (verse 20). He didn't do that to identify himself, for they already knew who he was. He did it so they would see the nail prints in his hands and the spear wound in his side and be reminded of what he'd suffered on the cross in order to make for them the peace that he was now bringing to them.

The disciples, we're told, were overjoyed when they saw the Lord among them. But then Jesus repeated his greeting: "Peace be with you" (verse 21). The very fact that he repeated it shows that it was more than a mere greeting. Repetition in Scripture, as in daily life, is for emphasis and to enforce significant meaning. It was supremely important to Jesus that the disciples should understand all that he meant when he said to them, "Peace be with you."

Never Beyond Hope

TWO ROADS TOGETHER

For though the LORD is high,
he regards the lowly.

PSALM 138:6

Knowing that our Father God is in heaven, or (putting it the other way around) that God in heaven is our Father, is meant to increase our wonder, joy, and sense of privilege at being his children and being given a hotline of prayer for communication with him. Though he is Lord of the worlds, he always has time for us; his eye is on everything every moment, yet we always have his full attention whenever we call on him. Marvelous! But have we really taken this in? There are two roads along which our minds can travel to grasp it properly.

Think first of God's greatness as the infinite and eternal Creator who "dwells in unapproachable light" (1 Timothy 6:16), apparently remote. Think of Solomon's words to him: "Behold, heaven and the highest heaven cannot contain you" (2 Chronicles 6:18). Then think of God's words through Isaiah: "For thus says the One who is high and lifted up, who inhabits eternity, whose name is Holy: 'I dwell in the high and holy place, and also with him who is of a contrite and lowly spirit'" (Isaiah 57:15). Remind yourself that this promise finds its deepest fulfillment when God becomes the Father of insignificant sinful mortals like us, sinners who are *contrite* in repentance and *humble* in fleeing by faith to Jesus for refuge.

Or, thinking of God's fatherhood, remind yourself that he is "in heaven," which means he is free from all the limitations, inadequacies, and flaws found in earthly parents, and his fatherhood is from every standpoint absolutely ideal, perfect, and glorious. Dwell on the fact that there is no better father, no parent more deeply committed to his children's welfare or more wise and generous in promoting it, than God the Creator.

Praying the Lord's Prayer

LUTHER: REFORMATION HERO

*That which was from the beginning . . . concerning the word of life —
the life was made manifest, and we have seen it, and testify to it.*

1 JOHN 1:1-2

Luther was the Father of the Reformation in the same sense in which
George Stephenson was the Father of the Railways — that is, he pioneered
the whole subsequent development. Without Luther, the gospel would
not have been recovered, nor would Christian faith and life have been
renewed, nor would there have been any evangelical leaven to work in
the upsurging life of the new European national states. There would have
been no Bucer, Tyndale, Cranmer, or Calvin, for all these were disciples of
Luther. Apart from Luther, the historical Reformation is as unintelligible
as Hamlet without the Prince.

Luther put forward the idea that whenever God means to move deci-
sively in his church, he raises up a wonder-man *(Wundermann),* a hero
(vir heroicus), a great individual leader, to be his instrument. Certainly
this principle was exemplified in Luther himself.

The phrase "the Word of God," or simply "the Word," is a key phrase
in Luther's thought. It meant to him not just the Scriptures formally, but
something wider — namely, the message and content of the Scriptures,
that is, the gospel concerning the Lord Jesus Christ, which is the sum and
substance of what God has to say to man.

Luther's constant aim was to inculcate the biblical knowledge of God,
and to this end he constantly rang the changes on the following five staple
themes: the authority of the biblical Word of God, the greatness of sin, the
graciousness of Christ, the vitality of faith, and the spiritual nature of the
church. These five themes made up the central content of "the Word" as
Luther understood it. It was in this field that all Luther's main concerns
lay. It was here that he made his abiding contribution to theology, holding
that "the Word," under God, must reform the church.

Honouring the People of God

STEPS TO REVIVAL

Your work, O LORD, do I fear. In the midst of the years revive it; in the midst of the years make it known; in wrath remember mercy.

The first step, perhaps, to the renewal of the Christian people is that leaders should begin to repent of their too-ready acceptance of too-low levels of attainment both in themselves and in those whom they lead, and should learn to pray from their hearts the simple-sounding but totally demanding prayer in Edwin Orr's chorus: *Send a revival — start the work in me.*

The second step, perhaps, is for leaders to challenge their followers as to whether they are not too much like the Laodiceans of Revelation, and whether Jesus' searing words to these latter — "You are lukewarm.... You say, I am rich, I have prospered, and I need nothing, not realizing that you are wretched, pitiable, poor, blind, and naked.... So be zealous and repent. Behold, I stand at the door and knock" (Revelation 3:16-17,19-20) — do not apply directly to themselves, here and now.

The third step, perhaps, is for us all, leaders and led together, to become more serious, expectant, and honest with each other as we look to God in our use of the means of grace — sermon and sacrament, worship and witness, praise and prayer, meditation and petition — and as we seek to make our own the psalmist's plea: "Search me, O God, and know my heart! Try me and know my thoughts! And see if there be any grievous way in me, and lead me in the way everlasting!" (Psalm 139:23-24).

Then the fourth step, perhaps, will be to trust the Holy Spirit to lead us on from there.

Does this prospect strike awe into you? It has that effect on me, but that is no justification for drawing back from it, when our need of it is so plain.

Serving the People of God

JOIN THE CHORUS

All your works shall give thanks to you, O LORD,
and all your saints shall bless you!

PSALM 145:10

C. S. Lewis took notice of the kinds of people who praised (anything) and those who simply didn't; he observed that "cranks, misfits and malcontents praised least," while the "humblest, and at the same time most balanced and capacious minds, praised most."[6] He noticed that lovers seemed to praise most of all, and to delight in drawing others into their praise of the beloved one.

We see this in Psalm 96:1 where the psalmist invites all creation to "sing to the LORD a new song; sing to the Lord, all the earth!" He calls on the seas to roar, the heavens to be glad, the fields to exult, the trees to sing for joy, the earth to tremble and rejoice, and all people to "declare his glory among the nations" (verse 3). What a chorus of praise! We would have to be spiritually deaf not to want to join in such a symphony. We may never have thought of what we call the natural order, the created world around us, as our partner in praise; maybe it is time we did.

The fact is that in praise, as in other matters, companionship quells inhibitions and creates incentives. As the discipline of bodily exercise becomes easier to give your heart to in a gym, where you are surrounded by a whole crowd of people exercising already, and as sticking to a prescribed diet becomes easier when everyone at the table is on the diet with you, so you are swept up into personal praise much more quickly and powerfully when you realize that praise — from angels, from glorified saints, and from all creation — is going on all 'round you.

Praying

THE DEEPEST PROBLEMS

And he asked them, "But who do you say that I am?"
Peter answered him, "You are the Christ."

MARK 8:29

Dietrich Bonhoeffer, writing from Nazi imprisonment, posed for enquiry the theme "who Christ really is, for us today."[7] His question could be taken as a plea for Christological novelty, as if only a novel account of Jesus Christ could catch men's ears today. Certainly, in our time much Christological novelty has been provided—in the reduced Jesus of humanitarianism, the revolutionary "political Christ" drawn by some, and the concept of Christ as a principle of evolution which we find in Teilhard de Chardin, to look no further. But the Christ of whom the modern West, with its vast problems and growing alienation from its Christian roots, most needs to hear is precisely the Christ of the New Testament and of historic Christian teaching—the incarnate Son of God who lives, reigns, judges, and saves; the Christ who prompts the confession, "My Lord and my God!" (John 20:28).

For what, after all, are the world's deepest problems? They are what they always have been: the individual's problems—the meaning of life and death, the mastery of self, the quest for value and worthwhileness and freedom within, the transcending of loneliness, the longing for love and a sense of significance and for peace.

Society's problems are deep, but the individual's problems go deeper; Solzhenitsyn, Dostoevsky, or Shakespeare will show us that, if we hesitate to take it from the Bible. And Jesus Christ the God-man, who is the same yesterday, today, and forever, still ministers to these problems in the only way that finally resolves them. "Him we proclaim," said Paul, "warning everyone and teaching everyone with all wisdom, that we may present everyone mature in Christ" (Colossians 1:28). It is for us, Christ's twenty-first-century servants, to proclaim him still, for the same end.

Celebrating the Saving Work of God

THE INWARD JOURNEY

May the God of peace himself sanctify you completely,
and may your whole spirit and soul and body be kept blameless
at the coming of our Lord Jesus Christ.

1 THESSALONIANS 5:23

The journey of our lives is a double journey. There is an outward journey into external confrontations, discoveries, and relationships, and there is an inner journey into self-knowledge and the discovery of what for me as an individual constitutes self-expression, self-fulfillment, freedom, and contentment within. For the Christian, the outward journey takes the form of learning to relate positively and purposefully to the world and other people — that is, to all God's creatures — for God the Creator's sake, and the inward journey takes the form of gaining and deepening our acquaintance with God the Father and with Jesus the Son, through the mighty agency of the Holy Spirit.

Now in the hustling, bustling West today, life has become radically unbalanced, with education, business interests, the media, the knowledge explosion, and our go-getting community ethos all uniting to send folk off on the outward journey as fast as they can go, and with that to distract them from ever bothering about its inward counterpart. In Western Christianity the story is the same, so that most of us without realizing it are nowadays unbalanced activists, conforming most unhappily in this respect to the world around us. Like the Pharisees, who were also great activists (Matthew 23:15!), we are found to be harsh and legalistic, living busy, complacent lives of conforming to convention and caring much more, as it seems, for programs than for people. When we accuse businessmen of selling their souls to their firms and sacrificing their integrity on the altars of their organizations, it is the pot calling the kettle black. Perhaps there are no truths about the Spirit that Christian people more urgently need to learn today than those that relate to the inner life of fellowship with God.

Keep in Step with the Spirit

COMMITTED TO INERRANCY

I the LORD speak the truth;
I declare what is right.

ISAIAH 45:19

Though the confession of inerrancy does not help us to make the literary judgments that interpretation of Scripture involves, it commits us in advance to harmonize and integrate all that we find Scripture teaching, without remainder, and so makes possible a theological grasp of Christianity that is altogether believing and altogether obedient. Without this commitment, no such grasp of Christianity is possible. So despite its negative form, this disputed word fulfills in evangelical theology a most positive, enriching, and indeed vital function.

Why is the confession of inerrancy important? It is important that we should embrace a fully believing method of biblical interpretation and theological construction, and it is equally important that the fellowship of evangelical theologians — and all theologians, as far as possible — should be based on a common commitment to such a method.

And let it be added that this point is a substantial rather than a verbal one. Words are not magic; each man has a right to use them in the way that best expresses what he has in mind. So if we think the word *inerrant* tainted through its past associations with literary insensitiveness and an improper rationalism in interpreting Scripture, and so prefer not to use it but to say *infallible* instead, that is our privilege. But what, in any case, our colleagues in evangelical theology have a right to expect from us is a clear demonstration in both word and action that we are nonetheless committed to what may be called the "inerrancy method." Given this, we shall be able to walk together, whatever words we elect to use — not, however, otherwise.

Honouring the Written Word of God

TAKING OUR CALLING SERIOUSLY

Necessity is laid upon me.
Woe to me if I do not preach the gospel!
1 CORINTHIANS 9:16

Nehemiah felt himself under compulsion, once God's call to him was clear, and tackled the task of restoring Jerusalem with single-minded, wholehearted enthusiasm. He focused his goals, planned thoroughly for their accomplishment, worked hard for long hours, dealt patiently and wisely with each problem as it arose, resisted distractions, and refused to be discouraged at any stage. He took his calling seriously and fulfilled it gloriously, and in this he is a model to all who serve in God's church.

Do we start where he started, with the same passion for God's glory, the same burden of concern and distress when we contemplate the broken-down state of God's church? Are we willing to learn to pray for the struggling communities of God's people as Nehemiah prayed, and to accept with Nehemiah any change of circumstances and any risk involved in rendering the needed service?

Are we proceeding as he proceeded, putting God first, others second, and ourselves last as we seek to fulfill our call to ministry? Do we act in a disinterested way, not seeking ease or personal advantage but simply making it our business to love and serve our Lord by loving and serving our neighbor, leaving it to the Lord to look after us as we concentrate on the tasks he has given us?

And when God is pleased to use us as a means of good for his people, shall we with Nehemiah give him the glory and the praise for what has happened and decline to take the credit for ourselves? Shall we humbly acknowledge the gracious hand of our God upon us, and the gracious kindness of our God in using us, rather than conceitedly supposing that the result is due to our own skills, talents, wisdom, gifts, and experience?

A Passion for Faithfulness

ORIGINAL CHRISTIANITY

It is the Spirit who gives life; the flesh is of no avail.
The words that I have spoken to you are spirit and life.

John 6:63

Evangelicalism is the oldest version of Christianity; theologically regarded, it is just apostolic Christianity itself. Ideally, the evangelical would choose no title for himself but "Christian." If, however, he must use a further label, he accepts "evangelical" as one which by its very form bears witness to his belief that this form of Christianity is loyal to the nature and content of the Evangel.

The evangelical does not mean by this that he regards as unimportant the theological legacy of all the past centuries of the church's life. He recognizes that, through the guiding activity of the Holy Spirit who indwells the church to lead it into truth, there has been a legitimate and necessary advance in elucidating the contents and plumbing the depths of the revelation which God once for all delivered to the saints and deposited in the Scriptures. The evangelical will value the work of the church fathers in defining the doctrines of the Trinity and incarnation, of Anselm and the Reformers in drawing out the doctrine of atonement, of Luther in expounding justification by faith, of Calvin and the Puritans in tracing out the work of the Holy Spirit, and of all others, past and present, who have contributed to the church's doctrinal heritage. He will acknowledge also that the church now sees further into the political and social implications of the gospel than it did at the beginning, having been repeatedly forced to reexamine these implications as society has grown more complex. But he insists that this whole process of growth in understanding, which still goes on, must be controlled and judged by that very Word of God which it seeks to elucidate, so as to ensure that it serves simply to display, and not in any way to alter, the distinctive doctrines of Christianity.

"Fundamentalism" and the Word of God

WHAT WOULD JESUS DO?

*Whoever says he abides in him ought to walk
in the same way in which he walked.*

1 JOHN 2:6

To move toward wisely applying Scripture is to grasp the true wavelength and inner unity of the moral law. Often God's law is thought of as a series of separate commands, and because it is the nature of the human mind to concentrate on one thing at a time, we easily slip into pursuing one virtue, or practicing one imperative, at the expense of others. The truth, however, is not only that all our doings should express love to God and neighbor, as Jesus insisted, but also that Jesus himself, the embodiment of all the virtues, must be our model, for he is God's law incarnate. Law-keeping is in truth imitation of Christ, and vice versa: The two are one. The implications are far-reaching.

To start with, the law is not telling us simply to do this or that, but rather to aim at being a certain type of person who behaves in a certain way. Ingenious Bible teachers have expressed this by saying that as all the promises of God to Christians analyze as beatitudes (assurances of blessings to come) so all the commands of God to Christians analyze as "be-attitudes" (calls for Christlike character) — that blend of virtues that are all to be expressed in Christlike behavior. Within this frame, the question "What would Jesus do?" becomes pertinent over and over again.

Imitating Christ means more than merely aping him as comedians do when they impersonate politicians; for as the qualities of vivid imagination and sometimes breathtaking ingenuity and creativity appeared in Jesus' dealings with the many people, and many sorts of people, whom his heart was loving all along, so we need to ask him to enable us to show the same qualities as we deal with others on his behalf.

Guard Us, Guide Us

CONTINUAL REASON FOR CONTINUING REPENTANCE

You shall love the Lord your God with all your heart
and with all your soul and with all your mind.

MATTHEW 22:37

God's purpose in our creation, as in our new creation, is that we should be holy. Therefore, moral casualness and unconcern as to whether or not we please God is in itself supremely evil. No expressions of creativity, heroism, or nice-guy behavior can cancel God's displeasure at being disregarded in this way.

God searches our hearts as well as weighing our actions. For this reason, guilt for sin extends to deficiencies in our motives and our purposes, as well as in our performances. God observes and assesses our reasons for action as thoroughly as he does the actions themselves. In one sense, indeed, he focuses more attention on the heart—the thinking, reacting, desiring, decision-making core and center of our being—than he does on the deeds done, for it is by what goes on in our hearts that we are most truly known to him.

God is good and gracious to all his creatures, and he has so loved the world as to give his only Son to suffer on the cross for our salvation. Active thanksgiving that expresses thankfulness of heart is the only proper response, and is in fact one of God's permanent requirements. Unthankfulness and unlove toward him are as culpable in his sight as are any forms of untruthfulness and unrighteousness in dealing with our fellow humans. Transgressing the first and greatest commandment has to be the first and greatest sin (Matthew 22:34-40).

God promises to pardon and restore all who repent of their sin. Because sin, both of omission and of commission, in motive, aim, thought, desire, wish, and fantasy even if not in outward action, is a daily event in Christians' lives (you know this about yourself, don't you?), regular repentance is an abiding necessity.

Rediscovering Holiness

THE BLESSING OF BELIEVING

Unless I see in his hands the mark of the nails,
and place my finger into the mark of the nails,
and place my hand into his side, I will never believe.

JOHN 20:25

What we see in Jesus' ministry to Thomas in John 20:27-29 is quite simply overwhelming kindness. Jesus was gentle with Thomas. The Savior's way of helping him to assurance about the ongoing reality of his resurrection life is a model of how today he works in the lives of many coming to faith out of total spiritual darkness.

Thomas had painted himself into a corner, and Jesus affirmed him by taking him at his word, meeting him where he was, and saying in effect, "If it is going to help you to finger the wounds in my body, then finger them. Only stop acting the unbeliever, Thomas. Acknowledge the reality of my rising. Believe."

We're not told whether Thomas actually did what Jesus was inviting him to do. Maybe he stood, bowed, even knelt; we don't know. What is apparent, though, is that Thomas was absolutely broken. "My Lord and my God!" he said (verse 28). He made the perfect confession of faith, the fullest and clearest that is found anywhere in the Gospels. Thomas's confession stated in effect, "Yes, Lord Jesus, I believe! Jesus, I take you afresh as all that you are, my Lord and my God, Author of my being, Savior of my soul. Here and now I vow to be yours, Lord."

Jesus responded by saying to Thomas, "Have you believed because you have seen me?" (verse 29). Then he spoke the last and in one way the most wonderful of all the beatitudes, for it leads us into the life and enjoyment of the rest of the beatitudes, which without Thomas-like faith you and I will never know: "Blessed are those who have not seen and yet have believed" (verse 29).

Never Beyond Hope

CALVIN: ECHOER OF GOD'S WORD

> *Great is the LORD, and greatly to be praised,*
> *and his greatness is unsearchable.*
>
> PSALM 145:3

The amount of misrepresentation to which John Calvin's theology has been subjected is enough to prove his doctrine of total depravity several times over. How we hate those who squelch our pride by demolishing our self-righteousness and exalting God's sovereign grace!

Calvin was, in fact, the finest exegete, the greatest systematic theologian, and the profoundest religious thinker that the Reformation produced. Bible-centered in his teaching, God-centered in his living, and Christ-centered in his faith, he integrated the confessional emphases of Reformation thought — by faith *alone,* by Scripture *alone*, by grace *alone*, by Christ *alone*, for God's glory *alone* — with supreme clarity and strength. He was ruled by two convictions written on every regenerate heart and expressed in every act of real prayer and worship: God is all and man is nothing, and praise is due to God for everything good. Both convictions permeated his life, right up to his final direction that his tomb be unmarked and there be no speeches at his burial, lest he become the focus of praise instead of his God. Both convictions permeate his theology too.

Calvin was a biblical theologian — not a speculator, but an echoer of the Word of God. Also, Calvin was a *systematic* theologian — not a taker of haphazard soundings, but an integrator of earlier gains. The final version of Calvin's *Institutes of the Christian Religion* (1559), in which the consistent teaching of the sixty-six canonical books is topically spelled out, is a systematic masterpiece, one that has carved out a permanent niche for itself among the greatest Christian books.

The bodies of four centuries of Calvinists lie moldering in the grave, but Calvinism goes marching on.

Honouring the People of God

TO RELIGHT THE FIRE

*Do not quench
the Spirit.*

1 THESSALONIANS 5:19

Why do we know so little of the power of the Spirit in our churches today? Both Testaments tell us that to enjoy a rich outpouring of the Holy Spirit is a characteristic privilege of the New Testament church. To lack the Spirit's powerful working in a church's life is therefore by biblical standards unnatural, just as heresy is; and this unnatural state of affairs can be accounted for only in terms of human failure.

The New Testament has a phrase for the failure in question: We may, it says, *quench* the Spirit by resisting or undervaluing his work, and by declining to yield to his influence (Acts 7:51; Hebrews 10:29). The image is of putting out a fire by pouring water on it. Note that in 1 Thessalonians 5:19 the words "do not quench the Spirit" are flanked, on the one hand, by exhortations to follow the good, and to rejoice, pray, and give thanks at all times, and on the other hand, by warnings against disregard for prophecies (the messages of God, however and by whomsoever declared), failure to discriminate, and evil involvement. It is natural to suppose that these things were connected in Paul's mind, and he wished his readers to see that heedlessness of these exhortations and warnings at any point was likely to quench the Spirit, not only in the Christian's personal life but also in the common life of the church.

While one may effectively put out a fire by dousing it, one cannot start it burning again simply by no longer pouring water; it has to be lighted afresh. Similar, when the Spirit has been quenched, it is beyond man's power to undo the damage he has done; he can only cry to God in penitence to revive his work.

Serving the People of God

DELIGHTING IN THE DUTY OF PRAISE

Sing the glory of his name;
give to him glorious praise!
PSALM 66:2

Praise, in Scripture, appears both as a duty and also as an expression of joy and delight. In everyday life, the word *duty* regularly signifies an unwelcome obligation, like paying taxes, so our delight is ordinarily found in something other than what we think of as the doing of our duty. But we are fallen creatures, and for sinners as such, duty, which is first God-centered and then others-centered, can never be a delight. And to the extent that original sin still shapes us, praise of God, though an acknowledged duty, will not be a delight.

But Christians, believers in Jesus Christ, are regenerate — born again, new creatures, dead and risen with Christ, alive to God in Christ. We have been changed, supernaturally renovated in the core of our personal being, and the nature of this change, which has been brought about through union with the risen Christ, is that now our hearts have become in a decisive way a transcript of his. In the days of his flesh, as the gospel stories show, the incarnate Lord was controlled — we might even say, driven — by the life-unifying desire to please, honor, exalt, and glorify his heavenly Father in all things by obedient service, and his joy was to do his Father's will and magnify his Father's name always and everywhere — in other words, to live a life that expressed worship and adoration of the one who had sent him to earth. That same desire, with the Son and the Spirit joined to the Father as its object, is now implanted in Christian hearts. The desires of the renewed heart are now dominant within, and that means that the duty of praise will increasingly become a delight — indeed, the supreme delight — of our life.

Praying

CHRISTIANITY IS CHRIST

Grow in the grace and knowledge of our Lord and Savior Jesus Christ.
To him be the glory both now and to the day of eternity. Amen.

2 PETER 3:18

Whatever cultural shifts take place around us, whatever sociopolitical concerns claim our attention, whatever anxieties we may feel about the church as an institution, Jesus Christ crucified, risen, reigning — and now in the power of his atonement, calling, drawing, welcoming, pardoning, renewing, strengthening, preserving, and bringing joy — remains the heart of the Christian message, the focus of Christian worship, and the fountain of Christian life. Other things may change; this does not.

Thus it was from the beginning. "Jesus is Lord" (Romans 10:9) was, by scholarly consensus, the first Christian confession of faith. Invoking and worshipping "our Lord and Savior Jesus Christ" (2 Peter 1:11) alongside the Father (his and ours) was the primary form of Christian devotion. Celebrating Jesus as "our great God and Savior" (Titus 2:13) was a basic focus of early Christian doctrinal teaching. "Believe in the Lord Jesus, and you will be saved" (Acts 16:31) was the original Christian message to the world. The apostles' staple themes were reconciliation with God and pardon of sin through Christ's atoning death; adoption and new birth into God's family through regeneration in Christ and co-resurrection with Christ; life in the power of the Spirit of Christ; and hope of everlasting glory in the presence of Christ.

When the hymnwriter Henry Francis Lyte wrote, "O how blest the congregation / Who the gospel know and prize," it was of the gospel of salvation from sin and death through Jesus Christ that he was thinking — the gospel that finds us lost and broken and leaves us "ransomed, healed, restored, forgiven." Thus Lyte anchored himself in the center of the Christian mainstream, glorying in "the old, old story / Of Jesus and his love." That is the place where today's Christians, with you and me among them, should be anchored also.

Celebrating the Saving Work of God

SPIRITUAL GIFTS FROM CHRIST

Since you are eager for manifestations of the Spirit,
strive to excel in building up the church.

1 CORINTHIANS 14:12

Our thinking about spiritual gifts is shallow. We say, rightly, that they come from the Spirit; Paul calls them "manifestations of the Spirit" (1 Corinthians 12:4-11). However, we go on to think of them in terms either of what we call "giftedness" (human ability to do things skillfully and well) or of supernatural novelty as such (power to speak in tongues, to heal, to receive messages straight from God to give to others, or whatever). We have not formed the habit of defining gifts in terms of Christ, the head of the body, and his present work from heaven in our midst. In this we are unscriptural. At the start of 1 Corinthians, Paul gives thanks "because of the grace of God that was given you *in Christ Jesus* . . . so that you are not lacking in any spiritual gift" (1:4,7, emphasis added). Paul's wording makes it clear that spiritual gifts are given in Christ; they are enrichment received from Christ. First Corinthians 12 assumes this Christ-oriented perspective that 1:4-7 established. It is vital that we should see this, or we shall be confusing natural with spiritual gifts to the end of our days.

Nowhere does Paul or any other New Testament writer define a spiritual gift for us, but Paul's assertion that the use of gifts *edifies* ("builds up," 1 Corinthians 14:3-5,12,17,26; see also Ephesians 4:12,16) shows what his idea of a gift is. For Paul, it is only through Christ, in Christ, by learning Christ, and by responding to Christ that anyone is ever edified. For Paul, edification is precisely a matter of growing in the depth and fullness of one's understanding of Christ and all else in relation to him and in the quality of one's personal relationship with him, and it is not anything else.

Keep in Step with the Spirit

CLEARLY SPOKEN, CLEARLY AUTHORITATIVE

God spoke to our fathers by the prophets,
but in these last day she has spoken to us by his Son.

HEBREWS 1:1-2

Christianity from the start has been based on the biblical conviction that in and through words spoken to and by prophets and apostles, and supremely by Jesus Christ, the Word made flesh, God has spoken, in the precise sense of using language to tell people things. To assume, with the liberals, that the biblical vocabulary of divine speech is metaphorical, in the sense of signifying nonverbal communication, or is simply the spontaneous discernment by sensitive souls of spiritual values, is incorrect.

God's word of direct self-disclosure to individuals in history — to Noah, Abraham, Moses, Jonah, Elijah, Jeremiah, Peter, Paul, and others — was directly authoritative for their own belief and behavior. God having spoken to them, they were bound to believe what he had told them, knowing it to be true (because he is a God of truth), and bound also to do all that God had told them to do.

The same direct divine authority attached to all that God prompted his chosen spokesmen — prophets, wisdom writers, poets, apostles, and Jesus Christ himself — to declare orally to others in his name. Their authority was not just that of deep human religious insight. Primarily and fundamentally, their authority was that of the God whose truth they were relaying in the verbal form to which he himself had led them. Paul declares that "we [apostles] have received . . . the Spirit who is from God, that we might understand the things freely given us by God. And we impart this in words . . . taught by the Spirit" (1 Corinthians 2:12-13). Verbal inspiration conferred direct divine authority on the words God's messengers spoke, requiring their hearers to receive what they heard as from God himself. The same authority belongs to what they wrote, in the books that now constitute our canonical Scriptures.

Honouring the Written Word of God

ETERNAL WELFARE AT STAKE

*Who hindered you
from obeying the truth?*
GALATIANS 5:7

The problem of authority is the most fundamental problem that the Christian church ever faces. This is because Christianity is built on truth — that is to say, on the content of a divine revelation. Christianity announces salvation through faith in Jesus Christ, in and through whom that revelation came to completion; but faith in Jesus Christ is possible only where the truth concerning him is known.

The New Testament tells us that God has made provision for the communication of this saving truth. He entrusted to the apostles, and through them to the whole church, a message from himself which conveys it. This is called "the word of God," "the word of the Lord," or sometimes simply "the word" (Acts 4:31; 1 Thessalonians 1:8; Acts 8:4). Its contents denominate it "the word of Christ," "the word of the cross" (Colossians 3:16; 1 Corinthians 1:18); and its divine origin guarantees it to be "the word of truth" (Ephesians 1:13).

Men come to faith through receiving this word, and such faith is specifically described as "obeying the truth" (Galatians 5:7). "The faith of God's elect" goes with "their knowledge of the truth" (Titus 1:1). But if this truth is rejected or perverted, faith is overthrown (2 Timothy 2:18) and men come under the power of a lie (2 Thessalonians 2:10-12), with terrible results.

Modern man, skeptical and indifferent as he is to dogmatic pronouncements about the supernatural order, may find it hard to take seriously the idea that one's eternal welfare may depend on what one believes; but the apostles were sure that it was so. Theological error was to them a grim reality, as was the spiritual shipwreck which comes in its wake.

"Fundamentalism" and the Word of God

WISDOM'S WALK

Look carefully then how you walk,
not as unwise but as wise.

EPHESIANS 5:15

Seeking to live in wisdom, to be wise in the way we make our decisions and plan our lives, is one aspect of biblical obedience. Scripture requires us to have this concern. In Paul's letter to the Colossians, we find him saying, "Conduct yourselves *wisely* toward outsiders, making the best use of the time" (4:5, emphasis added). Then he adds some exposition of that thought in the next verse: "Let your speech always be gracious, seasoned with salt, so that you may know how you ought to answer each person" (verse 6). The verb "to answer" here simply means how we respond to what outsiders say, whatever that is. Speech, the way we speak to each other and to those outside our circle, is the great index of whether we are *living* in wisdom.

"Conduct yourselves wisely" has been rendered "Walk in wisdom." *Walk* is a word Paul regularly uses for "live," as did the Old Testament writers before him. This image of putting one foot in front of another as you move steadily from your starting point toward your destination is in fact a brilliant picture of how human life should be lived, and Paul has already used it in a weighty way. Earlier in the letter to the Colossians he had said, "As you received Christ Jesus the Lord, so *walk* in him, rooted and built up in him and established in the faith, just as you were taught, abounding in thanksgiving" (2:6-7, emphasis added). Those great words are in truth the central message of Colossians; they establish the frame within which learning to behave wisely in our relation to other people is now being set. Wise behavior is one particular aspect of what it means to walk in Christ.

Guard Us, Guide Us

CONTINUOUS CONVERSION

> *Repent therefore, and turn again . . . that times of refreshing*
> *may come from the presence of the Lord.*
> ACTS 3:19-20

Growth in holiness cannot continue where repenting from the heart has stopped.

For many Christians, there is a moment of conscious conversion, and this "sudden" experience is a great blessing. There has to be for all of us some form of entry into the converted state, in which none of us is found by nature. It is a happy thing to be able to recall how one's own entry into that state took place. But there is more: Following on from "the hour I first believed," conversion must now become a lifelong process. *Conversion* has been defined as a matter of giving as much as you know of yourself to as much as you know of God. This means that as our knowledge of God and ourselves grows (and the two grow together), so our conversion needs to be repeated and extended constantly.

To think in these terms is to catch up with John Calvin, who in his *Institutes of the Christian Religion* set forth a concept of conversion as the practice of lifelong active repentance, the fruit of faith, springing from a renewed heart:

> The whole of conversion to God is understood under the term "repentance.". . . The Hebrew word for "repentance" is derived from conversion or return, the Greek word from mind and purpose: and the thing itself fits each derivation, for the essence of it is that departing from ourselves we turn to God, and putting off our former mind we put on a new one. So I think repentance may well be defined as a true conversion of our life to God, issuing from pure and heartfelt fear of him, and consisting in the mortification of our flesh and old man and the vivification of the Spirit.[8]

Exactly!

Rediscovering Holiness

FROM COLLAPSE TO STABILITY

*I have written briefly to you, exhorting and declaring
that this is the true grace of God. Stand firm in it.*
1 PETER 5:12

At the end of his life, Simon Peter writes two letters to churches. It's striking to see that stability and steadiness are prominent ideals enforced in both. As we look back over Peter's career and think again of the denial, the foolishness, and the failures, we can hardly be surprised that now, as a leader and teacher and apostle seeking to build up the saints, fulfilling a truly apostolic ministry, he is concerned about stability.

Near the end of 1 Peter he writes,

Be sober-minded; be watchful. Your adversary the devil prowls around like a roaring lion, seeking someone to devour [just as once he had come after Peter himself]. Resist him, firm in your faith, knowing that the same kinds of suffering are being experienced by your brotherhood throughout the world. And after you have suffered a little while, the God of all grace, who has called you to his eternal glory in Christ, will himself restore, confirm, strengthen, and establish you. (5:8-10)

That's his call to stability in 1 Peter.

Now hear him again in the closing section of 2 Peter, after he speaks of "ignorant and unstable" people (3:16) who twist the Scriptures:

You therefore, beloved, knowing this beforehand, take care that you are not carried away with the error of lawless people and lose your own stability. But grow in the grace and knowledge of our Lord and Savior Jesus Christ. To him be the glory both now and to the day of eternity. Amen. (verses 17-18)

Having experienced something of the spiritual disaster and personal wretchedness into which the Devil can plunge the unstable, Simon Peter the pastor is understandably anxious to make sure no one else lapses or collapses that way.

Never Beyond Hope

BAXTER: CALM CONCENTRATION ON GOD

Be still,
and know that I am God.

PSALM 46:10

Richard Baxter was a great and holy man, naturally gifted and super-naturally sanctified beyond most; humble, patient, realistic, and frank to an unusual degree. He was an endlessly active man whose soul was at rest in God all the time he labored in prayer Godward and in persuasion manward. The poise of his spirit is all the more impressive when we recall that of all the great Puritan sufferers, none had a heavier load of pain and provocation to endure than did he.

Baxter appears throughout his ministry as the epitome of single-minded ardor in seeking the glory of God through the salvation of souls and the sanctification of the church. To contemplate the independence, integrity, and zeal with which the public Baxter fulfilled his ministry is fascinating and inspiring; but even more fascinating and inspiring is contemplation of the private Baxter, the man behind the ministry, who in an elaborate self-analysis, written when he was fifty, opens his heart about the changes he sees in himself since his younger years in Christian service. He delineates a progress from raw zeal to ripe simplicity, and from a passionate narrowness that was somewhat self-absorbed and majored in minors to a calm concentration on God and the big things, with a profound capacity to see those big things steadily and whole.

Baxter's brand of spiritual straightforwardness in the service of the Triune God regularly affects Christians; it makes one seek to be energetic and businesslike in one's discipleship and service, just as he was, and gives one a conscience about aimlessness and casualness and spiritual drift. For this reason alone it is good for us to remember Baxter. I say to all: Get to know Baxter, and stay with Baxter. He will always do you good.

Honouring the People of God

BROKEN AND DISTORTED

For the desires of the flesh are against the Spirit,
and the desires of the Spirit are against the flesh.

GALATIANS 5:17

God in redemption finds us all more or less disintegrated personalities. Disintegration and loss of rational control are aspects of our sinful and fallen state. Trying to play God to ourselves, we are largely out of control of ourselves and also out of touch with ourselves, or at least with a great deal of ourselves, including most of what is central to our real selves. God's gracious purpose, we know, is to bring us into a reconciled relationship with himself through Christ, and through the outworking of that relationship to reintegrate us and make us whole beings again. The relationship itself is restored once for all through what Luther called the "wonderful exchange" whereby Christ was made sin for us and we in consequence are made the righteousness of God in him (2 Corinthians 5:21). But the work of re-creating us as psychophysical beings on whom Christ's image is to be stamped — the work of sanctification — is not the work of a moment. Rather, it is a lifelong process of growth and transformation.

Indeed, it extends beyond this life, for the basic disintegration, that between psychic (conscious personal) life and physical life, will not be finally healed till "the redemption of our bodies" (Romans 8:23). Not till then (we may suppose) shall we know all that is now shrouded in the mysterious reality of the "unconscious," or know the end of the split-self dimension of Christian experience — reactions and responses which Paul diagnoses as the continuing energy of "sin that dwells within me" (Romans 7:20), dethroned but not destroyed, doomed to die but not dead yet. But the indwelling Holy Spirit abides and works in us to lead us toward the appointed goal, and he deals with each one's broken and distorted humanity as he finds it.

Serving the People of God

SELF-EXAMINATION, NOT INTROSPECTION

> *Examine yourselves, to see whether you are in the faith.*
> *Test yourselves.*
>
> 2 CORINTHIANS 13:5

For centuries, exponents of Christian devotion were in agreement on the importance of regular self-examination as a necessity for spiritual health. What they had in view was a measuring of ourselves, morally and spiritually, positively in terms of things done and negatively in terms of things left undone, by the behavioral ideals that God sets before us in his Word. Whereas introspection, whether it ends in euphoria or in the gloom of self-pity and self-despair, can become an expression of self-absorbed pride, self-examination is the fruit of God-centered humility, ever seeking to shake free of all that displeases the Father, dishonors the Son, and grieves the Holy Spirit, so as to honor God more. Thus self-examination is a fundamentally healthy process, leading into repentance, where mere introspection can leave us just feeling sorry for ourselves. The distinction between the two is clear, and it is a bad sign that so many evangelical Christians today seem unable to practice spiritual self-examination.

It is generally agreed that introspection without intent to change is basically unhealthy, but the claim that spiritual self-examination is truly health-giving often has to be fought for, and it becomes all too apparent that the practice of this discipline is rare.

The paradoxical truth about self-examination is that we do it precisely by asking God to do it, and laying ourselves open to him for that purpose. At school we do not grade ourselves but are graded by our instructors, and we do not perform our own medical checkups but arrange for our physician to do them; in this case we go to God to admit our lack of self-knowledge and to have him show us and tell us how we are doing spiritually. Our praying in this process begins with submitting and ends with listening.

Praying

STUNNING INTELLECTUAL ACHIEVEMENT

I write these things to you who believe in the name of the Son of God that you may know that you have eternal life.

1 JOHN 5:13

It is hardly possible to overstress the magnitude of the intellectual achievement embodied in the New Testament. The New Testament, as we know, is a consensus collection of apostolic writings that were brought together after each had been separately produced as particular needs required. None of these twenty-seven books was written to be part of any such collection, or to back up any other items that are part of it, and all of them were produced within seventy years — indeed most, if not all, within forty years — of Jesus' resurrection when Christian theology might have been expected to be still in a rudimentary stage. But in fact they have within them a coherent body of thought that is fully homogenous in its substance and thrust, despite the independent individuality of each writer and the way in which all their thinking cuts across the dogmas of the Judaism out of which it came. The central place of Jesus Christ in creation, providence, the divine plan of salvation, the history of our race, and the coming universal judgment and new creation of the cosmos is the theme throughout, and amazingly there are no internal contradictions or loose ends.

This revolutionary consensus, involving as it does Trinitarian and incarnational beliefs within a monotheistic frame — perhaps the hardest bit of thinking that the human mind has ever been asked to do — is so stunning that it is hard to doubt its supernatural origin. As from one standpoint the person, power, and performance of the Lord Jesus is its main focus, so from another standpoint all the books dilate in their different ways on the need and glory of the saving grace that he gives, thus furnishing a wealth of material to guide us in our enquiry.

Celebrating the Saving Work of God

GOD'S CONDESCENSION

For the foolishness of God is wiser than men,
and the weakness of God is stronger than men.

1 CORINTHIANS 1:25

Paul calls the divine ordaining and encompassing of the cross of Jesus Christ the *foolishness* and *weakness* of God (1 Corinthians 1:25). He is being ironical, of course, for he knows Christ to be God's wisdom and power (verse 24). He is insisting that the word of the cross appears as folly only to those who have not understood it. He is making a positive theological point as well, namely, that the death of God's Son on Calvary shows how completely God, in love to mankind, was willing to hide his glory and become vulnerable to shame and dishonor. Now God in love calls men to embrace and boast of this foolish-seeming, weak-looking, disreputable event of the Cross as the means of their salvation. It is a challenge to sinful pride of both mind and heart.

Similarly, God in love calls us to humble ourselves by bowing to Holy Scripture, which also has an appearance of foolishness and weakness when judged by some human standards, yet is truly his Word and the means of our knowing him as Savior. God first humbled himself for our salvation in the Incarnation and on the cross and now he humbles himself for our knowledge of salvation by addressing us in and through the often humanly unimpressive words of the Bible.

The classical name for the quality in God whereby he lovingly identifies with what is beneath him is *condescension,* and the etymological significance is "coming down to be with." The condescension of God in becoming a baby Jew, in being executed on a Roman gibbet, and in proclaiming his goodness and his gospel to us via the down-to-earth, unliterary, often rustic words of the sixty-six canonical books, is one and the same and spells the same reality throughout: love to the uttermost.

Honouring the Written Word of God

TOWARD CHRISTIAN UNITY

Sanctify them in the truth;
your word is truth.
JOHN 17:17

We must not be surprised that the problem of authority still divides Christian people. Clearly it is the most far-reaching and fundamental division that there is, or can be. The deepest cleavages in Christendom are doctrinal, and the deepest doctrinal cleavages are those which result from disagreement about authority. Some of these divisions presuppose a common view of authority; some do not. Those who disagree as to the principle of authority and, in consequence, as to the right method in theology, can reach no significant agreement on anything else.

Today this is largely overlooked. Christian bodies of all sorts are urged to sink their differences and present a united front to the forces of secularism. It is taken for granted that the differences in question are small and trifling — unsightly little cracks on the surface of an otherwise solid wall. But this assumption is false. Some of the cracks are the outward signs of lack of structural integration. The wall is cracked because it is not all built on the same foundation.

Nothing is gained just by trying to cement up the cracks; that only encourages the collapse of the entire wall. Sham unity is not worth working for, and real unity, that fellowship of love in the truth which Christ prayed that his disciples might enjoy (John 17:17-23), will come only as those sections of the wall which rest on unsound foundations are dismantled and rebuilt. Till this happens, the question of authority must remain central in discussion between the dissident groups, and the best service one can do to the divided church of Christ is to keep that question at the center.

"Fundamentalism" and the Word of God

THE QUALITY OF OUR DEVOTION

Repent and turn from all your transgressions,
lest iniquity be your ruin.
EZEKIEL 18:30

The churches of the West present a spectacle of confused disorder in both faith and morals. In view of the way that pluralism of belief and behavior is currently generated and applauded in centers of theological study, the confusion seems certain to continue. It is a fact, unhappy but undeniable, that repentance nowadays rarely gets mentioned in evangelism, nurture, and pastoral care, even among evangelicals and Christian traditionalists. The preoccupations of stirring congregational excitement, sustaining believers through crises, finding and honing gifts and skills, providing interest-based programs, and counseling people with relational problems have displaced it. As a result, the churches themselves, orthodox and heterodox together, lack spiritual reality, and their members are all too often superficial people with no hunger for the deep things of God.

No, ours is not a good time for trying to promote the discipline of constant repentance. However, this emphasis is always needed, doubly so when repenting has gone out of fashion.

I believe that even as we who are Christians ought to praise God, give him thanks, and make requests to him daily, so we ought to repent daily. This discipline is as basic to holiness as any. Whatever else was wrong with the old practice of penance, its requirement of regular reporting in the confessional at least kept believers aware that facing, forsaking, and fighting sins is a constant task. The further one goes in holy living, the more sin one will find in the attitudes of one's own heart, needing to be dealt with in this way. As the single-mindedness of our inward devotion is the real index of the quality of our discipleship, so the thoroughness of our daily repentance is the real index of the quality of our devotion. There is no way around that.

Rediscovering Holiness

WHITEFIELD AND THE DRAMA OF THE SOUL

Having received from the Father the promise of the Holy Spirit,
he has poured out this that you yourselves are seeing and hearing.

ACTS 2:33

George Whitefield's preaching sparked and sustained revival — reflective, assured, joyful, powerful, and life-transforming — in tens of thousands of lives on both sides of the Atlantic for more than thirty years in the 1700s.

His preaching called for present response, and located every such response as part of the drama of the soul's ongoing journey to heaven or to hell. Whitefield's instinct for drama led him to preach sermon after sermon that dramatized the issues of eternity and summoned his hearers to seek, in his phrase, a "felt Christ." We can sum up the substance of Whitefield's sermons in a series of imperatives:

1. *Face God.* People live thoughtlessly, drifting through their days, never thinking of eternity. But God has revealed a coming day of judgment. So wake up, and reckon here and now with God!

2. *Know yourself.* The doctrine of original sin answers the question, Why am I no better than I am? It confirms that we are all spiritually impotent and helpless.

3. *See Jesus.* Whitefield's preaching centered on "the dear Jesus," the embodiment of divine mercy.

4. *Understand justification.* He denounced self-righteousness, insisted that nothing we do is free from sin, and called on his hearers to come to Christ as guilty, helpless, hell-deserving offenders, and find righteousness and life in him.

5. *Welcome the Holy Spirit.* Whitefield insisted that the Spirit's presence in human lives would always be consciously felt, because of the change in experience the Spirit would bring about. Without the Spirit there is no transformation through new birth; without this there is no salvation for anyone. Though God has his own sovereign ways of breaking into people's lives, only those who seek the Spirit's influence, and open themselves deliberately to it, can expect to undergo it in a converting way.

Honouring the People of God

OFFENDED BY GOD'S HUMILITY

In the wisdom of God . . . it pleased God through the folly
of what we preach to save those who believe.

1 CORINTHIANS 1:21

God's humility offends man's pride, and hence both incarnation and inspiration are rejected by some as incredible. It is instructive to note the parallel here. The pagan philosopher Celsus (ca. AD 150) led the van in ridiculing the Incarnation. How could God the Son, the supposedly infinite, eternal, and unchangeable Creator, become man — let alone become a Jew! — and make himself known within the limitations of human finitude? Surely the idea is absurd! Scripturally instructed Christians are content to reply that it must be possible, since God has actually done it. The Incarnation is a wise and glorious mystery, despite its attendant weakness and shame, and from it comes salvation.

At the end of the eighteenth century the deist philosopher Kant turned away in comparable contempt from belief in inspiration, and thus pioneered a stance that has become typical of Western intellectual culture ever since. How could the infinite, transcendent, and incomprehensible Creator reveal himself in the words of folk from the primitive Near East thousands of years ago? This, too, seems absurd! Again the Christian will reply, as in regard to the Incarnation, that it must be possible, since God has done it. In fact he still reveals himself by so applying to us what he said to others in the past that we come to know with certainty what he says to us in the present. This also is a wise and glorious mystery, and from it flows saving knowledge.

In both cases, the correct reply to criticism is found in confession of God's salvation: how it was wrought in the first case, and how it is grasped and enjoyed in the second. In neither case, however, does the correct answer remove the offense that the criticism expresses.

Honouring the Written Word of God

THE PROBLEM OF AUTHORITY

*This is the one to whom I will look: he who is humble
and contrite in spirit and trembles at my word.*

ISAIAH 66:2

All Christians agree that Christianity is a religion of authority, requiring
that its adherents conform themselves to the revelation on which it rests.
This revelation was given in history, in the course of a process of redemptive action which centered upon the life, death, and resurrection of Jesus
Christ. What God says to man and does for man in the present is no more
than a particular application of what he said to the world and did for the
world once for all through the man Christ Jesus. It is God, speaking in
Christ, and God's word spoken through Christ, that is ultimately authoritative. These general conceptions are common ground.

The problem arises when we try to be more specific and practical.
How should we go about discovering just what this word of God is? By
what channel exactly is it mediated from the past to the present? When
Christian opinions differ, where should be the final court of appeal? This
is the problem of authority.

Final appeal might be made to one of three distinct authorities: Holy
Scripture, church tradition, or Christian reason — that is to say, Scripture
as interpreted by itself; Scripture as interpreted (and in some measure
amplified) by official ecclesiastical sources; and Scripture as evaluated
in terms of extra-biblical principles by individual Christian men. The
problem of authority can be answered in three ways, and three only,
according to which of those authorities is given precedence. We call these
three types of answer the evangelical (giving precedence to Scripture),
the traditionalist (leaning toward tradition), and the subjectivist (leaning
toward reason).

The evangelical view was first formally stated in opposition to the
other two at the time of the Reformation, but it is in fact the original
Christian position.

"Fundamentalism" and the Word of God

WHITEFIELD: GRAND-SCALE REVIVALIST

Him we proclaim . . . that we may present everyone mature in Christ.
For this I toil, struggling with all his energy
that he powerfully works within me.

COLOSSIANS 1:28-29

With his Oxford education, natural ease of manner, and slight West-country twang, which made him seem attractively human (his resonant speech was always somewhat nasal, and he pronounced "Christ" as "Chroist" all his life), George Whitefield, having been ordained at twenty-one in 1736, shot quickly into prominence as a Bible-preaching pastoral evangelist on the grand scale. At a time when other Anglican clergy were giving flat sermons of a mildly moralistic and apologetic sort, Whitefield preached extempore about heaven and hell, sin and salvation, the dying love of Christ, and the new birth, clothing his simple expository outlines with glowing dramatic conscience-challenging rhetoric and reinforcing his vocal alternations of soothing and punching with a great deal of body movement and gesture. At a time when other Anglican clergy were watching their churches empty, Whitefield went out to preach in the open air, loved the experience, and saw vast crowds gather to hear him and many come to faith.

Whitefield was first, a born orator; second, a natural actor; third, an English Protestant pietist; fourth, a disciplined, somewhat ascetic clergy-man of inflexible single-mindedness and integrity, childlike in humility, and passionately devoted to his Lord; fifth, a transparently friendly, forthcoming, care-giving man, as far from standoffishness as could be, to whose spontaneous goodwill was added the evangelist's gift of making all his hearers feel they were being addressed personally; and sixth, a Christian of catholic and ecumenical spirit whose vision of continuous revival throughout the English-speaking world led him to renounce all forms of institutional leadership and control so that he might be entirely at the service of all.

A good dose of Whitefieldian revivalism, should God raise up a preacher capable of imparting it, would do today's churches more good than anything I can imagine.

Honouring the People of God

THE ESSENCE OF THE ATONEMENT

For our sake he made him to be sin who knew no sin,
so that in him we might become the righteousness of God.

2 CORINTHIANS 5:21

How did Christ's sacrificial death actually save us — that is, rescue us from jeopardy and ruin? By *redeeming* us, effecting our transfer from a state of bondage without hope to a state of freedom with a future, by paying the price that the transfer required (Romans 3:24; Galatians 3:13; 4:5; Ephesians 1:7).

How then did the cross actually redeem us, through Jesus' death? By *reconciling* us to God, ending the alienation and estrangement that were previously there, linking God and us together in new harmony, replacing enmity between us with friendship and peace, by means of the putting away of our sins (Romans 5:11; Colossians 1:19-22).

So how did the cross actually reconcile us to God, and God to us? By being a *propitiation*, ending God's judicial wrath against us (Romans 3:25).

And how did the cross actually propitiate God? By being an event of *substitution*, whereby at the Father's will the sinless Son bore the retribution due to us guilty ones (2 Corinthians 5:21; Galatians 3:13; Colossians 2:14).

For Paul, this substitution, Christ bearing our penalty in our place, is the essence of the atonement. Certainly he celebrates the cross as a victory over the forces of evil on our behalf (Colossians 2:15) and as a motivating revelation of the love of God toward us (2 Corinthians 5:14-15), but it would not for him have been either of these had it not been an event of penal substitution. As Galatians 2:20 declares, Paul's life of responsive faith was wholly formed and driven by the knowledge that his Savior had revealed divine love to him by giving himself to die on the cross in order to save him.

In My Place Condemned He Stood

TRUE EVANGELISM

In this way there will be richly provided for you an entrance
into the eternal kingdom of our Lord and Savior Jesus Christ.

2 PETER 1:11

Evangelizing means *declaring a specific message*. It is not evangelism merely to teach general truths about God's existence or the moral law; evangelism means to *present Christ Jesus*, the divine Son who became man at a particular point in world history in order to save a ruined race.

Nor is it evangelism merely to present the teaching and example of the historical Jesus, or even the truth about his saving work; evangelism means to present *Christ Jesus himself*, living Savior and reigning Lord.

Nor again is it evangelism merely to set forth the living Jesus as Helper and Friend, without reference to his saving work on the cross; evangelism means to present Jesus as Christ, God's anointed Servant, fulfilling the tasks of his appointed office as Priest and King. "The man Christ Jesus" is to be presented as the "one mediator between God and men" (1 Timothy 2:5), who "suffered once for sins . . . that he might bring us to God" (1 Peter 3:18), the one through whom, and through whom alone, men may come to put their trust in God, according to his own claim: "I am the way, and the truth, and the life. No one comes to the Father except through me" (John 14:6).

He is to be proclaimed as the *Savior*, the one who "came into the world to save sinners" (1 Timothy 1:15) and "redeemed us from the curse of the law by becoming a curse for us" (Galatians 3:13) — "Jesus who delivers us from the wrath to come" (1 Thessalonians 1:10). And he is to be set forth as *King*: "For to this end Christ died and lived again, that he might be Lord both of the dead and of the living" (Romans 14:9).

There is no evangelism where this specific message is not declared.

Evangelism and the Sovereignty of God

MODERN MAN'S OBSESSION

To the Lord our God belong mercy and forgiveness,
for we have rebelled against him.

DANIEL 9:9

"Freedom" is today almost a magic word — a worldwide passion, encouraged and catered to at every level.

Longings for freedom from restrictions, from the dead hand of the past, from disliked pressures, obligations, systems, and whatnot are for many people the strongest of life's driving forces. It has become modern man's obsession. It has its roots in philosophy: in dreams of the perfectibility of man, in Rousseau's idea that civilization squeezes you out of shape, in the educationists' fancy that inside each little demon is a little angel waiting to come out as soon as mechanical pressures relax and interest is wooed. It is rooted in experience too. Bad experiences of harsh and stifling authority at home, at school, in church, with the boss or the police, or elsewhere in the body politic have fueled fires of revolt. Who can wonder when rebels are hostile to what hurt them?

The effect is that all forms of authority are seen as cell walls, which makes the quest for freedom feel like a Great Escape from some ideological prison camp, and anyone who respects authority stands out as odd. Modern man may claim to have come of age, but from this standpoint he seems to have regressed to adolescence. (Adolescents, of course, are always first to insist on their own adulthood.) Surely today's rebellion against authority is a sign not of maturity but of its opposite. It is a form of folly, not of wisdom. It leads only to decadence and spoiled lives.

The truth, paradoxical yet inescapable, is this: There is no freedom apart from external authority. To say "I am my own authority" is to enslave myself to myself — the worst bondage of all. Only as I bow to an authority which is not myself am I ever free.

Freedom and Authority

PURPOSEFUL WORK

They said, "Let us rise up and build."
So they strengthened their hands for the good work.

NEHEMIAH 2:18

When the Bible talks about work, it has in view much more than what we call our job or our employment. In the Bible, *work* as such means any exertion of effort that aims at producing a new state of affairs. Such exertions involve our creativity, which is part of God's image in us and which needs to be harnessed and expressed in action if our nature is to be properly fulfilled. So, for instance, homemaking, sweeping snow, obeying orders, practicing for a performance, darning socks, and answering letters are all focused, intentional exertions that count as work, though none of them necessarily involves contractual employment. Conversely, warbling under the shower to express your euphoria at the feel of the hot water is not work, no matter how much energy you put into it. If, however, your warbling was learning a part to sing in a choir, that would be work, because of its purpose. Work in the biblical sense is always goal-oriented; it is action with an end in view.

The Bible envisages life as a rhythm of work and rest (generally, labor by day and sleep by night; labor for six days and rest on the seventh) and does not distinguish between spiritual and secular work as if these belonged in separate compartments. The Bible teaches, rather, that we should plan and live our life as a unity in which nothing is secular and everything is in a real sense sacred, because everything is being done for the glory of God — that is, to show appreciation for what he has made, to please him by loving obedience to his commands, and to advance his honor and praise among his creatures, starting with the homage and adoration that we render to him ourselves.

A Passion for Faithfulness

CLEAR AND COMPLETE

*I am watching over my word
to perform it.*
JEREMIAH 1:12

The teaching of the written Scriptures is the Word which God spoke and speaks to his church, and is finally authoritative for faith and life. To learn the mind of God, one must consult his written Word. What Scripture says, God says.

The Bible is inspired in the sense of being word-for-word God-given. It is a record and explanation of divine revelation which is both complete *(sufficient)* and comprehensible *(perspicuous)* — that is to say, it contains all that the church needs to know in this world for its guidance in the way of salvation and service, and it contains the principles for its own interpretation within itself.

Furthermore, the Holy Spirit, who caused it to be written, has been given to the church to cause believers to recognize it as the divine Word that it is, and to enable them to interpret it rightly and understand its meaning. He who was its Author is also its Witness and Expositor. Christians must therefore seek to be helped and taught by the Spirit when they study Scripture, and must regard all their understanding of it, no less than the book itself, as the gift of God. The Spirit must be acknowledged as the infallible Interpreter of God's infallible Word.

The Bible, therefore, does not need to be supplemented and interpreted by tradition, or revised and corrected by reason. Instead, it demands to sit in judgment on the dictates of both, for the words of men must be tried by the Word of God. The church collectively, and the Christian individually, can and does err, and the inerrant Scripture must ever be allowed to speak and correct them.

"Fundamentalism" and the Word of God

UNDERSTANDING HOW TO LIVE

Blessed is the one who finds wisdom,
and the one who gets understanding.

PROVERBS 3:13

Wisdom is about understanding. Wisdom, in the book of Proverbs and elsewhere, is constantly contrasted with folly. Proverbs devotes its first nine chapters to a general exhortation to seek wisdom as the supreme value of life, since the quest for wisdom is the most important thing we can ever engage in.

Understanding means specifically knowing how to live as a response to God's revelation. Wisdom includes understanding, but wisdom is larger, for it includes also the prudent doing of what we understand that we should do. In other words, it is *practical*. In some eras and cultures, practical wisdom has been thought of as separate from understanding in a way which might be caricatured as "I don't need no book learnin'; God gives me all the wisdom I need when I need it," but the writer of Proverbs (and therefore God) disagrees. Wisdom for the business of living is gained through the labor of learning to understand; understanding is learned from the book of God and books about the book of God, as well as from live teachers who help us in this.

Throughout Proverbs, wisdom and understanding are the key thoughts. Wisdom in the heart starts in the mind and is thus about thinking and about learning and also about unlearning. One mark of a wise person, according to Proverbs, is that one is willing to accept instruction and correction and to learn to know things better than one does at the moment. The life of wisdom is a life of constant learning: constant evaluating, constant discerning, constant extension of one's understanding.

WHEN WE'RE PROVOKED

Put to death therefore what is earthly in you.

COLOSSIANS 3:5

Holiness means, among other things, forming good habits, breaking bad habits, resisting temptations to sin, and controlling yourself when provoked. No one ever managed to do any of these things without effort and conflict.

How do we form the Christlike habits which Paul calls the fruit of the Spirit? By setting ourselves, deliberately, to do the Christlike thing in each situation. "Sow an act, reap a habit; sow a habit, reap a character."[9] That might sound very simple and straightforward, but in practice it does not prove so. The test, of course, comes when the situation provokes us to cut loose with some form of ungodly tit for tat. We should think out our behavioral strategy with such situations directly in view. Thus, we should think of:

- *Love* as the Christlike reaction to people's malice
- *Joy* as the Christlike reaction to depressing circumstances
- *Peace* as the Christlike reaction to troubles, threats, and invitations to anxiety
- *Patience* as the Christlike reaction to all that is maddening
- *Kindness* as the Christlike reaction to all who are unkind
- *Goodness* as the Christlike reaction to bad people and bad behavior
- *Faithfulness* and *gentleness* as the Christlike reactions to lies and fury
- *Self-control* as the Christlike reaction to every situation that goads you to lose your cool and hit out

The principle is clear: The Spirit is with us to empower us, and we know that Christlike behavior is now in the profoundest sense natural to us. But still, maintaining Christlikeness under this kind of pressure is hard.

Rediscovering Holiness

BECOMING LIKE THE ROCK

And I tell you, you are Peter,
and on this rock I will build my church,
and the gates of hell shall not prevail against it.
MATTHEW 16:18

"Everybody loves Peter," a veteran cross-cultural missionary said to me. What she meant, I think, was that everybody identifies with a great deal of what they see in Simon Peter: his eager thoughtlessness, his cheerful and naive self-confidence, his warm-hearted big-brotherliness, his readiness to ask questions when he did not know something, and the occasional goofiness of things he blurted out. People empathize too with the depth of his fall when he denied his Lord and with the glory of his restoration as Jesus talked graciously to him at the lakeside and the Holy Spirit came powerfully upon him at Pentecost. They feel that if God could do so much by way of transforming that man, then there is surely more hope than perhaps they realized for themselves.

But we need to be honest with ourselves and with God. Can we say to Jesus with Simon Peter, "Lord . . . you know that I love you" (John 21:15-17, NIV)? No doubt we are compelled to say with him, "Lord, I know I've let you down. What I have done is terrible, and the memory of it is awful — yet in my heart I do love you, and what I want more than anything is to love you more and better."

Becoming honest, realistic, and responsive to the Son of God was the path of Simon's progress. It was how he came to know God the Father. It was as he traveled this path that God transformed him from Simon the unstable into Peter the rock. Following this path is in one very basic sense the real apostolic succession. This is the track for Jesus' true disciples. This is the way you and I must go. May the Lord lead us this way.

Never Beyond Hope

LLOYD-JONES: PROCLAIMER OF GRACE

The grace of our Lord overflowed for me
with the faith and love that are in Christ Jesus.

1 TIMOTHY 1:14

David Martyn Lloyd-Jones was the greatest man I have ever known, and I am sure there is more of him under my skin than there is of any other of my human teachers.

He was a saint, a holy man of God — a naturally proud person whom God made humble; a naturally quick-tempered person to whom God taught patience; a naturally contentious person to whom God gave restraint and wisdom; a natural egoist, conscious of his own great ability, whom God set free from self-seeking to serve the servants of God. The moral effects of grace in his life were plain to see. His self-control was marvelous; only the grace of God suffices to explain it.

He was essentially a preacher. No one who has ever heard him preach the gospel from the Gospels and show how it speaks to the aches and follies and nightmares of the modern heart will doubt that this was where his own focus was, and where as a communicator he was at his finest. He was bold enough to believe that because inspired preaching changes individuals it can change the church and thereby change the world, and the noble purpose of furthering such change was the whole of his life's agenda. As for force in pursuing his goal, the personal electricity of his pulpit communication was unique. All his energy went into his preaching: not only animal energy, of which he had a good deal, but also the God-given liveliness and authority that in past eras was called *unction*. He effectively proclaimed the greatness of God, and of Christ, and of the soul, and of eternity, and supremely of saving grace — the everlasting gospel, old yet ever new, familiar yet endlessly wonderful.

Honouring the People of God

IS CHRISTIANITY CREDIBLE?

The natural person does not accept the things of the Spirit of God,
for they are folly to him, and he is not able to understand them.

1 CORINTHIANS 2:14

The intellectual credentials of thorough-going Christianity are very strong, much stronger than is often allowed, and it is only when Christians cease to be thorough-going that their faith ever sounds or looks forlorn. When it *feels* forlorn and dubious (and I suppose all Christians know such feelings on occasion), it is because, for whatever reason, relevant facts are not making their proper impact.

If thorough-going Christianity be thought incredible, it is a case of pots calling the kettle black, for the rival convictional systems which present themselves are less credible still. Skepticism, solipsism, and nihilism, being philosophies of ultimate negation, cannot be refuted in the ordinary way but can yet be shown to be paradoxical and unnecessary, while affirmations of alternative absolutes — Marxist, humanist, Freudian, or whatever — prove on inspection to be inadequate to fit all the facts.

The difficulties which much contemporary Protestantism finds in commending Christianity as a believable option for folk today spring directly from the way in which, following in the methodological footsteps of Schleiermacher, we habitually scale Christianity down so as to represent it to its cultured despisers as the fulfillment of their own best thoughts, instincts, and longings. Scaled-down Christianities are both the fruit and the root of uncertainty, and the supposition that the less we commit ourselves to maintain, the easier it will be to maintain never proves true.

The inescapable plurality of notions and insights has spawned so wide a range of diverse beliefs about Christian essentials (God, Jesus Christ, salvation) as to make anyone who wants to communicate Christianity to the wider world feel completely stymied. Looked at from this standpoint, the Schleiermacherian tradition of theological subjectivity has much to answer for.

Serving the People of God

THE DIVINE PHYSICIAN

Prove me, O LORD, and try me;
test my heart and my mind.
PSALM 26:2

When God puts us through a spiritual checkup, he takes notice of all aspects of our inner life, about which only we and he knows.

He checks up on our *faith*. Do we really know what we should about God? Do we trust in Christ as we should? Do we take careful note of God's promises found in Scripture, claim them in our prayers, and rely on him to keep them?

God checks our *repentance*. Real Christianity is serious about penitently tracking down and turning from all the false steps of the past.

He checks our *love*. Sin in our system enslaves our natural self-love to unnatural pride, keeping us from loving God and others. So God exposes to our conscience our self-absorption and self-centeredness, our tendency to focus entirely on our own concerns.

God checks up on our *humility* — our honest realism and realistic honesty. Humility cannot be fully detected by direct inspection, for trying to inspect our own humility is itself a yielding to pride. The most we can do is concentrate on negating and mortifying the various expressions of pride we are aware of, and on asking our Lord to show us what more needs to be done.

God also checks up on us in the matter of *wisdom*. Christlike wisdom forms strategies, calculates consequences, channels passion, sustains sobriety, discerns and avoids foolishness, and cherishes peace and harmony at all times. Without wisdom there is no God-pleasing life.

Summarizing these, we may say that *God checks our focus*: how far our faith, repentance, love, humility, and wisdom have combined to make us clear-sighted about our goal in life and the priorities that it imposes. Thus the divine physician probes us, and his probing goes on all the time.

Praying

PACKED AND READY

Always carrying in the body the death of Jesus,
so that the life of Jesus may also be manifested in our bodies.

2 Corinthians 4:10

As I see it, the Puritans are giants compared with us, giants whose help we need if ever we are to grow. Learning from the heroes of the Christian past is in any case an important dimension of that edifying fellowship for which the proper name is the communion of saints. The great Puritans, though dead, still speak to us through their writings, and say things to us that we badly need to hear at this present time.

The Puritans have taught me to see and feel the transitoriness of this life, to think of it, with all its richness, as essentially the gymnasium and dressing room where we are prepared for heaven, and to regard readiness to die as the first step in learning to live.

The Puritans' awareness that in the midst of life we are in death, just one step from eternity, gave them a deep seriousness, calm yet passionate, with regard to the business of living that Christians in today's opulent, mollycoddled, earthbound Western world rarely manage to match. Few of us, I think, live daily on the edge of eternity in the conscious way that the Puritans did, and we lose out as a result. For the extraordinary vivacity, even hilarity, with which the Puritans lived stemmed directly, I believe, from the unflinching, matter-of-fact realism with which they prepared themselves for death, so as always to be found, as it were, packed up and ready to go. Reckoning with death brought appreciation of each day's continued life, and the knowledge that God would eventually decide, without consulting them, when their work on earth was done brought energy for the work itself while they were still being given time to get on with it.

A Quest for Godliness

IS THERE ONENESS IN WORLDWIDE RELIGIONS?

Whoever does not obey the Son shall not see life,
but the wrath of God remains on him.

JOHN 3:36

What should we say of *pluralism,* the relativistic notion that all theological clashes between religions can be transcended and that an ultimate oneness of worldwide religious outlooks can be demonstrated? Speaking in general terms, three points seem to stand insuperably against it.

First, the accounts of the religious ultimate (God), the human predicament (sin), and the nature and path of true life (salvation) that the world's religions offer are neither compatible nor convergent, but diverge radically. Second, all attempts to achieve an umbrella account of what they say on these three issues (the highest-common-factor quest in multifaith theology) have so far failed to produce anything substantial for which the exponents of the various world religions can settle, and the most careful analysis yields no likelihood of any greater success in the future. Third, New Testament theology is explicitly exclusivist.

"I am the way, and the truth, and the life," said Jesus. "No one comes to the Father" — that is, no one comes to know God as Father, however strong he or she is on God's reality — "except through me" (John 14:6). "There is no other name under heaven given among men," preached Peter, "by which we" — who? clearly in context, anybody and everybody — "must be saved" (Acts 4:12). *Must* implies that people both need to be saved and may be saved through Jesus: this is the universality of the Christian claim. Pluralism, however, is categorically ruled out by such statements as these.

Our future depends on how faithfully we maintain faith in, and fidelity to, Jesus Christ the only Savior. The way is clear; the only question is whether we will walk in it.

Celebrating the Saving Work of God

OUR PENTECOST

> *For in one Spirit we were all baptized into one body . . .*
> *and all were made to drink of one Spirit.*
>
> 1 CORINTHIANS 12:13

What should we say of the often-heard view, based on Acts 2, that God means every Christian's life to be a two-stage, two-level affair, in which conversion is followed by a second event (called Spirit baptism on the basis of Acts 1:5 or Spirit-filling on the basis of 2:4), which raises one's spiritual life to new heights?

Though individual Christians need, and again and again are given, "second touches" of this kind (and third, fourth, and any number more), the idea that this is God's program for all Christians as such is mistaken. God means all Christians to enjoy the full inward blessing of Pentecost (not the outward trimmings necessarily, but the communion of heart with Christ and all that flows from it) right from the moment of their conversion.

The only reason the first disciples had to be taken through a two-stage pattern of experience was that they became believers before Pentecost. But for folk like you and me, who became Christians nearly two thousand years after Pentecost, the revealed program is that fullest enjoyment of the Spirit's New Covenant ministry should be ours from the word go. This is already clear in the New Testament, where Paul explains Spirit baptism as something that happened to the Corinthians — and, by parity of reasoning, happens to all other post-Pentecost converts — at conversion (1 Corinthians 12:13). He describes Spirit-filledness in terms of a lifestyle that all Christians should have been practicing from conversion (Ephesians 5:18-21). If it has not worked out that way for any of us, the reason is not that God never meant it to, but rather that somehow, whether or not we realize it, we have been quenching God's Spirit (1 Thessalonians 5:19), which is a state of affairs that has to be changed.

Keep in Step with the Spirit

OUR INTELLECTUAL PRIDE

Now the serpent . . . said to the woman,
"Did God actually say . . . ?"
GENESIS 3:1

Whence comes the impulse — common, indeed, to us all — to trust and follow the leading of human reason in religion, rather than be content simply to take God's word for things? Whence comes the impulse to exalt reason over revelation, and the sense of outrage which is so widely felt when the authority of reason in religion is challenged? Answer: This spirit springs from *sin*.

To doubt revelation in favor of a private hunch was the sin into which Satan led Eve, and Eve's children have been committing the same sin ever since. The impulse to indulge oneself in believing something other than what God has said is an expression of the craving to be independent of God, which is the essence of sin. The attempt to know all things, including God, by reason, without reference to revelation, is the form this craving for independence takes in the intellectual realm, just as the attempt to win heaven by works and effort, without grace, is the form it takes in the moral realm. Pride prompts fallen mankind to go about, not merely to establish their own righteousness, but also to manufacture their own wisdom. The quest all along is for self-sufficiency: Our sinful arrogance prompts us to aspire after independence of God in the realm of knowledge. We want to be intellectually autonomous, intellectually self-made men.

The gospel, fundamentally, is a message that tells us it is useless to seek for truth about God by speculation, and it comes to us as a command to stop speculating and to put faith in what God has said, simply on the grounds that he, the God of truth, has said it. The gospel, in other words, repudiates absolutely the authority of reason and demands implicit subjection to God's revealed truth.

Honouring the Written Word of God

OUR FAMILY CODE

> *Bear one another's burdens,*
> *and so fulfill the law of Christ.*
> GALATIANS 6:2

Scripture shows that God intends his law to function in three ways, which Calvin crystallized in classic form for the church's benefit as the law's threefold use.

Its first function is to be a mirror reflecting to us both the perfect righteousness of God and our own sinfulness and shortcomings. Thus "the law bids us, as we try to fulfill its requirements, and become wearied in our weakness under it, to know how to ask the help of grace."[10] The law is meant to give knowledge of sin and, by showing us our need of pardon and our danger of damnation, to lead us in repentance and faith to Christ (Galatians 3:19-24).

Its second function is to restrain evil. Though it cannot change the heart, the law can to some extent inhibit lawlessness by its threats of judgment, especially when backed by a civil code that administers present punishment for proven offenses. Thus it secures some civil order and goes some way to protect the righteous from the unjust.

Its third function is to guide the regenerate into the good works that God has planned for them (Ephesians 2:10). The law tells God's children what will please their heavenly Father. It could be called their family code. Christ was speaking of this third use of the law when he said that those who become his disciples must be taught to keep the law and to do all that he had commanded (Matthew 5:18-20; 28:20), and that it is obedience to his commands that will prove the reality of one's love for him (John 14:15). The Christian is free from the law as a supposed system of salvation but is "under Christ's law" as a rule of life.

Concise Theology

FASCINATING WORK

> *There is nothing better than that a man should*
> *rejoice in his work, for that is his lot.*
> Ecclesiastes 3:22

Human nature finds fulfillment and contentment only when we have work to do. The creation story tells us that God put Adam "in the garden of Eden to work it and keep it" (Genesis 2:15). The work would have given him great pleasure and no pain; thorns and thistles, and sweat and tears because of barren fields and failed harvests, came in only through the curse that followed the Fall (3:17-19). The work would have required constant thought and effort, yet it would have been happy partnership with God all the way, and Adam would have perceived himself as fulfilling his human calling to be, in Tolkien's word, a "sub-creator" under God.

God, it seems, has ordained work to be our destiny, both here and hereafter. What was his reason for planning our lives this way? I think we see the answer when we note what happens as we work. We discover our potential as craftsmen, learning to do things and developing skills, which is fascinating. We also discover the potential of God's world as raw material for us to use, manage, and bring into shape, which is fascinating too.

Work as a way of life that we approve, embrace, and pursue for the glory of God generates within us a spirit of praise to him, both for the wonders of creation outside us and for the creativity that our work draws out of us. Furthermore, work brings joy in the experience of making and managing; fosters wisdom and maturity in the way we run things, including our relationships with other people; leads to an increase of affection and goodwill toward others as we harness our skills to serve them; and develops ingenuity and resourcefulness in finding ways to tap into the powers and processes that surround us.

A Passion for Faithfulness

RIGHTLY USING TRADITION AND REASON

The sum of your word is truth,
and every one of your righteous rules endures forever.

PSALM 119:160

The proper ground for believing a thing is not that the church or reason says it. Both these authorities may err, and in any case it is not to them that God has told us to go for authoritative indications of his mind. The proper ground for believing a thing is that God says it in his written Word, and a readiness to take God's Word and accept what he asserts in the Bible is thus fundamental to faith.

Not that church tradition is unimportant. On the contrary, it yields much valuable help in understanding what Scripture teaches. The Spirit has been active in the church from the first, doing the work he was sent to do: guiding God's people into an understanding of revealed truth. The history of the church's labor to understand the Bible forms a commentary on the Bible which we cannot despise or ignore without dishonoring the Holy Spirit. Tradition may not be lightly dismissed, but neither may it be made a separate authority apart from Scripture. Like every commentary on the Bible, it must itself be tested and, where necessary, corrected by the Bible which it seeks to expound.

Nor may reason be viewed as an independent authority for our knowledge of God's truth. Reason's part is to act as the servant of the written Word, seeking in dependence on the Spirit to interpret Scripture scripturally, to correlate its teaching and to discern its application to all parts of life. We may not look to reason to tell us whether Scripture is right in what it says (reason is not in any case competent to pass such a judgment); instead, we must look to the Scriptures to tell us whether reason is right in what it thinks on the subject with which Scripture deals.

"Fundamentalism" and the Word of God

NO PANIC IN FEARING GOD

Work out your own salvation with fear and trembling,
for it is God who works in you.

PHILIPPIANS 2:12-13

The word *fear* in the phrase "fear of the Lord" does not imply panic; what it implies is reverence, yet not the sort of reverence that rules out boldness. Christians know that through God's grace their sins are forgiven and that they are in God's favor, so they can be bold in invoking him, looking to him, and asking for his teaching and his help. Panicky fear would inhibit all of that. Panic, shaking-in-your-boots fear is not the sort of fear that the biblical writers are talking about. This fear of the Lord is reverence — with boldness, yes — but reverence linked with awe at God's greatness, and an active, deep concern to obey and please him.

That, incidentally, is what the reference to fear and trembling means in Philippians 2:12-13, where Paul directs his readers to actively express their salvation with awe and reverence. Paul states the reason for this: "For it is God who works in you, both to will and to work for his good pleasure" (verse 13). It is awesome to know that God works in our hearts as we seek to use our minds to think for him, to discern his will, to work out what is the best we can do to advance his kingdom and his praise, and to program ourselves for doing that. Every right thought we manage to think, and every right action we manage to perform, is God's work in us and his gift to us. This realization evokes deep awe and deep gratitude and an ongoing sense of humble dependence on the God who thus confirms to us that he is ours and we are his. This state of mind is at the heart of the human reality labeled "the fearer of the Lord."

Guard Us, Guide Us

KILLING OUR SINS

> *Those who belong to Christ Jesus have crucified the flesh*
> *with its passions and desires.*
>
> GALATIANS 5:24

How do we "by the Spirit . . . put to death the misdeeds of the body" (Romans 8:13, NIV)? It is a matter of negating, wishing dead, and laboring to thwart the inclinations, cravings, and habits that have been in you for a long time. Pain and grief, moans and groans, will certainly be involved, for your sin does not want to die, nor will it enjoy the killing process. Jesus told us vividly that mortifying a sin could well feel like plucking out an eye or cutting off a hand or foot — in other words, self-mutilation. You will feel you are saying good-bye to something so much a part of you that without it you cannot live.

Both Paul and Jesus assure us that this exercise, however painful, is a necessity for life, so we must go to it. How? Outward acts of sin come from inner sinful urges, so we must learn to starve these urges of what stimulates them. And when the urge is upon us, we must learn, as it were, to run to our Lord and cry for help, asking him to deepen our sense of his holy presence and redeeming love, to give us the strength to say no to that which can only displease him. It is the Spirit who moves us to act this way, and who actually drains the life out of the sins we starve.

Thus, habits of self-indulgence, spiritual idolatry, and abuse of others can be broken. But while surrendering sins into which you drifted casually is not so hard, mortifying what the Puritans called "besetting" sins — dispositional sins to which your temperament inclines you, and habitual sins that have become addictive and defiant — is regularly a long, drawn-out, bruising struggle. No one who is a spiritual realist will ever pretend otherwise.

Rediscovering Holiness

MADE TO BURN

*My zeal
consumes me.*
PSALM 119:139

When we read how the Lord Jesus made a multithonged whip and cleared the temple of the businessmen, we're seeing something so rare nowadays that we've hardly got a word for it. And when the regular biblical word for it is used, we hardly know what it means. That word is *zeal*.

The disciples, watching Jesus' fury in awe, realized that they were now seeing fulfilled in Jesus what was written in Scripture, "Zeal for your house will consume me" (literally, "eat me up"; see John 2:14-17). That's the Lord Jesus, who is our model and our standard in the service of God.

Bishop J. C. Ryle, one of the great men of the church of England at the end of the nineteenth century, defines zeal as "a burning desire to please God, to do his will, and to advance his glory in the world in every possible way." He describes a person of zeal as one who "only sees one thing . . . cares for one thing . . . lives for one thing . . . is swallowed up in one thing. . . . He burns for one thing, and that one thing is to please God, and to advance God's glory. . . . He feels that, like a lamp, he is made to burn; and if consumed in burning, he has but done the work for which God appointed him."

The path of zeal is one trod by Jesus as well as men like Nehemiah and Paul, and in this, it seems to me, they set a benchmark and a standard that all believers should aim at. We cannot justify ourselves in not being zealous. We are called to be zealous for our God, as an expression of our love for him, and we don't please him unless we are zealous for him in this way.

Never Beyond Hope

PASSIONATE THINKER, PASSIONATE PREACHER

I did not shrink from declaring to you
the whole counsel of God.

ACTS 20:27

David Martyn Lloyd-Jones rightly believed that preachers are born rather than made, that preaching is caught more than it is taught, and that the best way to vindicate preaching is to preach. And preach he did, almost greedily, till the very end of his life — "this our short, uncertain life and earthly pilgrimage," as by constant repetition in his benedictions he had taught Christians to call it.

His concern was always with the flow of thought, and the emotion he expressed as he talked was simply the outward sign of passionate thinking. He never put on any sort of act, but talked in exactly the same way from the pulpit, the lecture desk, or the armchair, treating everyone without exception as fellow enquirers after truth. Always he spoke as a debater making a case, as a physician making a diagnosis, as a theologian blessed with what he once recognized in another as a "naturally theological mind," thinking things out from Scripture in terms of God.

When he preached, he usually eschewed the humor which bubbled out of him so naturally at other times and concentrated on serious, down-to-earth, educational exposition. His preaching always took the form of an argument — biblical, evangelical, doctrinal, and spiritual — starting most usually with the foolishness of human self-sufficiency, as expressed in some commonly held opinions and policies, moving to what may be called the Isaianic inversion whereby man who thinks himself great is shown to be small and God whom he treats as small is shown to be great, and always closing within sight of Christ — his cross and his grace. When he came to the awesome and magnificent thing he had to declare about our glorious, self-vindicating God, he would let loose the thunder and lightning with a spiritual impact that was simply stunning.

Honouring the People of God

WONDERING WHAT WE ARE

What is man that you are mindful of him,
and the son of man that you care for him?
PSALM 8:4

What is man? This is an inescapable question which no one who thinks at all can avoid asking about himself or herself. We find ourselves to be self-transcendent, because we are self-conscious and self-aware. We can stand back from ourselves and look at ourselves and judge ourselves and ask basic questions about ourselves, and, what is more, we cannot help doing these things. The questions ask themselves, unbidden; willy-nilly, one finds oneself wondering what life means, what sense it makes, what one is here for. And such questions must be squarely faced.

What is man? The mainstream Christian answer, as given in the Bible and maintained in the church against eccentric extremes ever since Christianity began, is essentially as follows: Every human individual has infinite worth, being made by God for nobility and glory; but every human individual is currently twisted out of moral shape in a way that only God can cure. Each of us by nature is God's image-bearer, but is also fallen and lives under the power of sin, and now needs grace. Sin, the anti-God allergy of the soul, is a sickness of the spirit, and the tragic sense of life, the inner tensions and contradictions, plus our inveterate unrealism, egoism, and indisposition to love God and our neighbor, are all symptoms of our disorder.

Sometimes Christians have expressed this thought by saying that man, though good, is terribly weak. That, however, seems hardly adequate, and I side with those who speak more strongly and say that each of us is radically bad, though providentially kept from expressing our badness fully. But in human nature, viewed morally, as God views it, everything is out of true to some extent. It is beyond us to straighten and integrate the human character. Man needs God for that.

Serving the People of God

ALL BEGGARS

Every good gift and every perfect gift is from above,
coming down from the Father of lights.

JAMES 1:17

Martin Luther's last written words were "We are all beggars. That is true."[11] Two days later he died. He was right, of course. If we think of ourselves as achievers, creators, reformers, innovators, movers and shakers, healers, educators, benefactors of society in any way at all, we are at the deepest level kidding ourselves. We have nothing and have never had anything that we have not received, nor have we done anything good apart from God who did it through us. In ourselves we are destitute, bankrupt, and impotent, totally dependent on God in every respect. This is true, as Luther constantly insisted, with regard to the pardon of our sins and the justification of our persons. And it is equally true of life, health, food, clothing, a job, a home, a family, a car, a bank balance in the black, and every other good thing that comes our way. So before God's throne we *are* all beggars, and begging good gifts from God is what petitionary prayer is all about.

We ask God, as beggars, for what we need because he explicitly invites us to do so in Scripture. The very nature of prayers of petition emphasizes our true relationship with God. He is the provider; we the receivers. He is the master of the universe; we are small. And though, from our own standpoint, we are important and truly valued by God as his image-bearers, yet from another standpoint we are quite unimportant subjects within his universe. God is the maker of all things; we are completely dependent on what he gives. Could he get on without us? Yes. Does this fact make his actual generosity to us more and more marvelous to contemplate? Yes again.

Praying

WHOLENESS IN CHURCH RENEWAL

Pay careful attention to yourselves and to all the flock . . .
to care for the church of God,
which he obtained with his own blood.

ACTS 20:28

The Puritans shaped my churchly identity, by imparting to me their vision of the wholeness of the work of God that they called reformation, and that we would more likely nowadays call renewal. Today, as in my youth, some conservative Anglicans (I speak as one of them) care about orthodoxy, some about liturgy and corporate life, some about individual conversion and nurture, some about aspects of personal sanctity, some about central and congregational structures, some about national moral standards, some about compassionate social witness, some about the reviving of piety amid our Laodiceanism. But each of these concerns gets outflanked, undermined, and ultimately trivialized if it is not linked with all the others. Divided, they fall and run into the sand. I have seen this happen across the board, both inside and outside Anglicanism, in my own lifetime. The Puritans gave me a concern for all these things together, as all sustaining each other, and all bearing on the honor and glory of God in his church, and I am thankful to be able to say that inside me they are together still.

I could have learned this ideal of overall evangelical renewal from others; but, in fact, I got most of it from the Puritans, and principally from Richard Baxter, to whom I owe so much. Following this gleam as a reforming Anglican has sometimes put me in places where I seemed not to be in step with anyone, and I do not suppose that my judgment on specific questions was always faultless, but looking back I am sure that the comprehensive, non-sectarian lead that Baxter gave me was the right one. I continue to be grateful for it, and expect that gratitude to last for eternity.

A Quest for Godliness

VIVID EXPERIENCE OF LIFE

> *For because he himself has suffered when tempted,*
> *he is able to help those who are being tempted.*
>
> HEBREWS 2:18

John's statement that the Word became flesh (John 1:14) means more than that he encased himself in a physical body. It means he took to himself, and entered right into, everything that contributes to a fully human experience.

By virtue of what he experienced as a healthy first-century Jewish male before his death at thirty-three, he can now enter sympathetically into all human experiences, those of girls and women, sick folk, the aged, and addicts (for instance) no less than those of young males like himself. Thus he is able to give to all the help toward right living that we all need (Hebrews 2:18; 4:15-16).

The church has always known this. That is why such ideas as that Jesus was not really human (though he appeared to be), or that the incarnate Son had no human mind or will, have always been condemned as heresy. And that is why Christians have been constantly asking Jesus to help them in their struggles ever since the day of the apostles, and constantly declaring that he does.

The Jesus of the New Testament experienced everything in the unity of his divine-human person, and his experiencing of life was more vivid than ours because his sensitivity had not been dulled at any point.

The true Christian claim here is that incarnation made direct entry into human frustration and pain possible for the Son of God, who then out of love actually entered in person into the agony of crucifixion and the greater agony of God-forsakenness (Mark 15:34) in order to bear our sins and so redeem us. Never let this claim be played down.

Celebrating the Saving Work of God

THE CURES FOR INTELLECTUAL PRIDE

We . . . take every thought
captive to obey Christ.
2 Corinthians 10:5

What will break men of the habit of looking to the authority of reason in religion? Answer: Only *regeneration* will break it in the natural man; only *revival* will break it in a regenerate church.

Fallen man cannot of himself escape from bondage to sin. Sin he must, whatever he does. It is not in him to acknowledge God's authority, or to receive God's truth when presented to him. "The natural person does not accept the things of the Spirit of God, for they are folly to him, and he is not able to understand them because they are spiritually discerned" (1 Corinthians 2:14). What can cure his condition? Only *regeneration.* Only the man who is born again of the Spirit of God will repent of the sin of intellectual self-sufficiency and consent to be taught of God through his written Word.

But sin remains in the regenerate, in the mind no less than in the members. And when the fires of spiritual life burn low in the church, the sinful lust for intellectual autonomy reasserts itself. The intellectual apostasy of Western Christendom in recent years is not unconnected with its spiritual lethargy and barrenness: each has fostered the other. What can cure this condition? Only *revival.*

Only a new outpouring of spiritual life can clear the spiritual vision and bring home to the minds of Christians the power, the authority, and the meaning of "God's Word written" and enable them to see their mental sins, their intellectual compromises and betrayals of truth, for what they are, and give them strength of mind to repent and cast out the sinful ways of thinking.

May God revive his work in his church, that his people may once again learn to think and live to his honor and glory.

Honouring the Written Word of God

THE DOOR STOOD OPEN

We have seen his glory,
glory as of the only Son from the Father.

JOHN 1:14

Recorded in three of the Gospels, and evidently planned by Jesus for Peter, James, and John to see and, later, to testify to, the Transfiguration was significant in the revelation of Jesus' deity. The transformation that the divine-human Lord underwent as he prayed (Luke 9:29) was from one standpoint a taste of things to come: It was a momentary transition from the concealing of his divine glory that marked his days on earth to the revealing of that glory when he returns and we see him as he is.

The bright light that shone from Jesus through his clothes as his face changed was the glory intrinsic to him as the divine Son, "the radiance of the glory of God" (Hebrews 1:3). The voice from the cloud confirmed the identification that the vision had already given.

The Transfiguration was also a significant event in the revelation of God's kingdom — the kingdom of the Messiah, God's prophesied Savior-King. Moses and Elijah represented the law and the prophets witnessing to Jesus and being superseded by him. The "departure" (Greek: *exodos)* of which they and Jesus talked (Luke 9:31) must have been his death, resurrection, and ascension. This was not just a way of leaving this world but also a way of redeeming his people, just as the *exodos* from Egypt that Moses led was to redeem Israel from bondage.

Following the Transfiguration, Jesus veiled his glory and went down from the mount to minister once more, and in due course to suffer for our salvation. Comments F. B. Meyer: "The door though which Moses and Elijah had come stood open, and by it our Lord might have returned. But he could never, under those circumstances, have been the Savior of mankind. He knew this, so he set his face toward Calvary."

Concise Theology

152

AWESOME, SHOCKING AUTHORITY

They were astonished at his teaching, for he taught them
as one who had authority, and not as the scribes.

MARK 1:22

The authority to which Jesus laid claim was absolute and unqualified. He appealed to no human authority, but put his teaching forward as divine in origin, and therefore eternally valid in its own right. "My teaching is not mine, but his who sent me" (John 7:16); "I have not spoken on my own authority, but the Father who sent me has himself given me a command-ment — what to say and what to speak. . . . What I say, therefore, I say as the Father has told me" (12:49-50). Therefore, "heaven and earth will pass away, but my words will not pass away" (Mark 13:31). Jesus told his hearers that their eternal destiny depended on whether, having heard his words, they kept them (Matthew 7:24-27); for "the one who rejects me and does not receive my words . . . the word that I have spoken will judge him on the last day" (John 12:48). He taught "as one who had authority" (Mark 1:22).

Some were awed by his authoritative manner; others were shocked. He did not hesitate to challenge and condemn, on his own authority, accepted Jewish ideas which seemed to him false. But he never opposed his personal authority to that of the Old Testament. He never qualified the Jewish belief in Scripture's absolute authority. The fact we have to face is that Jesus Christ, the Son of God incarnate, who claimed divine authority for all that he did and taught, both confirmed the absolute authority of the Old Testament for others and submitted to it unreservedly himself. He treats arguments from Scripture as having clinching force. When he says, "it is written," that is final.

His whole ministry, as recorded in the Gospels, may justly be described as a prolonged and many-sided affirmation of the authority of the Old Testament.

"Fundamentalism" and the Word of God

WISDOM SETS GOALS

The wisdom of the prudent is to discern his way,
but the folly of fools is deceiving.

PROVERBS 14:8

Wisdom is also about goals, the aims and targets that one sets for oneself. Wisdom teaches us how to set our sights on objectives that are truly worth aiming at. Goal number one (which all the Bible insists on) is that the knowledge of God, the enjoyment of God, the praise of God, and the honor of God should be our constant aim in everything we do, so that we may truly live to his glory. The consequent goals include love, goodwill, and care in all our personal relationships with family, friends, acquaintances, and casual contacts; faithfulness in all business dealings; integrity in all community involvements and all enterprises in which we lead and direct others; and creativity, the quest for order and beauty, in pursuing whatever interests and hobbies we embrace. Wisdom enables us to formulate and focus our goals in our various fields of activity.

In Ecclesiastes 2:13-14 the wise man says, "I saw that there is more gain in wisdom than in folly, as there is more gain in light than in darkness. The wise person has his eyes in his head, but the fool walks in darkness." Part of the implication of "eyes in his head" and "darkness" is that while the wise person sets goals and knows where he or she is going, the fool practices a random kind of living. A fool walks through life as if he were blind. Aimlessness in the most fundamental sense is the sad word that has to be written over the life of a fool. Wise persons, by contrast, have clear purposes and make thoughtful plans. They do not simply drift through life as the fool does.

Guard Us, Guide Us

HOLINESS AND USEFULNESS

*You will receive power
when the Holy Spirit has come upon you.*

ACTS 1:8

It is noteworthy that most speakers and books on holiness say little about ministry, while most speakers and books on ministry say little about holiness. It has been this way for over a century. But to treat holiness and ministry as separate themes is an error. God has linked them, and what God joins man must not put asunder.

One regular result of ongoing sanctification is that concern for others, with recognition of what they lack, and wisdom that sees how to help them is increased. Ministry blossoms naturally in holy lives. In effective ministry, God's power is channeled through God's servants into areas of human need. A saintly person of limited gifts is always likely to channel more of it than would a person who is more gifted but less godly. So God wants us all to seek holiness and usefulness together.

Out of this awareness I venture to formulate five theses that bear on *the manifesting of the power of God* among his people today, because I want the power of God to be manifested to God's glory in your life, in my life, and in our churches: (1) It is right to bring the supernatural into prominence and to raise Christians' expectations with regard to it. (2) It is right to aspire to use one's God-given gifts in powerful and useful ministry. (3) It is right to want to be a channel of divine power into other people's lives at their points of need. (4) It is right to want to see God's power manifested in a way that has a significant evangelistic effect. (5) It is right to want to be divinely empowered for righteousness, for moral victories, for deliverance from bad habits, for loving God, and for pleasing God.

Rediscovering Holiness

SCHAEFFER: CELEBRATING WHOLENESS UNDER GOD

Whatever is true ... honorable ... just ... pure ...
lovely ... commendable, if there is any excellence ...
anything worthy of praise, think about these things.

PHILIPPIANS 4:8

Francis Schaeffer embodied to an outstanding degree qualities of which English-speaking evangelicalism at the time was very short. Schaeffer did seven things (at least) that other evangelicals, by and large, were not doing.

First, with his flair for didactic communication, he coined new and pointed ways of expressing old thoughts (the "true truth" of revelation, the "mannishness" of human beings, the "upper story" and "lower story" of the divided Western mind). Second, with his gift of empathy he listened to and dialogued with the modern secular world as it expressed itself in literature and art, which most evangelicals were too cocooned in their own subculture to do. Third, he threw light on things that secularists take for granted by tracing them to their source in the history of thought, a task for which few evangelicals outside the seminaries had the skill.

Fourth, he cherished a vivid sense of the ongoing historical process of which we are all part, and offered shrewd analysis concerning the likely effect of current Christian and secular developments. Fifth, he felt, focused, and dwelt on the dignity and tragedy of sinful human beings rather than their grossness and nastiness. Sixth, he linked the passion for orthodoxy with a life of love to others as the necessary expression of gospel truth, and censured the all-too-common unlovingness of frontline fighters for that truth.

Seventh, he celebrated the wholeness of created reality under God and stressed that the Christian life must be a corresponding whole—a life in which truth, goodness, and beauty are valued together and sought with equal zeal. Having these emphases institutionally incarnated at L'Abri, his ministry understandably attracted attention. For it was intrinsically masterful, and it was also badly needed.

Honouring the People of God

REBUILDING THE RUINS

Whoever believes in the Son has eternal life;
whoever does not obey the Son shall not see life,
but the wrath of God remains on him.

JOHN 3:36

It is the way of human nature as God designed it to live in and by one's hopes, and part of the real Christian's joy, increasing with age, is to look forward to eternal life in resurrection glory with the Father and the Son. Christians have sometimes described this present life, first to last, as preparation for dying, which might sound to modern ears like a gruesome and neurotic fancy; but in light of God's design of us as hoping animals, the statement is really no more than a matter-of-fact realization of the truly natural outlook for us all.

But the children of our secular, materialistic culture decline to live, even to think of living, in terms of the world to come, and this, along with actual irreligion and egocentric immorality, constitutes the inward deformity which Christianity sees in fallen human beings. However handsome the face and however beautiful the body, the soul — that is, the real person — is out of shape and ugly. This deformity leads to a constant diffused discontent with things as they are, a miserable old age (because one has less and less to look forward to), and, one fears, a yet more miserable eternity. The Christian vision of each unregenerate person is accordingly of a tragic ruin — a noble creation originally, but one now spoiled and wasted, and tragically so by reason of the great potential for good and for joy that has thus been lost.

This shows why thoughtful Christians have always seen missionary ministry as the church's top priority in this world. Since it is only as individuals become Christians that the ruins of their lives get rebuilt, evangelism is service of each person's deepest need, and is thus the truest love of one's neighbor.

Serving the People of God

WHAT WE REALLY WANT

If we ask anything according to his will
he hears us.

1 JOHN 5:14

How are we to formulate petitions according to God's will? The answer is twofold: by following the guidelines of, first, observed need and, second, inner inclination.

In asking God to meet observed needs, the Lord's Prayer stands as a model. Here we pray for daily provision ("our daily bread"), daily pardon ("forgive us our debts"), and daily protection ("deliver us from evil") (Matthew 6:11-13). Beyond this, questions still arise. When we have told God what we would most like to see happen, some degree of uncertainty must remain as to whether we prayed according to his will. What to do then? Two things. First, we should lay before God, as part of our prayer, the reasons why we think that what we ask for is the best thing. Second, we should tell God that if he wills something different, we know it will be better, and that is what we really want him to do.

Giving God reasons shows the boldness of humility; embracing God's will shows the submissiveness of humility. In the former, faith engages with God's wisdom; in the latter, it bows to his authority. What that means is most tellingly shown us by the account of Jesus praying in Gethsemane, as he said, "My Father, if it be possible, let this cup pass from me; nevertheless, not as I will, but as you will" (Matthew 26:39). We walk in the footsteps of our Savior when we tell him and the Father that however much we find ourselves longing for something else, the Father's will has priority for us; we do not want to receive what is not part of that will; we want our Father's will and only his will, whether or not at the moment we know how much it involves.

Praying

EVERYTHING FOR CHRISTIAN LIVING

His divine power has granted to us all things
that pertain to life and godliness.

2 PETER 1:3

The Puritans made me aware that all theology is also spirituality, in the sense that it has an influence, good or bad, positive or negative, on its recipients' relationship or lack of relationship to God. If our theology does not quicken the conscience and soften the heart, it actually hardens both; if it does not encourage the commitment of faith, it reinforces the detachment of unbelief; if it fails to promote humility, it inevitably feeds pride.

Theologians are called to be the church's water engineers and sewage officers; it is their job to see that God's pure truth flows abundantly where it is needed, and to filter out any intrusive pollution that might damage health. The sociological remoteness of theological colleges, seminaries, and university faculties of theology from the true life of the church makes it easy to forget this, and the track record of professional teachers in these units has in my time been distinctly spotty so far as concerns their responsibility to the church and to the world. In fact, anyone could learn the nature of this responsibility from the church fathers, or Luther, or Calvin, but it was given to me to learn it through watching the Puritans put every "doctrine" (truth) they knew to its proper "use" (application) as a basis for life.

It seems in retrospect that by virtue of this Puritan influence on me, all my theological utterances from the start, on whatever theme, have really been spirituality (i.e., teaching for Christian living), and that I cannot now speak or write any other way. Am I glad? Frankly, yes. It is a happy inability to suffer from.

A Quest for Godliness

JESUS' HUMAN LIMITATIONS

The Son can do nothing of his own accord,
but only what he sees the Father doing.

JOHN 5:19

An unhappy speculation that mesmerized many during the past century is the so-called "kenosis theory," which suggests that in order to enter into a fully human experience of limitation, the Son of God at his incarnation forfeited his natural powers of omnipotence and omniscience; as a result, there were things he wanted to do that he could not do, and mistakes due to ignorance could enter into his teaching. Four comments seemed to be called for by way of reaction.

First, there is no hint of any such forfeiture in Scripture. Second, the suggestion seems to undermine Jesus' authority as a teacher and thus dishonor him. Third, it raises a problem about Jesus' present heavenly life. If Jesus' exercise of the two abilities mentioned (natural power to *do* and to *know)* is incompatible with a fully human experience, it would seem to follow that *either* — having in heaven affirmed these powers — his experience is not now fully human, *or*, since his heavenly experience remains fully human, he has not regained these powers, and never will. I leave it to proponents of the kenosis theory to struggle with this dilemma; it is not my problem, nor I hope yours.

Fourth, the natural explanation of the one bit of evidence from the Gospels cited in support of the theory — Jesus' acknowledged ignorance of the time of his return (Mark 13:32) — is that since the Son's nature is not to take initiatives but to follow his Father's prompting, his reason for not doing certain things, or bringing to conscious knowledge certain facts, was simply that he knew that his Father did not wish this done.

Jesus' human limitations should be explained in terms not of the special conditions of the Incarnation, but of the eternal life of the Trinity.

Celebrating the Saving Work of God

HOW GOD REVEALS

*Flesh and blood has not revealed this to you,
but my Father who is in heaven.*

MATTHEW 16:17

It has long been Christian custom to equate *revelation* with the Bible. This equation is not wrong, but it is so foreshortened and oversimplified that it hinders clear analysis, and thus it is misleading. Certainly the Bible is central and crucial to divine communication, but that is because, first, it records, interprets, and shows the right response to God's revelation of himself in history, and, second, it is the means whereby God brings all subsequent believers to recognize, receive, and respond to that revelation for themselves. For clear thought about revelation from the beginning to the present day, we need to distinguish within the revelatory process three interconnected stages.

First, *God's redemption revealed in world history* (the long series of saving acts of God recorded in history); second, *God's redemption recounted in public records* ("public records" is a phrase of John Calvin's indicating the significance of Holy Scripture as a testimony and memorial for all time of God's redemptive work in Christ, and all that led up to it and now flows from it); third, *God's redemption revealed to, and received by, individuals in the church,* involving inward enlightenment from God whereby the meaning and truth of divinely inspired witness to redemptive realities are grasped and those realities are themselves embraced in responsive faith. This is the stage without which neither of the first two would constitute actual revelation to anyone. Revelation in this subjective sense is the work of the Holy Spirit. In this sense (but in no other, it seems) revelation continues at the present time.

These three elements in the work of revelation must be bound together in our mind, for they are three stages in the single process whereby God in mercy brings spiritually blind sinners to know him.

Honouring the Written Word of God

THE KEY AND THE FULFILLMENT

Do not think that I have come to abolish the Law or the Prophets;
I have not come to abolish them but to fulfill them.

MATTHEW 5:17

In life and death, our Lord devoted himself to fulfilling the Scriptures. And it was as the fulfiller of Scripture that he presented himself to the Jews. He claimed to exhibit in himself what the Old Testament actually meant. He saw himself as the key to it, and it as the key to himself. Indeed, he held that anyone who really believed the Old Testament would know who he was, and come to trust him. In short, the Gospels assure us that the historic Israelite belief in the divine authority of the Old Testament was the foundation of Christ's whole ministry.

Jesus forbade men to view him as anything other than the fulfiller of the law and the prophets, for he did not believe himself to be anything other than that. He was the divine Messiah of whom the Old Testament spoke; he had come into the world to fulfill the Scriptures, and that was what he was doing. He appealed to Scripture as the sole and sufficient warrant for the things that he said and did because it was in conscious obedience to Scripture that he said and did them.

If we reject his attitude toward the Old Testament, we are saying in effect that he founded Christianity on a fallacy. And if we say he was wrong here, we really imply that he was wrong everywhere; for his view of the nature and authority of the Old Testament underlies all he said and did. If, on the other hand, we believe that his claims and ministry were comprehensively vindicated by his resurrection, we are bound to say that his view of the Old Testament was thereby vindicated also.

"Fundamentalism" and the Word of God

POWER ON DISPLAY

*Now to him who is able to do far more abundantly than all
that we ask or think, according to the power at work within us.*

EPHESIANS 3:20

As God exerted great power in creation, and exerts great power in his
providential upholding and shaping of things, so he has committed
himself to exert great power in the saving and upbuilding of his people.
In Ephesians 3:10, Paul, having declared that the riches of Christ are
unsearchable, explains the divine intent in the economy of grace: "that
through the church the manifold wisdom of God might now be made
known to the rulers and authorities in the heavenly places."

The vivid picture these words conjure up is one of the church as
God's display area, where he shows an audience of watching angels what
a breathtaking variety of wonderful things he can do in and through sin-
damaged human beings. My three Greek dictionaries render the Greek
word translated "manifold" as much variegated, very many-sided, and of
greatly differing colors — giving us some idea of the range and resourcefulness of God's ongoing work of power in the church. This word, writes
John Stott, "was used to describe flowers, crowns, embroidered cloth, and
woven carpets. . . . The church as a multiracial, multicultural community
is like a beautiful tapestry."[12] Yes — and also as a multi-repair shop, where
disordered and broken-down lives, made ugly by sin, are being recon-
structed in Christlike shape. The wisdom of God that Paul has in view is
not just the wisdom that brings Jew and Gentile together in the body of
Christ, but is also the wisdom that directs the power that quickens the
spiritually dead and makes new creatures of them in a new and lovely
fellowship of holiness and love.

Great is the power of God in the lives of the people of God! The
potential of his power in our lives is incalculable. Do we reckon with this
fact?

Rediscovering Holiness

LUTHER VERSUS ERASMUS

For by grace you have been saved through faith.
And this is not your own doing; it is the gift of God.

EPHESIANS 2:8

The question whether or not man has free will, in Erasmus's sense of the term, was to Luther the hinge of the whole Reformation debate. To Luther, what he and his opponents were really arguing about was whether the Christian message tells man how, with God's help, he may save himself, or whether Christianity declares that it is God in Christ who saves, and God alone. Luther's fundamental purpose as theologian and churchman was to explicate and establish the second view against the medieval habit of taking the first for granted.

Luther saw that denying Erasmus's position undercuts at a stroke every form of the gospel of self-salvation and shuts us up to the second view, forcing us to recognize that unless God freely works our whole salvation, we cannot be saved at all.

Luther's exposition of his thesis has two parts. The better-known part is his insistence that we are justified not on the ground of any merit of our own (for we have none) but through God's own gift of righteousness, freely bestowed on us in virtue of Christ's obedience and sacrifice and received through faith alone. The second part, often underemphasized today, is his equally vigorous insistence that our very faith depends not on any natural ability to trust God (again, we have none) but on God's calling — his supernatural work by the Spirit of creating in us a response to the word of the gospel.

God in grace gives not only righteousness but also faith to receive it. First to last, salvation is of the Lord. The importance of Luther's doctrine of the enslaved will is that it clears the road for this account of salvation by grace by establishing the inability of sinners to supply either works or faith from their own natural resources.

Honouring the People of God

THE MAKINGS OF MATURITY

They went about . . . destitute, afflicted, mistreated—
of whom the world was not worthy.
HEBREWS 11:37-38

Maturity is a compound of wisdom, goodwill, resilience, and creativity.
The Puritans exemplified maturity; we don't. We are spiritual dwarfs.
A much-traveled leader has declared that he finds North American
Protestantism — man-centered, manipulative, success-oriented, self-
indulgent, and sentimental, as it blatantly is — to be 3,000 miles wide and
half an inch deep. The Puritans, by contrast, as a body were giants. They
were great souls serving a great God. In them, clear-headed passion and
warm-hearted compassion combined. Visionary and practical, idealistic
and realistic too, goal-oriented and methodical, they were great believers,
great hopers, great doers, and great sufferers. But their sufferings (on both
sides of the Atlantic) seasoned and ripened them till they gained a stature
that was nothing short of heroic.

Ease and luxury, such as our affluence brings us today, do not make
for maturity; hardship and struggle however do, and the Puritans' battles
against the spiritual and climatic wildernesses in which God set them
produced a virility of character, undaunted and unsinkable, rising above
discouragement and fears, for which the true precedents and models are
men like Moses, Nehemiah, Peter after Pentecost, and the apostle Paul.

Spiritual warfare made the Puritans what they were. They accepted
conflict as their calling, seeing themselves as their Lord's soldier-pilgrims,
just as in Bunyan's allegory, and not expecting to be able to advance a
single step without opposition of one sort or another.

The moral and spiritual victories that the Puritans won by keeping sweet, peaceful, patient, obedient, and hopeful under sustained and
seemingly intolerable pressures and frustrations give them a place of high
honor in the believers' hall of fame, where Hebrews 11 is the first gallery.
Out of this constant furnace experience their maturity was wrought and
their wisdom concerning discipleship was refined.

A Quest for Godliness

HOW NECESSARY ARE THE SCRIPTURES?

> *I have written briefly to you, exhorting and declaring that this is the true grace of God. Stand firm in it.*
>
> 1 PETER 5:12

It is clear that God was under no absolute necessity to reveal himself savingly to sinful men. God owes sinners nothing; if he does them good, it is an exercise of free grace on his part; he was not obliged to show it. One may still ask, however, whether God's plan of redeeming, calling, sanctifying, and perfecting a worldwide church through the mediation of one man, Christ Jesus, whose universally significant ministry took place at one particular point in the total space-time structure of world history, did not require the giving of the Scriptures as a necessary means to God's end.

Is the Bible *necessary* for the preservation and propagation of the gospel, the securing and spreading of true knowledge of God? Protestant divines of the sixteenth and seventeenth centuries answered this question with an emphatic yes.

Calvin argued that the revealed Word is necessary for the knowledge of God, because, on one hand, God has given and appointed it for this purpose, and commands that it be used accordingly. On the other hand, sin has so darkened human minds that they cannot know God apart from the light (information plus inner illumination) that Scripture brings, or rather (to indicate Calvin's full thought) apart from the light that the Holy Spirit brings by sealing Scripture on men's hearts.

A pervasive conviction of the necessity of Scripture lies at the heart of evangelicalism, and it is no accident that evangelicals have always been the backbone of the world's Bible Societies, and the pioneers of Bible translation. The self-conscious Bible-centeredness of evangelical culture in all its forms during the past three centuries is further testimony to the strength of the evangelical conviction that Scripture alone can and must guide us in living to the praise and pleasure of God.

Honouring the Written Word of God

SCRIPTURE, OR CHRIST?

So whatever you wish that others would do to you,
do also to them, for this is the Law and the Prophets.

MATTHEW 7:12

Some will say that the final authority for Christians is not Scripture, but Christ, whom we must regard as standing apart from Scripture and above it. He is its Judge; and we, as his disciples, must judge Scripture by him, receiving only what is in harmony with his life and teaching and rejecting all that is not. But who is this Christ who judges Scripture? Not the Christ of the New Testament and of history. That Christ does not judge Scripture; he obeys it and fulfills it. By word and deed he endorses the authority of the whole of it. Certainly, he is the final authority for Christians; that is precisely why Christians are bound to acknowledge Scripture's authority. Christ teaches them to do so.

A Christ who permits his followers to set him up as Scripture's judge, one by whom its authority must be confirmed before it becomes binding and by whose adverse sentence it is in places annulled, is a Christ of human imagination, made in the theologian's own image, and whose attitude to Scripture is the opposite to that of the Christ of history.

If the construction of such a Christ is not a breach of the second commandment, it is hard to see what is. It is sometimes said that to treat the Bible as the infallible Word of God is idolatry. If Christ was an idolater, and if following his teaching is idolatry, the accusation may stand, not, however, otherwise. But to worship a Christ who did not receive Scripture as God's unerring Word, nor require his followers to do so, would seem to be idolatry in the strictest sense.

We must reckon seriously with the fact that Christ accepted the Jewish principle of biblical authority and embodied it unchanged in Christianity.

"Fundamentalism" and the Word of God

EVERYTHING SACRED

Who is wise and understanding among you? By his good conduct
let him show his works in the meekness of wisdom.

JAMES 3:13

Through the legacy of their literature, the Puritans can help us today
toward the maturity that they knew, and that we need.

First, there are lessons for us in the integration of their daily lives.
As their Christianity was all-embracing, so their living was all of a piece.
Nowadays we would call their lifestyle holistic: all awareness, activity, and
enjoyment, all development of personal powers and creativity, were integrated in the single purpose of honoring God by appreciating all his gifts
and making everything "holiness to the Lord." There was for them no
disjunction between sacred and secular; all creation, so far as they were
concerned, was sacred, and all activities, of whatever kind, must be sanctified—that is, done to the glory of God. So, in their heavenly minded
ardor, the Puritans became men and women of order, matter-of-fact and
down-to-earth, prayerful, purposeful, practical. Seeing life whole, they
integrated contemplation with action, worship with work, labor with rest,
love of God with love of neighbor and of self, and personal with social
identity, in a thoroughly conscientious and thought-out way.

In their blending of the whole wide range of Christian duties set
forth in Scripture, they were eminently balanced. They lived by "method"
(we would say, by a rule of life), planning and proportioning their time
with care, not so much to keep bad things out as to make sure they got all
good and important things in—necessary wisdom, then as now, for busy
people! We today, who tend to live unplanned lives at random in a series
of non-communicating compartments and who hence feel swamped and
distracted most of the time, could learn much from the Puritans at this
point.

A Quest for Godliness

BEING FULLY ALIVE TO GOD

God has not destined us for wrath,
but to obtain salvation through our Lord Jesus Christ,
who died for us so that . . . we might live with him.

1 THESSALONIANS 5:9-10

Thirty years ago I wrote an analysis of insights basic to personal religion that faith in Christ as one's penal substitute yields. Since I cannot today improve on it, I cite it as it stands.

1. God "condones nothing," but judges all sin as it deserves: which Scripture affirms, and my conscience confirms, to be right.

2. My sins merit ultimate penal suffering and rejection from God's presence (conscience also confirms this), and nothing I do can blot them out.

3. The penalty due to me for my sins, whatever it was, was paid for me by Jesus Christ, the Son of God, in his death on the cross.

4. Because this is so, I through faith in him am made "the righteousness of God" (Romans 3:22), i.e., I am justified. Pardon, acceptance, and sonship to God become mine.

5. Christ's death for me is my sole ground of hope before God. "If he fulfilled not justice, I must; if he underwent not wrath, I must to eternity."[13]

6. My faith in Christ is God's own gift to me, given in virtue of Christ's death for me: i.e., the cross procured it.

7. Christ's death for me guarantees my preservation to glory.

8. Christ's death for me is the measure and pledge of the love of the Father and the Son to me.

9. Christ's death for me calls and constrains me to trust, to worship, to love, and to serve.[14]

Only where these nine truths have taken root and grow in the heart will anyone be fully alive to God.

In My Place Condemned He Stood

PURPOSEFUL EVANGELISM

Whoever captures souls
is wise.

PROVERBS 11:30

In our work of evangelism, Christians are sent to convert, and they should not allow themselves, as Christ's representatives in the world, to aim at anything less. Evangelizing, therefore, is not simply a matter of teaching, and instructing, and imparting information to the mind. There is more to it than that. Evangelizing includes the endeavor to elicit a response to the truth taught. It is communication with a view to conversion. It is a matter not merely of informing, but also of inviting. It is an attempt to *gain* (KJV), or *win,* or *catch* our fellow men for Christ (1 Corinthians 9:19-23; 1 Peter 3:1; Luke 5:10). Our Lord depicts it as fishermen's work (Matthew 4:19; 13:47).

Paul is our model here. Paul knew himself to be sent by Christ, not only to open men's minds by teaching them the gospel (though that must come first), but also to turn them to God by exhorting and applying the truth to their lives. Accordingly, his avowed aim was not just to spread information, but to save sinners: "that by all means I might save some" (1 Corinthians 9:22; see also Romans 11:14). Thus, there was in his evangelistic preaching both instruction — "in Christ God was reconciling the world to himself" — and entreaty — "we implore you on behalf of Christ, be reconciled to God" (2 Corinthians 5:19-20).

Evangelism and the Sovereignty of God

170

OUR NEED FOR WORK

For we are his workmanship,
created in Christ Jesus for good works.
EPHESIANS 2:10

Had God not required us, made as we are, to work in his world, the experience of fulfillment that these things engender would not be ours; and if, made as we are, we should become work-shy and give ourselves to pursuing leisure and amusement instead, we should sentence ourselves to deep-level dissatisfaction with life.

No form of work can guarantee that virtue, love, and joy will become ours, but we need not expect that virtue, love, and joy will ever mark us out if our lives have in them no forms of work. Nehemiah, Moses, David, Paul, and Jesus beckon us down a different path, a path of purposeful effort, as indeed does the entire New Testament, with its insistence that Christians must constantly practice "good works" (Matthew 5:16; 2 Corinthians 9:8; Ephesians 2:10; 1 Timothy 6:18; 2 Timothy 3:17; Titus 2:7,14; 3:1,8,14; Hebrews 10:24).

I am here thinking of work, as I have said, in a much wider and more basic sense than paid employment, but it would be wrong not to notice that one great social evil in the modern West is the ongoing lack of paid employment for something like 10 percent of the workforce — in other words, the actual unemployment of many millions at any one time. Inability to find paid work is demoralizing and depressing, as well as financially and spiritually impoverishing. The unemployed need all the sympathy and help that Christians can give, both to retain their self-respect and also to go on using their natural creativity in informal ways, which their inner frustration tempts them not to do.

A Passion for Faithfulness

THE CHURCH'S TWO CONSTANT NEEDS

> *My people know not*
> *the rules of the LORD.*
> JEREMIAH 8:7

Those who acknowledge the lordship of Christ are bound to accept the principle of biblical authority. This principle has far-reaching practical implications as it dictates our approach to the church's life.

Because the church on earth consists of imperfectly sanctified sinners, there are always two defects in the lives of its members, both corporately and individually. These are ignorance and error, which cause omissions and mistakes in belief and behavior. The church, therefore, has two constant needs: instruction in the truths by which it must live, and correction of the shortcomings by which its life is marred.

Scripture is designed to meet this twofold need; it is "profitable for teaching . . . and for training in righteousness" on one hand, and for "reproof" and "correction" on the other (2 Timothy 3:16). It is the church's responsibility to use Scripture for its intended purpose. This it does by the complementary activities of exposition followed by reformation.

To accept the authority of Scripture means in practice being willing first to believe what it teaches, and then to apply its teaching to ourselves for our correction and guidance. The Reformers saw that this was what God demanded of the church in the sixteenth century, and the truth is that he demands the same in every age of the church's life. The words and lives of Christian men must be in continual process of reformation by the written Word of their God.

This means that ecclesiastical traditions and private theological speculations may never be identified with the word which God speaks, but are to be classed among the words of men which the Word of God must reform.

"Fundamentalism" and the Word of God

AVOIDING LIFE'S PITFALLS

Do you see a man who is wise in his own eyes?
There is more hope for a fool than for him.

PROVERBS 26:12

Wisdom has to do with strategies — the establishing of means to achieve our goals so we don't slip into pitfalls and places of disaster through imprudences that we could have avoided. Think of the mountain climber whose goal is to get to the top; he has to be very careful about the way he goes or he may fall into a crevasse or lose his footing on a slope or a rock face and come to great grief.

The book of Proverbs is from one standpoint a very prudent book, constantly teaching how to avoid life's pitfalls, so that all the time we are achieving the practice of God-honoring wisdom in all its fullness. This is where willingness to accept advice comes in. Proverbs 10:17 says, "Whoever heeds instruction is on the path to life, but he who rejects reproof leads others astray." The fool (one who has chosen not to walk in God's wisdom nor accept advice and correction from anybody, but to be led by his own mother wit) is going to go astray himself, and he will persuade others to follow him. Everyone has spheres of influence, for better or for worse, and in those spheres of influence others will follow our example. We are wise to be aware that our way of living and believing will influence others whether or not we intended it so — and therefore to humbly heed advice from others about avoiding pitfalls on our own chosen path.

"The way of a fool is right in his own eyes, but a wise man listens to advice" (Proverbs 12:15). "By insolence comes nothing but strife, but with those who take advice is wisdom" (13:10). "Listen to advice and accept instruction, that you may gain wisdom in the future" (19:20).

Guard Us, Guide Us

PERSON OF POWER

> *For all who are led by the Spirit of God*
> *are sons of God.*
>
> ROMANS 8:14

Power is a word associated in everyday English with impersonal forces, but the power of the Holy Spirit is the effective agency of a person, who personally relates himself to those in whose lives he works. "Even when the New Testament speaks of the Spirit in impersonal images, the chief of which are wind, fire, and water," writes Tom Smail, "the images are used dynamically to show that they are pointing to one who has the will and the power to control us rather than to something we ourselves can control."[15] The Holy Spirit is not an impersonal force at our disposal or harnessed to our wills; rather, the Spirit is a sovereign person with his own will, which is also the will of the Father and the Son.

The Spirit operates in and through our thinking (he convinces us of God's truth), our decision-making (he leads us to will the will of God), and our affections (he draws forth from us love and hate, hope and fear, joy and sorrow, and other feeling-laden dispositions, all responding to the realities of the gospel).

His blessing on the Bible we read, and on the Christian instruction we receive, persuades us of the truth of Christianity. He shows us how God's promises and demands bear on our lives. His new creative action at the center of our personal being so changes and energizes us that we do in fact obey the truth. The persuasion at conscious level is powerful. The heart-changing action that produces Christian commitment is almighty. First to last, however, the power exercised is personal. The Holy Spirit is a living person, not a mere force.

Rediscovering Holiness

DEEP EXPERIENCE OF THE SPIRIT

The anointing that you received from him abides in you . . .
just as it has taught you—abide in him.

1 JOHN 2:27

The Reformers set their faces against any trust in natural theology, basing their distrust on a denial of fallen man's ability to apprehend general revelation correctly. Fallen man's proud intellect (so the Reformers held) always distorts what comes through to him from general revelation by his own self-willed speculation or self-induced obtuseness. The Reformers argued constantly that those who do not in humility and self-distrust allow the Bible to teach them its message about God and grace will never have their false notions of God corrected, nor see the light of saving truth, but will walk in darkness forever; only those who become pupils of Scripture will find the true God and eternal life.

This point is bound up with another: the clear understanding of the ministry of the Holy Spirit which blossomed at the Reformation in a way that was quite without precedent since the apostles Paul and John laid down their pens. Theologically, the Reformers' grasp of the nature and power of the Spirit's ministry sprang straight from the Scriptures, which as scholarly Renaissance men they read not to allegorize in terms of inherited ideas as medieval preachers had done, but to enter into the thinking of the authors. Reading them thus, they learned from God's penmen of the Spirit's covenanted work in Christians and in the church.

Subjectively, however, what determined the emphasis they gave to the Spirit's ministry was the fact that, reading the Scriptures not just as scholars but as Christians, conscious of the darkness of their own minds and praying for light, they had enjoyed in answer to their prayers a deep personal experience of the Spirit's inner witness to the authenticity of Scripture as God's Word, and of the Spirit's power to use it as a source of instruction, hope, and strength.

Honouring the People of God

WE'RE DIFFERENT NOW

Consider how I love your precepts!
Give me life according to your steadfast love.

PSALM 119:159

Holy Scripture, which is Law and Light, is also Life, in the very precise sense that it bestows life through the Holy Spirit because the Holy Spirit writes it in our hearts. James 1:21 actually gives us this thought: "Receive with meekness the implanted word." God implants the Word in our hearts, just as we implant bulbs and seeds in our flowerpots.

The implanted Word, continues James, "is able to save your souls." The Word takes root in our hearts, and changes us in ways of which we are not at first conscious; in due course, however, we become aware that we are different from the way we were. Once I didn't see Jesus in his glory and now I do. Once I didn't love my heavenly Father or my Savior, and now I do. Once I didn't honor the Holy Spirit and now I do. Once I didn't find worship a joy and now I do. Once I didn't desire to please God more than I desire anything else in the world, once I didn't desire God's fellowship at all, but that has changed.

What's happened? What has happened is that the Word has been implanted and taken root, and through the Holy Spirit it has become the means of life to my heart; yours too, I trust. It's the fulfillment of the New Covenant prophecy of Jeremiah 31:33: God writes his words on our hearts.

Bible truth imparts spiritual life, and we need to soak ourselves in Scripture if we are ever to learn how to know and love and serve and honor and obey our Lord. God grant you to share in the excitement and in a full measure of that divine life to which the love of God's Word opens the door.

Serving the People of God

A HEART THAT HALLOWS GOD'S NAME

Among those who are near me I will be sanctified,
and before all the people I will be glorified.

LEVITICUS 10:3

With God — the Searcher of hearts — the inner realities of motivation, purpose, and desire that prompt and energize our actions are just as important as the performance of the actions themselves, viewed from the outside. Prayer that is performed mechanically, without any focused thought (as when we clean our teeth) and in a state of suppressed resentment, perhaps, at having to do it, is prayer from a heart that is not as it should be, and so the performance is in God's eyes hypocritical to a degree. God assesses all our actions from the inside as well as the outside, as Jesus tried (unsuccessfully) to teach the Pharisees.

The basic petition of the entire Lord's Prayer is "Hallowed be your name" — which means, May you, God, be always and everywhere honored, exalted, magnified, and praised for all that you are and do. This is the global ideal and desire that all the other petitions in the Lord's Prayer are actually spelling out and specifying in one way or another. Just as this petition is the controlling thought of the Lord's Prayer as a whole, so the longing to see this petition fulfilled should be the controlling desire of the heart whenever God's children pray. We have been given the Lord's Prayer so that we might learn from it not just the wording but the spirit, the animating attitude, of this authoritative model.

So we are to pray to God in order to further the praise of God first and foremost, not to gratify selfish concerns in which God has no place. Why then should we ask for what we do ask for? Our honest answer to that question should point toward God: his name, his glory, his nature, his kingdom.

Praying

PASSIONATE PIETY

I will meditate on your precepts
and fix my eyes on your ways.
PSALM 119:15

The Puritans also offer lessons for us in the quality of their spiritual experience. They sought to live by Scripture, as God's word of instruction about divine-human relationships, and here, too, they were conscientiously methodical. Knowing themselves to be creatures of thought, affection, and will, and knowing that God's way to the human heart (the will) is via the human head (the mind), the Puritans practiced meditation, discursive and systematic, on the whole range of biblical truth as they saw it applying to themselves.

Puritan meditation on Scripture was modeled on the Puritan sermons; in meditation the Puritan would seek to search and challenge his heart, stir his affections to hate sin and love righteousness, and encourage himself with God's promises, just as Puritan preachers would do from the pulpit. This rational, resolute, passionate piety was conscientious without becoming obsessive, law-oriented without lapsing into legalism, and expressive of Christian liberty without any shameful lurches into license. The Puritans knew that Scripture is the unalterable rule of holiness, and never allowed themselves to forget it.

Knowing also the dishonesty and deceitfulness of fallen human hearts, they cultivated humility and self-suspicion as abiding attitudes, and examined themselves regularly for spiritual blind spots and lurking inward evils. They found the discipline of self-examination by Scripture, followed by the discipline of confessing and forsaking sin and renewing one's gratitude to Christ for his pardoning mercy, to be a source of great inner peace and joy. We today, who know to our cost that we have unclear minds, uncontrolled affections, and unstable wills when it comes to serving God, and who again and again find ourselves being imposed on by irrational, emotional romanticism disguised as super-spirituality, could profit much from the Puritans' example at this point too.

A Quest for Godliness

THE KEYSTONE OF THE ARCH

No one has ever seen God; the only God,
who is at the Father's side, he has made him known.

JOHN 1:18

We should watch like hawks against any fragmenting of the seamless robe of scriptural testimony to Jesus Christ as God incarnate, our prophet, priest, and king, our wisdom and righteousness, our Lord, our life, our way, and our end.

The worship of Jesus Christ alongside the Father, to which the New Testament leads us, the Christian's saving relationship with him, and the church's corporate solidarity with him in his risen life — all assume that he died as an effective sacrifice for our sins, rose again as proof that his atoning work was done, reigns here and now and will one day return to judge the living and the dead. None of this can be convincingly affirmed if his divine-human glory as God incarnate be denied.

It really is not true that the less of New Testament Christology you set yourself to defend, the easier it will prove to defend it. On the contrary, if you take away any of its component bricks, and particularly the reality of the Incarnation, which is the keystone of the arch, the whole structure falls down. Only when the whole New Testament story concerning Christ is told in all its parts will credibility attach to any of it.

If the Incarnation is denied, the whole New Testament account of Jesus the Christ should certainly be categorized as mythological fantasy. But then there is no reason why it should any longer claim our interest; the proper place for it then would be the dustbin. We need to realize the interlocking and interdependent character of the truths concerning Jesus, to see that divided they fall, and to make it a matter of deliberate care to tell the whole story when bearing testimony to the Son of God in this clashing, confused, and disordered age.

Celebrating the Saving Work of God

THE CHARISMATIC CHALLENGE

> *For the love of Christ controls us . . . he died for all,*
> *that those who live might no longer live for themselves*
> *but for him who for their sake died and was raised.*
>
> 2 CORINTHIANS 5:14-15

The central charismatic quest is not for any particular experience as such, but for what we may call thoroughgoing and uninhibited *totality* in realizing God's presence and responding to his grace. In worship, this totality means full involvement of each worshipper and the fullest openness to God. In ministry, it means not only nor even chiefly the use of sign gifts, but the discerning and harnessing of all capacities to serve. In Christian expression and communication, it means a great deal of singing, both from books and "in the Spirit"; clapping, arm raising, hand stretching; muttering together in group prayer, delivering of prophecies from God to the fellowship, passing the lead from glossolalics to interpreters, loose improvisatory preaching and corporate dialogue with the preacher by interjection and response hugging, dancing, and so on. In fellowship, it means giving oneself and one's substance generously, even recklessly, to help others.

The charismatic quest for totality is surely right, and even if this way of pursuing it is not one which all believers can happily buy into, it comes as a salutary challenge to the muddleheaded ideals of restraint and respectability that have bogged down so many within our older churches in a sort of conscientious half-heartedness. This challenge must be received as from God.

Specifically, then, those who stand aloof, while doubtless not obliged to adopt the charismatic ethos or forbidden to think that some of what they see in the movement is childish and zany, must face this question: How are you, in your church and fellowship, proposing to realize comparable totality before the Lord?

Keep in Step with the Spirit

THEOLOGY AND WISDOM

I have taught you statutes and rules,
as the LORD my God commanded me. . . .
Keep them and do them, for that will be
your wisdom and your understanding.
DEUTERONOMY 4:5-6

Up to the seventeenth century, theology (*theologia*) was conceived primarily as a personal quality, "a cognitive disposition and orientation of the soul, a knowledge of God and what God reveals."[16] But since the seventeenth century the word has come increasingly to signify sharing one's own ideas about other people's ideas about God — basically a conversational agenda that often leads nowhere. Thus has theology trivialized itself. Theology has become simply the voicing and discussing of any and every notion about God and religion — good and bad, old and new, familiar and strange, conventional and eccentric, true and false — and it is clear that many institutions of the theological trade wish to keep it that way.

For the best part of a century now, many theology-teaching institutions have employed instructors less for the orthodoxy of their views than for their technical prowess and their penchant for stabbing sleepy minds awake. Moreover, many of these teachers seem to have operated on the assumption that their students' education was best served by challenging whatever confessional, Bible-based certainties were brought into the classroom. This has had the knock-on effect of impoverishing churches, for though it is a truism that congregations want to hear their preachers' certainties rather than their doubts, this kind of theological education makes the proclamation of certainties impossible, thus undermining the morale of believers and churches alike.

Where do we go from here? The answer is, back to the Bible. There we see the striking likeness between the *theologia* of the medieval and Reformational believer and the wisdom of the truly wise person as pictured in the Bible. True theology is essentially identical with God's gift of wisdom.

The Way of Wisdom

THE COMPLEXITY OF TRUTH

I still have many things to say to you,
but you cannot bear them now.

JOHN 16:12

The revealed Word — the Bible as we have it — is necessary because of the complexity of revealed truth.

From the moment man sinned, God the Creator began to show himself a God of grace, accepting responsibility to do all that was necessary to restore human beings to himself. It was necessary that his work of restoration should have an educational, instructional aspect. In addition to making redemptive provision for sinners, God must speak to them, to teach them his character, aims, standards, and proposals. He must explain to them what his purpose is for themselves as individuals, and also for the church, the redeemed community, and the whole cosmos, so that they may know his mind at least in principle regarding every issue and situation with which they have to deal, and in which he has to deal with them.

To move us by external physical force alone, as men move sticks or stones, would not answer God's restorative purpose. Only as God addresses us directly, and works on and in us in conjunction with his message, can our activity take the form of rational, personal response to himself. Therefore a revealed Word from God to mankind, embracing a wide range of instruction, was necessary from the start. Such a revealed Word cannot avoid being complex if it is to deal adequately with the complexity of human life, "that the man of God may be competent, equipped for every good work" (2 Timothy 3:17).

Furthermore, the heart of the knowledge which God seeks to impart is knowledge of the risen Jesus, understood in terms of the triunity of God, incarnation of the Son, the mediatorial office, and saving union with Christ — perhaps the most complex and elusive concepts in the whole history of human thought.

Honouring the Written Word of God

REIGNING HIGH

> *While he blessed them, he parted from them*
> *and was carried up into heaven.*
>
> LUKE 24:51

Jesus' ascension was his Father's act of withdrawing him from his disciples' gaze upward (a sign of exaltation) into a cloud (a sign of God's presence). This was not a form of space travel, but part two (the Resurrection being part one) of Jesus' return from the depths of death to the height of glory.

Paul celebrated Christ's ascension and affirmed his consequent lordship (Ephesians 1:20; 4:8-10; Philippians 2:9-11; 1 Timothy 3:16), and the writer of Hebrews applied this truth for encouragement of the fainthearted (Hebrews 1:3; 4:14; 9:24). The fact that Jesus Christ is enthroned as master of the universe should be of enormous encouragement to all believers.

The Ascension was from one standpoint the restoration of the glory that the Son had before the Incarnation, from another the glorifying of human nature in a way that had never happened before, and from a third the start of a reign that had not previously been exercised in this form. The Ascension establishes three facts:

1. Christ's personal ascendency. Jesus went up to the place of power, pictured as a throne at the Father's right hand.

2. Christ's spiritual omnipresence. In the heavenly sanctuary in heavenly Zion, Jesus is accessible to all who invoke him, and he is powerful to help them, anywhere in the world.

3. Christ's heavenly ministry. The reigning Lord intercedes for his people (Romans 8:34; Hebrews 7:25). The essence of Christ's intercession is intervention in our interest from his throne. In sovereignty he now lavishes upon us the benefits that his suffering won for us. From his throne he sends the Holy Spirit constantly to enrich his people (John 16:7-14; Acts 2:33) and equip them for service (Ephesians 4:8-12).

Concise Theology

PRAYER FROM PURE MOTIVES

Hear the prayer of your servant
that I now pray before you day and night.
NEHEMIAH 1:6

Our praying determines the quality of our working, just as our working reflects the quality of our praying. Nehemiah's narrative seems to illustrate this very clearly.

William Temple said somewhere that whereas we think our real work is our activity, to which prayer is an adjunct, our praying is our real work, and our activity is the index of how we have done it. Temple is surely right. For real prayer — prayer, that is, that centers on the hallowing of God's name and the doing of his will — has, among its other effects, a reflex effect. It purifies the heart; it purges our attitudes and motives; it melts down all the self-centeredness, self-sufficiency, and self-reliance that as fallen creatures we bring to it, and programs us to work humbly, in a God-honoring, God-fearing, God-dependent way. We need to remember that in God's sight motivation is an integral element in action; the Lord looks not only on the outward behavior but also on the heart, and any motivation that exalts itself will render our work rotten at the core from his point of view. (Remember the Pharisees, and Jesus' words about them!) Because of the self-absorbed habits of our sinful hearts, the only way to anything like pure motives is to pray persistently about the things we do and ask ourselves constantly before the Lord why we are doing them and how they fit in with God's glory and the good of his people. This is the path to purer hearts than we could hope to have otherwise.

I see Nehemiah as an example of this, for it looks as if he followed the above procedure all the time. Nehemiah's rule of action seems to have been: first pray, then act, then pray again.

A Passion for Faithfulness

TRADITION'S HOLD ON US ALL

*You leave the commandment of God
and hold to the tradition of men.*

MARK 7:8

Whether or not we belong to a communion that treats tradition as an authoritative source of teaching, we are all in fact children of tradition in our religion. We do not start our Christian lives by working out our faith for ourselves; it is mediated to us by Christian tradition, in the form of sermons, books, and established patterns of church life and fellowship. We read our Bibles in the light of what we have learned from these sources; we approach Scripture with minds already formed by the mass of accepted opinions and viewpoints with which we have come into contact, in both the church and the world. Inevitably, we grow up children of our own age, reflecting in our outlook the mental environment in which we were reared. The process is as natural as breathing in the air around us, and as unconscious. It is easy to be unaware that it has happened; it is hard even to begin to realize how profoundly tradition in this sense has molded us. But we are forbidden to become enslaved to human tradition, either secular or Christian, whether it be "catholic" tradition, or "critical" tradition, or "ecumenical" tradition, or even "evangelical" tradition. We may never assume the complete rightness of our own established ways of thought and practice and excuse ourselves the duty of testing and reforming them by Scripture.

Christ deals with the question of the authority of tradition in Mark 7:6-13. He tells the Pharisees that by bowing to man-made tradition rather than God-given Scripture, they show that their hearts are far from God. To Christ, ecclesiastical tradition was no part of the Word of God; it must be tested by Scripture and, if found wanting, dropped.

"Fundamentalism" and the Word of God

WISDOM AND MEEKNESS

He leads the humble in what is right,
and teaches the humble his way.

PSALM 25:9

James, wisdom writer of the New Testament, amplifies Proverbs on the subject of wisdom and humility by saying, "Who is wise and understanding among you? By his good conduct let him show his works in the meekness of wisdom" (James 3:13). Meekness accepts things the way they come at us; it doesn't quarrel with God when discerning aspects of his providence. Instead, meekness acknowledges that God knows what he is doing and that he makes all things work together for good for those who love him — even if at this present moment things do not appear to be working well at all. A person who is meek accepts the way God orders things, and such meekness, James says, is a mark of wisdom.

As we read further in James 3, we come to verse 17 and find this: "The wisdom from above [that is, the wisdom that God gives, the wisdom of Christlikeness, the wisdom imparted by God's Spirit that we ought to be seeking constantly] is first pure, then peaceable, gentle, open to reason, full of mercy and good fruits, impartial and sincere." To enter into the quest for wisdom, which means the quest for Christlikeness in all these ways, is thus to pursue a life of holiness, godliness, and sanctity, marked by prudence, good sense, discretion, purity, meekness, mercy, and thoughtful self-control. In this fashion, God leads us in paths of righteousness — that is, right paths — for his name's sake, in other words, for his own glory as the God who keeps his covenant promises and beautifully blesses his people in doing so.

Guard Us, Guide Us

GOD'S POWER AND HIS PURPOSES

His divine power has granted to us all things
that pertain to life and godliness.

2 PETER 1:3

Scripture is full of references to the power of God. In all these acts of power, we are told, God shows himself sovereign. He is working out his own purpose for each individual person, human or angelic, and for the history of the universe, over which he rules and which he directs toward its climax according to his eternal plan.

With regard to the history of this world, the church is at the center. The Bible tells us what the essence of the plan is: Jesus Christ, already this world's reigning Lord, will continue to reign until, one way or another (opinions among believers differ as to just how), all created rational beings come to acknowledge his lordship. In the broadest sense, God is exerting his power here and now in order, step by step, to bring about this final consummation.

God has made his purpose a matter of promise to us. The Bible is full of particular promises in which aspects of his purpose are spelled out as a basis for our responsive trust. Were it not so, you could hardly call our contact with God a personal relationship at all. Real, personal relationships always involve personal commitments, and promises are the utterances that regulate such commitments. A promise is a word that reaches into the future, creating a bond of obligation on the part of the one who gives it and of expectation on the part of the one who receives it. In this sense it brings about a new state of affairs for those by whom and to whom it is spoken. That our mighty Creator should have bound himself to use his power in fulfilling promises to us — "precious and very great promises," as 2 Peter 1:4 puts it — is one of the wonders of biblical religion.

Rediscovering Holiness

THE EXCELLENCE OF SCRIPTURE

The law of the LORD is perfect, reviving the soul;
the testimony of the LORD is sure, making wise the simple.

PSALM 19:7

The Reformers' whole understanding of Christianity depended on the view that Scripture is the *only* guide for conscience and the church, the *only* source of true knowledge of God and grace, and the *only* qualified judge of the church's testimony and teaching. This view rests upon a further series of principles:

1. God's people need God's instruction because their minds are blind and ignorant through sin, and it is beyond their power to work out any true knowledge of God for themselves.

2. God intends to enlighten and teach us, bringing us to faith and knowledge of himself in Christ, by the Spirit through the Scriptures. That is why the Scriptures exist.

3. The Scriptures were so directly produced by the Holy Spirit that whatever they teach, God himself teaches.

4. The Scriptures are essentially clear in their meaning and do not need an authoritative human voice to speak for them, as if they were intrinsically obscure.

5. Scripture's teaching is sufficient for our guidance in all matters of faith and life; there is no need or possibility of supplementing the Bible from any other source of revelation.

6. Through the inner witness of the Spirit, Christians recognize that the Scriptures "breathe out something divine" and come with God's own authority to all who hear or read them.

7. The Spirit enables us to understand the Scriptures in their true theological sense, as a complex unity of witness to our Lord and Savior Jesus Christ.

8. The biblical message stands over the church and over individual Christians at all times to judge, correct, and amplify their understanding of God's works and ways.

9. The people of God must wait on the ministry of his Word by those whom he has qualified for this task.

Honouring the People of God

SEEKING AND COMING

All that the Father gives me will come to me,
and whoever comes to me I will never cast out.

JOHN 6:37

The Greek participle translated in our Bibles by the words "whoever *comes* to me" (John 6:37, emphasis added) could be translated "whoever is *coming*" or "whoever is *in process of coming* to me." The promise is that such a one will not be cast out.

There were some in the crowd listening to Jesus speak those words, and there are many more in our churches today, who were and are seeking Christ. They are coming to church, reading the Word, praying, trying to get the doctrines of grace clear — and finding it hard to do. Somehow things are not coming clear for them in the way they are for others. They think it marvelous to see others being converted suddenly and dramatically, like a cork being pulled out of a bottle, but it makes them frightened about their own situation. They ask, "Is there no mercy for me? Am I too late because I'm so slow?"

No! This is the precious truth this participle is teaching. Jesus says, "However difficult the journey to the foot of my cross, I will wait for you. And I shall go on helping you and will receive you when you do come." You can miss a plane by being too late at the terminal. You will not miss Jesus Christ by coming slowly, if you are seeking him with all your heart and in all your slowness are coming as fast as you can.

To seekers, then, I offer this word of encouragement: Go on seeking. As you seek, you will find the Lord waiting for you. May the Lord Christ draw us all to his feet, bring us all into the knowledge of the richness of his love, and lead us all into that joy of assurance which is every Christian's birthright.

Serving the People of God

RIGHTLY EXPECTING
ANSWERED PRAYER

For everyone who asks receives,
and the one who seeks finds.

MATTHEW 7:8

We weren't born God's children; nobody is. We become God's children through faith in Jesus Christ. He, who is the eternal Son of the Father by nature, brings us into the family as adopted children, and henceforth is our elder brother. Our relationship with the Father of Jesus as our own Father is basic to all that we ask in prayer. Fathers give good gifts to their children, and that should give us boldness in making our requests.

Matthew 6, where Jesus teaches the Lord's Prayer, is the midsection of the Sermon on the Mount and consists entirely of teaching on three of the realities that lie with our heavenly Father: practicing piety to please him alone (verses 1-18), living single-mindedly as his heirs and servants (verses 19-24), and trusting his fatherly care in daily life (verses 25-34). It is within that family frame that in Matthew 7, having warned us against sibling savagery in God's family (verses 1-5), Jesus invites us to offer petitions to our Father in heaven: "Ask, and it will be given to you; seek, and you will find; knock, and it will be opened to you. . . . If you then, who are evil, know how to give good gifts to your children, how much more will your Father who is in heaven give good things to those who ask him!" (verses 7,11).

Jesus addresses these words to all who know they are children of God through faith in himself, so with a humble boldness we can rightly say that our relationship with God as children to a Father is a solid basis for *expecting* that our asking will receive a positive answer.

Praying

ACTIVE CHANGE AGENTS

*Wake up, and strengthen what remains and is about to die,
for I have not found your works complete in the sight of my God.*

REVELATION 3:2

In the lives and writings of the Puritans there are lessons for us also in their passion for effective action. The Puritans had no time for the idleness of the lazy or passive person who leaves it to others to change the world. They were men of action in the pure Reformed mold — crusading activists without a jot of self-reliance; workers for God who depended utterly on God to work in and through them, and who always gave God the praise for anything they did that in retrospect seemed to them to have been right; gifted men who prayed earnestly that God would enable them to use their powers, not for self-display, but for his praise.

None of them wanted to be revolutionaries in church or state, though some of them reluctantly became such; all of them, however, longed to be effective change agents for God wherever shifts from sin to sanctity were called for. So Cromwell and his army made long, strong prayers before each battle, and preachers made long, strong prayers privately before ever venturing to the pulpit, and laymen made long, strong prayers before tackling any matter of importance (marriage, business deals, major purchases, or whatever).

Today, however, Christians in the West are found to be on the whole passionless, passive, and, one fears, prayerless. Where the Puritans prayed and labored for a holy England and New England — sensing that where privilege is neglected and unfaithfulness reigns, national judgment threatens — modern Christians gladly settle for conventional social respectability and, having done so, look no further. Surely it is obvious that at this point the Puritans have a great deal to teach us.

A Quest for Godliness

THE CLEANSING AGENT

You were ransomed . . . with the precious blood of Christ,
like that of a lamb without blemish or spot.

1 PETER 1:18-19

Paul tells us that God set forth his Son "as a propitiation by his blood" (Romans 3:25). "Blood" is New Testament shorthand, pointing to animal sacrifice as a type of the death of Christ and to Christ's death as coming in the category of sacrifice. "Blood" tells us that sacrifice is the clue we need for interpreting the nature of the atonement.

What does the sight of blood do to you? Some people find that it turns their stomachs and makes them feel faint. If you are one of those, you would have had a hard time in temple and tabernacle worship in ancient Israel, for much blood was spilled in the course of that worship. Most of the sacrifices offered to God were of animals ceremonially slaughtered. It was specifically stated in the Old Testament rituals that sin offerings and guilt offerings must take this form: an animal killed, the blood drained, and the blood thrown out at the base of the altars, as prescribed.

Paul often speaks of Christ's death in this way (Romans 5:9; Ephesians 1:7; Colossians 1:20). Each time the word *blood* occurs, it is theological shorthand expressing the thought of sacrifice for sin. Other New Testament writers speak similarly of Christ's death (for example, Hebrews 9:11-14; 1 Peter 1:19; Revelation 1:5-6; 5:9). In all these texts the atonement of Christ has the nature of sacrifice.

First John 1:7 tells us that "the blood of Jesus his Son cleanses us from all sin." As a literal idea it makes our imagination boggle — red blood, yet cleansing! Yes, but the theological meaning is right; Christ's blood, that is, his atoning sacrifice, does cleanse from sin.

Celebrating the Saving Work of God

A LOST REALITY

Be transformed by the renewal of your mind, that by testing
you may discern what is the will of God.

ROMANS 12:2

During the twentieth century, a number of streams of thought converged to produce what we now speak of as the post-Christian mindset. Among these were philosophical and scientific rationalism's claim of being the only way to knowledge; evolutionary theory's attempt to explain everything in progress terms; literary and historical criticism's challenge to the Bible's trustworthiness; and positivism's skepticism about any form of supernaturalism. These ideas stand in startling contrast to the view that they displaced.

Up to the seventeenth century, Christians everywhere had assumed, more or less explicitly and clearheadedly, that theology was a true science and indeed the Queen of the Sciences, in the sense of its offering an account of God that determines where the other sciences fit in and how they should be practiced. Christians believed that this theology constituted a cognitive apprehension — that is, actual knowledge — of the reality of God in Christ according to the Bible and the church's creeds and liturgies. By the same token, they also believed that the apprehension was not self-generated but was given by God through the means of grace that he provides in and via the church.

They believed, moreover, that this apprehension was marked by three integrated characteristics: that as it was factually instruction, so it was devotionally relational and morally transformational. In other words, knowledge of God is as much communion with him and obedience to him as it is grasping facts about him; and theology — that is, the formulation of this knowledge in orderly speech — is real and authentic only to the extent that it embodies these three elements with biblical accuracy and then expresses them in worship and holy living. This was the intellectual paradigm of the whole Christian world for a millennium and a half.

The Way of Wisdom

GOD'S UNIFIED CALL TO US ALL

> *I have spoken to them and they have not listened,*
> *I have called to them and they have not answered.*
>
> JEREMIAH 35:17

The way the Spirit of God creates, sustains, and renews our fellowship with our Creator is by applying to us the Word of God — that is, God's message as his inspired messengers set it forth, whether orally or in writing. The Old Testament use of the phrase "the word of the Lord" for each prophetic oracle points to the organic unity of all the particular "words" of God, as part of a single composite manifestation of a single speaker's mind. "Each individual revelation is not *a* word, but *the* word of Jahweh. . . . In every single revelation it is always the whole word of God that expresses itself."[17]

In the New Testament, apart from its Johanine application to the Son of God (John 1:1-14), the phrase "the word of God" denotes specifically the Christian message as a whole, the many-sided good news of divine grace through Jesus Christ, as proclaimed by Jesus and his apostles. The New Testament itself, and, indeed, in a large sense the whole Bible, may properly be called "the Word of God" in this material sense, as being proclamation of the gospel, no less than in the formal sense of having God as its source and speaker.

Two principles emerge: First, what God blesses to us is his truth, and only his truth — that is, the teaching of Scripture, as faithfully echoed and reproduced in the preaching and witness of the church. It is only with his truth that he feeds our souls.

Second, God's Word has the nature of a call. It comes as a summons to each hearer to respond to God in light of its application to himself, and the way the Holy Spirit blesses it is precisely by causing us to understand and receive it as God's call, and to answer accordingly.

Honouring the Written Word of God

IN THE SEAT OF AUTHORITY

After making purification for sins,
he sat down at the right hand of the Majesty on high.
HEBREWS 1:3

The New Testament can picture Jesus' heavenly activity as standing ready to act (Acts 7:56), walking among his people (Revelation 2:1), and riding to battle (Revelation 19:11-16), but it regularly expresses his present authority by saying that he sits at the Father's right hand—not to rest, but to rule. The picture is not of inactivity but of authority.

In Psalm 110, God sets the Messiah at his right hand as king and priest—as king to see all his enemies under his feet, and as priest to serve God and channel his grace forever. Though personally the Messiah may be out fighting, positionally he is always sitting at Yahweh's right hand. In Matthew 22:44, Acts 2:34-35, and Hebrews 1:13 and 10:12, this picture is applied directly to Jesus Christ, who since the Ascension actively reigns in the mediatorial kingdom of God.

Christ rules over all the spheres of authority that exist, both angelic and human (Matthew 28:18; 1 Peter 3:22). His kingdom in a direct sense is the church, which he leads as his body and governs by his Word and Spirit (Ephesians 1:22-23).

Christians take great comfort in knowing that Christ is Lord of all; they seek in every sphere of life to do his will and to remind themselves and others that all are accountable to Christ as judge, whether they be governors or governed, husbands or wives, parents or children, employers or employees. All rational beings will finally give account of themselves to Christ as judge (Matthew 25:31; Acts 17:31; Romans 2:16; 2 Corinthians 5:10).

Once final judgment has been executed, the work of the mediatorial kingdom will be over, and Christ will triumphantly deliver the kingdom to the Father (1 Corinthians 15:24-28).

Concise Theology

SUBJECTIVISM AFFECTS US ALL

We refuse to practice cunning or to tamper with God's word,
but by the open statement of the truth we would commend
ourselves to everyone's conscience in the sight of God.

2 CORINTHIANS 4:2

We are all inclined to subjectivism in our theology. God's thoughts are not our thoughts, and the God-centered approach which the Bible makes to problems of life and thought is in the highest degree unnatural to the minds of sinful and self-centered men. It calls for a veritable Copernican revolution in our habits of thought, and is slowly and painfully learned. On the other hand, it is entirely natural for sinners to think of themselves as wise, not by reason of divine teaching but through the independent exercise of their own judgment, and to try to justify their fancied wisdom by adjusting what the Bible teaches to what they have already imbibed from other sources ("modern knowledge"). Professed restatements of the faith in modern terms often prove to be revisions of the faith to make it square with popular intellectual fashions. This process of assimilating God's revealed truth to the current religious and philosophical opinions of men is the essence of the speculative method in theology which Scripture repudiates. Yet we all constantly do it, more or less; for sin is present with all of us. As usual with sinful habits of mind, we are largely unconscious of our lapses, and become aware of them only as we test ourselves by Scripture and ask God to search our minds and teach us to criticize our own thinking. This is a discipline that none may shirk.

Nor may speculative revisions of the faith by the light of secular thought be equated with the Word of God. No synthesis between the gospel and non-Christian systems is permissible. The gospel is complete in itself; to supplement it with extraneous ideas is not to enrich it, but to pervert it.

"Fundamentalism" and the Word of God

SAYING YES IS SAYING NO

Who is the man who fears the LORD?
Him will he instruct in the way that he should choose.

PSALM 25:12

It is amazing and almost unnerving to see how Jesus was able to make out of every situation something creative, ingenious, and genuinely helpful to the people with whom he was dealing.

When Jesus, God incarnate, walked in human sandals, each time he said yes to one use of his time, he was saying no to some other use. As we trace his actions, we can usually appreciate the priorities underlying his choices on how to use his humanly limited time and energies, and we can discern the loving wisdom that these choices reveal.

For example, once when Jesus was busily teaching a mass of people, including a number of hostile Pharisees looking for a chance to trip him up with some theological conundrum, a cluster of infatuated parents elbowed their way through the crowd, bringing their young children and even their noisy babies to him so he could "touch them" (Mark 10:13), as if his touch would impart some special magic. His disciples, fulfilling their duty in crowd control, told the parents to leave him alone so he could continue giving instruction on God's coming kingdom, his own imminent death, signs of the end times, divorce and remarriage, the nature of true prayer, and other matters of similar importance. But Jesus assessed how his time and effort would be best spent and interrupted what the disciples thought was his most important work. He stopped teaching the crowd, scolded his disciples for their mistaken assumption, took the children into his lap, and "blessed them, laying his hands on them" (Mark 10:16; see also Luke 18:15-17), meanwhile holding them up as illustrations of how by childlike faith and trust we are to enter God's kingdom — the theological topic that is perhaps the most vital of all.

Guard Us, Guide Us

WHERE EMPOWERMENT BEGINS

*My grace is sufficient for you, for my power
is made perfect in weakness.*

2 Corinthians 12:9

Being divinely empowered so that one grows stronger in Christ has nothing necessarily to do with performing spectacularly or, by human standards, successfully (that is for God to decide). It has everything to do, however, with knowing and feeling that one is weak. In this sense, we grow stronger only by growing weaker. God-given strength or power is a matter of being enabled by Christ himself, through the Spirit, to keep on keeping on in personal holiness before God, personal communing with God, personal service of God, and personal action for God.

One keeps on however weak one feels. One keeps on even in situations where what is being asked for seems to be beyond one, and one does so in the confidence that this is how God means it to be. For only at the point where the insufficiency of natural strength is faced, felt, and admitted does divine empowering begin.

So the power path is humble dependence on God to channel his power to the depths of our being so as to make and keep us faithful to our calling in sanctity and service. With that we depend on him to channel his power through us into others' lives to help them move forward at their points of need. The power pitfall is self-reliance and failure to see that without Christ we can do nothing that is spiritually significant, however much we do quantitatively, in terms of energetic activity. The power principle — God's power scenario — is that divine strength is perfected in conscious human weakness.

If I would accept that each day's frustrations, obstacles, and accidents are God's ways of making me acknowledge my weakness, so that growing stronger might become a possibility for me, what a difference it would make to me!

Rediscovering Holiness

BEING REAL ABOUT THE HUMAN CONDITION

It depends not on human will or exertion,
but on God, who has mercy.

Romans 9:16

No reader of Calvin's *Institutes of the Christian Religion* can fail to
be struck by the intensity of his stress on the wretchedness of fallen
man — corrupt, demented, defiled, beastly, vile, full of rottenness (these
are his regular epithets). Why such violent denigration? We can dismiss
the naive idea that Calvin's natural outlook was so jaundiced as to make
all human life appear to him brutish and nasty. Everything we know
about Calvin refutes that.

Nor are the true reasons far to seek. Writing against a humanistic
background — we must remember that he was a child of the Renaissance
before he became a son of the Reformation — Calvin wished to convey the
sense Scripture had given him of the tragic quality of the human predicament. Here was the noblest of this world's occupants, a creature made for
fellowship with God and given great intellectual and moral potentialities,
now spiritually ruined; he had lost his uprightness, the image of God in
which he was made, and had been banished from God's favor; and yet
in this condition he was so perverse as to be proud, vainglorious, and
self-satisfied!

Calvin knew that fallen man, because sin has darkened his mind, is
disinclined to take his fallen state seriously, and he knew too that shallow
views of sin are a barrier to true faith. He who thinks himself still good
at heart, still free to do good and please God, will trust in his own works
for salvation and never learn to look to Christ as his righteousness. Calvin
stressed the bondage of man to sin, and the vileness of man in sin, in
order that his readers might learn to be realistic about themselves, and in
self-despair go out of themselves to find peace with God through trusting
the blood of Christ.

Honouring the People of God

THE GOSPEL MUST BE PREACHED

Therefore, we are ambassadors for Christ,
God making his appeal through us.
We implore you on behalf of Christ, be reconciled to God.

2 CORINTHIANS 5:20

The content of the gospel must always control the method of its communication, and we must judge the value of various evangelism techniques by asking how far they can and do succeed in getting the message across.

The gospel's content includes a diagnosis of the hearers' state and needs before God, value judgments on the life they live as compared with that which might be theirs, and a call to judge themselves, to acknowledge the gracious approach and invitation of God in Christ, and to respond by a commitment more radical and far-reaching than any they will ever make. The gospel is not fully communicated unless all this comes over.

So the gospel must be *verbalized;* it must be preached — that is, set forth by a messenger who interprets and applies it to the hearers in a way which makes its implications for them plain. Since the gospel is a personal message from God to each hearer, the only appropriate and effective way of communicating it is for a messenger to deliver it on God's behalf, ambassador-style — that is, identifying with God's concerns and expressing the mind and heart of God, how he hates sin and loves sinners, and what he has done, is doing, and will do for the salvation of those who turn to him. God has shown us that preaching is the only natural and adequate way to communicate the content of the gospel by himself actually communicating it this way.

Two far-reaching conclusions clearly follow. First, preaching must continue as a main activity of the church. Second, whatever technical skills a Christian communicator may command, what will count ultimately is what he is in himself, whether or not his manner backs up his matter in making God's mind and heart known.

Serving the People of God

PATIENCE WITH GOD'S PROMISES

Yet a little while, and the coming one will come
and will not delay.

HEBREWS 10:37

One of the difficulties with promises is waiting. In New Testament times, some faithful believers thought God was delaying the fulfillment of the promises of Christ's return. Near the end of his second letter, Peter speaks directly to unrest and skepticism about Christ's reappearing, and does so in a way that throws light on the whole issue of God's apparent delays, whether in the past or as may arise in the future. Says Peter,

> The Lord is not slow to fulfill his promise as some count slowness, but is patient toward you, not wishing that any should perish, but that all should reach repentance. . . . Count the patience of our Lord as salvation, just as our beloved brother Paul also wrote to you according to the wisdom given him. (2 Peter 3:9,15)

Our desire for instant action in response to our prayers reflects the limitation and smallness of our view of things compared with God's. God fixes his time for doing what he has promised (and what his people look to him to do) in light of long-term purposes of goodness and wisdom involving far more than we can ever be aware of. "That *all* should reach repentance" is a case in point: Who were Peter's first readers, and who are you and we today, to compute God's "all"?

The principle that Bible believers must grasp is that it is God's prerogative to do what he promises in what he knows to be the best and wisest way, at what he knows to be the best and wisest time. Seeing this will help us to develop the patience and settled trust that God desires to shape in us, and will stabilize our hope when our hearts move us to pray, "Lord, how long?"

Praying

LESSONS FOR OUR HOMES

He will declare to you a message by which you will be saved,
you and all your household.

ACTS 11:14

It is hardly too much to say that the Puritans created the Christian family in the English-speaking world. The Puritan ethic of marriage was to look not for a partner whom you *do* love passionately at this moment, but rather for one whom you *can* love steadily as your best friend for life, and then to proceed with God's help to do just that.

The Puritan ethic of nurture was to train up children in the way they should go, to care for their bodies and souls together, and to educate them for sober, godly, socially useful adult living. The Puritan ethic of home life was based on maintaining order, courtesy, and family worship. Goodwill, patience, consistency, and an encouraging attitude were seen as the essential domestic virtues. In an age of routine discomforts, rudimentary medicine without painkillers, frequent bereavements (most families lost at least as many children as they reared), an average life expectancy of just under thirty years, and economic hardship for almost all save merchant princes and landed gentry, family life was a school for character in every sense, and the fortitude with which Puritans resisted the all-too-familiar temptation to relieve pressure from the world by brutality at home, and labored to honor God in their families despite all, merits supreme praise. At home the Puritans showed themselves mature, accepting hardships and disappointments realistically as from God and refusing to be daunted or soured by any of them.

In an era in which family life has become brittle even among Christians, with chicken-hearted spouses taking the easy course of separation rather than working at their relationship, and narcissistic parents spoiling their children materially while neglecting them spiritually, there is once more much to be learned from the Puritans' very different ways.

A Quest for Godliness

LOVE'S EXCELLENCE

And I will show you
a still more excellent way.
1 CORINTHIANS 12:31

In *The Four Loves,* C. S. Lewis distinguished *agape* (the New Testament Greek word for God's love and Christian love) from *storge* (the feeling of affection or fondness), *eros* (the feeling of desire and need for some person or thing that is felt to be attractive, especially in sexual or aesthetic contexts), and *philia* (the attitude of friendliness to one who is friendly to you). Each of these three is a blend of animal instinct, personal taste, appreciative awareness, and self-gratifying impulse, and in this all three differ radically from *agape.*

Agape is a "way" (1 Corinthians 12:31) — a path of action — of which four things are true. First, it has as its purpose doing good to others, and so in some sense making them great. *Agape* Godward, triggered by gratitude for grace, makes God great by exalting him in praise, thanksgiving, and obedience. *Agape* manward (love for neighbor) makes fellow humans great by serving their observed real needs. Thus, marital *agape* seeks fulfillment for the spouse and parental *agape* seeks maturity for the children. Second, *agape* is measured not by sweetness of talk or strength of feeling, but by what it does, and more specifically by what of its own it gives, for the fulfilling of its purpose. Third, *agape* does not wait to be courted, nor limit itself to those who appreciate it, but takes the initiative in giving help where help is required, and finds joy in bringing others benefit. The question of who deserves help is not raised; *agape* does good to the needy (however undeserving), not to the meritorious. *Agape* focuses on particular people with particular needs, and prays and works to deliver them from evil. In all of this it is directly modeled on the love of God revealed in the gospel.

Celebrating the Saving Work of God

HOW WE BECOME WISE

> *The fear of the LORD is the beginning of wisdom;*
> *all those who practice it have a good understanding.*
>
> PSALM 111:10

What is wisdom?

The first thing to say about it is that it begins with (derives from, is rooted in) *the fear of the Lord* (Psalm 111:10; Proverbs 9:10). It comes our way through reverence toward, dependence upon, humility before, worship of, and obedience to the God who presents himself in covenant to his people. He is the object of their faith, hope, love, and enjoyment, and he promises to fulfill for them the role of guide, benefactor, helper, and sustainer as they set themselves to meet his covenant claims upon them. To honor, adore, and trust God in this way, and to acknowledge in prayer that wisdom comes from him alone (James 1:5), is to be wise at the most basic level. For only God is wise in himself and always free of folly; and human wisdom is a gift of God every time, never an unaided human achievement.

Wisdom is a divine character quality that God graciously reproduces in sinful human beings by his generous grace. He imparts the gift to all who sincerely seek it from him and are ready for the changes that its coming may bring. In Proverbs 1–9, a wise man tells his son that seeking wisdom from God must be his life's priority (4:7; 8:11). To reinforce this perspective, personified Wisdom is introduced and allowed to speak for herself (1:20-33; 8:1–9:18). But the means (words of counsel) are not the source of wisdom; rather, wisdom is formed in us as the Holy Spirit opens the eyes of the mind and the heart, working with and through what is seen and said.

This is how we become wise in the full biblical sense of being prudent, patient, and God-honoring in all we do.

The Way of Wisdom

BEING SURE OF GOD'S PROMISES

No distrust made him waver concerning the promise of God,
but he grew strong in his faith as he gave glory to God.
ROMANS 4:20

Abraham's faith, which Paul proclaimed as a standard and model (Romans 4), was essentially an unyielding trust in God's promise. Abraham received God's promise by immediate revelation, but what of us, living nineteen centuries after immediate revelations ended?

If the Bible were not God's revealed Word — if, that is, no one could be sure that everything the biblical writers say of God, God also says of himself — we could not be sure either that any single statement in the Bible purporting to be a promise of God to Christian believers is really valid. No critical cross-examination on earth can tell us whether such statements are genuine divine commitments to which God has pledged himself to stand to all eternity, or whether the human writers were not perhaps astray in the words of promise they put into the mouths of Jesus and his Father, and the assurances they gave in God's name.

If the canonical Scriptures were only a mere fallible human witness to God's Word, no present-day Christian could emulate Abraham's faith, because none could be sure that he had a single definite promise from God on which to rest. The historic evangelical concept of the life of faith as a matter of living and dying in the strength which God's promises give would then have to be thrown away as a beautiful pipe dream. Those who jettison the evangelical concept of a totally trustworthy inspired Scripture must exchange the rational biblical notion of faith as walking in the light of God for the irrational existential idea of faith as a leap in the dark, and must abandon the firm foundation of the divine promises for the yawning abyss of a foggy uncertainty.

Surely it is plain that we do in fact need the revealed Word that God has given.

Honouring the Written Word of God

MYSTERY AT EVERY TURN

He reveals deep and hidden things;
he knows what is in the darkness,
and the light dwells with him.

DANIEL 2:22

All doctrines terminate in mystery; for they deal with the works of God, which man in this world cannot fully comprehend, nor has God been pleased fully to explain. "We know in part" (1 Corinthians 13:9) — and only in part. Consequently, however successful our attempt to state a biblical doctrine may be, it will not put us in a position where we "have all the answers."

A mere complaint that some problems have been left unsolved will not, of itself, be valid criticism of any theological exposition; for incompleteness is of the essence of theological knowledge. This, of course, is to a greater or less degree the case with all our knowledge of facts. We never know everything about anything. But clearly, when we creatures come to study the Creator and his ways, we must expect our knowledge to be more fragmentary and partial, and further from being exhaustive, than when we study created things.

No article of Christian faith admits of full rational demonstration as, say, geometrical theorems do; all the great biblical doctrines — the Trinity, the Incarnation, the Atonement, the work of the Spirit in man, the resurrection of the body, and the renewal of the creation — are partly mysterious, and raise problems for our minds that are at present insoluble. But that should not daunt, nor even surprise us; for it is the very nature of Christian faith to believe, on the authority of God, truths which may neither be rationally demonstrated nor exhaustively understood. God does not tell us everything about his acts and purposes, nor put us in a position to work them all out for ourselves. We are wholly dependent on him for our knowledge of his ways.

"Fundamentalism" and the Word of God

BE RIGHT AND PERSIST

May you be strengthened with all power, according to his glorious might,
for all endurance and patience with joy.

COLOSSIANS 1:11

Christian maturity, which is holiness full-grown, is the promised end product of *endurance* — both passive *(patience)* and active *(perseverance)*. The colloquial English word for endurance is "stickability." Its North American counterpart is "stick-to-it-iveness." The notion is summed up by the motto of the Christian institution: "Be right and persist."

Endurance is a major New Testament theme. And patience (the passive mode of endurance, whereby pain, grief, suffering, and disappointment are handled without inner collapse) is named as one facet, if we may so speak, of the fruit of the Spirit (Galatians 5:22-23). This means that it is not a natural endowment but a supernatural gift, a grace of character that God imparts to those whom he is transforming into the likeness of Christ.

Each aspect of the fruit of the Spirit that Paul mentions is a matter of divine command as well as of divine gift. Each is a habit of reaction that is most strikingly seen in situations where, humanly speaking, a different reaction would have been expected. Thus, love shines brightest when exercised for Jesus' sake toward the unlovely and seemingly unlovable; joy, when sure of God's sovereign providence, we stay calm instead of panicking or getting frazzled.

In the same way, patient endurance is most apparent when we stand steady under pain and pressure instead of cutting and running, or crumpling and collapsing. But hanging tough in this way is a habit that takes some learning. To endure Christianly is no casual agenda. Many of us have hardly begun to tackle it as yet. Integral to our holiness, our maturity, and our Christlikeness, however, is this habit of enduring. Forming the habit, and making sure we never lose it, is a necessary discipline for those who are Christ's.

Rediscovering Holiness

A WONDER TO ADORE

In this is love, not that we have loved God but that he loved us
and sent his Son to be the propitiation for our sins.

1 JOHN 4:10

Calvin's treatment of salvation in *Institutes of the Christian Religion* — a more thorough and systematic treatment than any previous theologian had written — is against the false gospel of synergism and self-help. Fallen men are spiritually helpless, Calvin insists; not only can they not obey God's truth, they cannot even properly understand it in their natural state; the work of saving them must therefore be God's work entirely. We can sum up his contention thus: *God* (alone) *saves sinners* (however bad) *in and through Jesus Christ.*

God saves *sinners*. Here is the *wonder* of grace. Like Romans, the *Institutes* is dominated by the biblical thought of the judgment seat of God, and of God himself as set to judge mankind retributively, giving evidence of personal pleasure or anger according to what the various parties before him deserve. The present wrath of the Judge against all sin, and the coming day of reckoning for every man, appear in the *Institutes* as vivid realities, constantly to be kept in view.

But if God is set to judge, what hope can any of us have? We are all sinners.

We have hope, says Calvin, because God has freely and undeservedly set his love upon us, and reconciled us to himself by propitiating his own wrath through the atoning sacrifice of his Son. "Of his mere goodpleasure he appointed a mediator to purchase salvation for us." "Christ . . . was destined to appease the wrath of God by his sacrifice." Calvin quotes 1 John 4:10, and comments, "There is great force in this word *propitiation*; for in a manner which cannot be expressed . . . God, at the very time when he loved us, was hostile to us until reconciled in Christ."[18] Here is the mystery of God's free grace — a wonder not to be pried into by speculation, but to be reverently adored.

Honouring the People of God

A CURE FOR THE RESTLESS

See if there be any grievous way in me,
and lead me in the way everlasting!
PSALM 139:24

In today's evangelical world, those whom I call restless experientialists are a familiar breed. Their outlook is one of casual haphazardness and fretful impatience, of grasping after novelties, entertainments, and "highs," and of valuing strong feelings above deep thoughts. They have little taste for solid study, humble self-examination, disciplined meditation, and unspectacular hard work in their callings and their prayers. They conceive the Christian life as one of exciting extraordinary experiences rather than of resolute rational righteousness. They dwell continually on the themes of joy, peace, happiness, satisfaction, and rest of soul with no balancing reference to the divine discontent of Romans 7, the fight of faith of Psalm 73, or the "lows" of Psalms 42, 88, and 102. And they scarcely give the scriptural virtue of steadiness a thought.

Such saints need the sort of maturing ministry in which the Puritan tradition has specialized.

1. The stress on God-centeredness as a divine requirement that is central to the discipline of self-denial.
2. The insistence on the primacy of the mind, and on the impossibility of obeying biblical truth that one has not yet understood.
3. The demand for humility, patience, and steadiness at all times, and for an acknowledgment that the Holy Spirit's main ministry is not to give thrills but to create in us Christlike character.
4. The recognition that feelings go up and down, and that God frequently tries us by leading us through wastes of emotional flatness.
5. The singling out of worship as life's primary activity.
6. The stress on our need of regular self-examination by Scripture, in terms set by Psalm 139:23-24.
7. The realization that sanctified suffering bulks large in God's plan for his children's growth in grace.

A Quest for Godliness

WISDOM'S WIDE RANGE

The beginning of wisdom is this: Get wisdom,
and whatever you get, get insight.

PROVERBS 4:7

The basic acts of wisdom — in humans as in God — are to choose good and praiseworthy goals along with honorable means of pursuing them. Believers who focus on God see his praiseworthy wisdom displayed in creation and providence, in the complex processes and variegated beauties of the natural order, as much in tiny lovely things as in huge awesome things. Also they see God's wisdom displayed in the measure of justice found in this fallen world and in acts of what appears as divine kindness toward undeserving humanity in the flow of events.

They see God's wisdom also, and supremely, in the plan of salvation: the eternal predestining of the Mediator; the long preparation for his coming; his incarnation, atonement, resurrection, and enthronement; the ministry of the Holy Spirit in individuals and churches; and the disciplines and delights of the Christian life.

To acknowledge God's wisdom in this way is their own wisdom in action. At the same time, wisdom teaches them to set their own good goals, to devise positive means of realizing them, to steer clear of all forms of foolish and evil behavior, and to help others to do the same.

It was, I think, Oswald Chambers who said that the Psalms teach you how to pray and praise, Proverbs teaches you how to behave, Job teaches you how to suffer, the Song of Solomon teaches you how to love, and Ecclesiastes teaches you how to enjoy. This statement, which is itself wisdom in the sense of discernment, indicates something of the versatility and range of wise living according to the Scriptures.

The Way of Wisdom

LIKE FATHER, LIKE CHILD

You therefore must be perfect,
as your heavenly Father is perfect.
MATTHEW 5:48

A basic principle of all biblical ethics is the principle of the family likeness — the principle that those who are God's by right of creation and redemption must strive to imitate him, so that their character will reflect his.

Christians, through their personal knowledge of forgiveness, new birth, and God's fatherhood, know more of the riches of God's free love to sinners than individual Israelites knew, or could know, in Old Testament days. Nowhere in the Old Testament did God reveal himself as the Father of the individual believer in the way that the gospel of the kingdom reveals him. The Christian knows much more of the height, and depth, and length, and breadth of God's free love to him personally than the Old Testament saint knew. Therefore the imitating of God will require of him correspondingly more in the way of generous and spontaneous love to others than was demanded of Israel.

Hence we find in the law of Christ emphases relating to the love of others which go beyond anything the Old Testament law contained. For instance, the Christian must love his enemies. Again, the Christian must be infinitely forgiving, because of the infinite debt of sin that has been forgiven him (Matthew 18:21-35). Again, the Christian must keep a "new" commandment — he must love his fellow Christians as Christ loved him (John 13:34); the love of Christ dying to redeem the ungodly creates an entirely new ideal of what mutual care and service among Christians ought to mean. These three examples are typical illustrations of how the subject matter of the gospel imparted a new depth and richness to our Lord's exposition of the law.

Honouring the Written Word of God

GOD'S SPEECH, IN CHOSEN WORDS

Hear the word of the LORD,
you who tremble at his word.

ISAIAH 66:5

When we hear or read Scripture, that which impinges on our mind (whether or not we realize it) is the speech of God himself.

Not that the church knows, or ever knew, or will know in this world, the full meaning of God's Word. The task of biblical interpretation never ends. There is no such thing as an exhaustive exegesis of any passage. The Holy Spirit is constantly showing Christians facets of revealed truth not seen before. To claim finality for any historic mode of interpretation or system of theology would be to resist the Holy Ghost; there is always more to be said; the Lord has more light and truth yet to break out of his holy Word. The church must receive all teaching that proves to be biblical, whether on matters of historical or of theological fact, as truly part of God's Word.

This shows the importance of insisting that the inspiration of Scripture is *verbal*. Words signify and safeguard meaning; the wrong word distorts the intended sense. Since God inspired the biblical text in order to communicate his Word, it was necessary for him to ensure that the words written were such as did in fact convey it. We do not stress the verbal character of inspiration from a superstitious regard for the original Hebrew and Greek words (like that of Islam for its Koran, which is held to consist essentially of Arabic words, and therefore to be untranslatable); we do so from a reverent concern for the sense of Scripture. If the words were not wholly God's, then their teaching would not be wholly God's.

"Fundamentalism" and the Word of God

THE SCIENCE OF LIVING TO GOD

The Lord GOD has given me the tongue of those who are taught,
that I may know how to sustain with a word him who is weary.

ISAIAH 50:4

Entrenched intellectualists in the evangelical world constantly present themselves as rigid, argumentative, critical Christians, champions of God's truth for whom orthodoxy is all. There is little warmth about them: Relationally they are remote; winning the battle for mental correctness is their one great purpose.

They need exposure to the Puritan heritage for their maturing. Several points from that tradition spring to view. First, true religion claims the affections as well as the intellect; it is essentially, in Richard Baxter's phrase, "heart-work." Second, theological truth is for practice. William Perkins defined theology as the science of living blessedly forever; William Ames called it the science of living to God. Third, conceptual knowledge kills if one does not move on from knowing notions to knowing the realities to which they refer — from knowing about God to a relational acquaintance with God himself. Fourth, faith and repentance, issuing in a life of love and holiness — of gratitude expressed in goodwill and good works — are explicitly called for in the gospel. Fifth, the Spirit is given to lead us into close companionship with others in Christ. Sixth, the discipline of discursive meditation is meant to keep us ardent and adoring in our love affair with God. Seventh, it is ungodly and scandalous to become a firebrand and cause division in the church, and it is ordinarily nothing more than spiritual pride in its intellectual form that leads men to create parties and splits.

The great Puritans were as humble-minded and warmhearted as they were clearheaded, as fully oriented to people as they were to Scripture, and as passionate for peace as they were for truth. They would certainly have diagnosed today's fixated Christian intellectualists as spiritually stunted, not in their zeal for sound words but in their lack of zeal for anything else.

A Quest for Godliness

THE RIGHTNESS OF GOD'S ANGER

It was to show his righteousness at the present time, so that he might be just and the justifier of the one who has faith in Jesus.

ROMANS 3:26

The wrath of God is as personal, and as potent, as his love; and just as the blood-shedding of the Lord Jesus was the direct manifesting of his Father's love toward us, so it was the direct averting of his Father's wrath against us.

What manner of thing is the wrath of God that was propitiated at Calvary?

It is not the capricious, arbitrary, bad-tempered, and conceited anger that pagans attribute to their gods. It is not the sinful, resentful, malicious, infantile anger that we find among humans. It is a function of that holiness which is expressed in the demands of God's moral law ("Be holy, for I am holy" [1 Peter 1:16]), and of that righteousness which is expressed in God's acts of judgment and reward. "We know who it is that has said, 'Justice is mine: I will repay'" (Hebrews 10:30, NEB).

God's wrath is "the holy revulsion of GOD's being against that which is the contradiction of his holiness"; it issues in "a positive outgoing of the divine displeasure."[19] And this is *righteous* anger — the *right* reaction of moral perfection in the Creator toward moral perversity in the creature. So far from the manifestation of God's wrath in punishing sin being morally doubtful, the thing that would be morally doubtful would be for him *not* to show his wrath in this way. God is not *just* — that is, he does not act in the way that is *right*, he does not do what is proper to a *judge* — unless he inflicts upon all sin and wrongdoing the penalty it deserves.

In My Place Condemned He Stood

EVANGELISM IN LOVE

*You are in
our hearts.*
2 CORINTHIANS 7:3

As an apostle of Christ, Paul was more than a teacher of truth; he was a shepherd of souls, sent into the world not to lecture sinners, but to love them. For he was an apostle second and a Christian first; and as a Christian, he was a man called to love his neighbor. This meant simply that in every situation, and by every means in his power, it was his business to seek other people's good. From this standpoint, the significance of his apostolic commission to evangelize and found churches was simply that this was the particular way in which Christ was calling him to fulfill the law of love to his neighbor. He might not, therefore, preach the gospel in a harsh, callous way, putting it before his neighbor with a contemptuous air of "there you are — take it or leave it," and excusing himself for his unconcern about people on the grounds of his faithfulness to the truth. Such conduct would be a failure of love on his part. His business was to present truth in a spirit of love, as an expression and implementation of his desire to save his hearers. The attitude which informed all of Paul's evangelism was this: "I seek not what is yours but you. . . . I will most gladly spend and be spent for your souls" (2 Corinthians 12:14-15).

And all our own evangelism must be done in the same spirit. As love to our neighbor suggests and demands that we evangelize, so the command to evangelize is a specific application of the command to love others for Christ's sake, and must be fulfilled as such.

Evangelism and the Sovereignty of God

GOD MAKES HIS PEOPLE HIS CHILDREN

> *When the fullness of time had come, God sent forth his Son . . .*
> *so that we might receive adoption as sons.*
>
> GALATIANS 4:4-5

Paul teaches that the gift of justification (i.e., present acceptance by God as the world's Judge) brings with it the status of sonship by adoption (i.e., permanent intimacy with God as one's heavenly Father, Galatians 3:26; 4:4-7). In Paul's world, adoption was ordinarily of young adult males of good character to become heirs and maintain the family name of the childless rich. Paul, however, proclaims God's gracious adoption of persons of bad character to become "heirs of God and fellow heirs with Christ" (Romans 8:17).

Justification is the basic blessing on which adoption is founded; adoption is the crowning blessing, to which justification clears the way. Adopted status belongs to all who receive Christ (John 1:12). The adopted status of believers means that in and through Christ, God loves them as he loves his only begotten Son and will share with them all the glory that is Christ's now (Romans 8:17,38-39). Here and now, believers are under God's fatherly care and discipline (Matthew 6:26; Hebrews 12:5-11) and are directed, especially by Jesus, to live their whole lives in light of the knowledge that God is their Father in heaven. They are to pray to him as such (Matthew 6:5-13), imitate him as such (Matthew 5:44-48; 6:12,14-15; 18:21-35; Ephesians 4:32–5:2), and trust him as such (Matthew 6:25-34), thus expressing the filial instinct that the Holy Spirit has implanted in them (Romans 8:15-17; Galatians 4:6).

Adoption and regeneration accompany each other as two aspects of the salvation that Christ brings (John 1:12-13), but they are to be distinguished. Adoption is the bestowal of a relationship, while regeneration is the transformation of our moral nature. Yet the link is evident; God wants his children, whom he loves, to bear his character, and he takes action accordingly.

Concise Theology

LEADERSHIP AND PARTNERSHIP

> *You see the trouble we are in. . . .*
> *Come, let us build the wall of Jerusalem.*
> NEHEMIAH 2:17

The particular work to which God had called Nehemiah was to get Jerusalem's ruined walls rebuilt. This was a huge job. The circuit of the walls was more than a mile, and the new wall needed to be three or four feet thick, more perhaps at ground level, and fifteen to twenty feet high. Rebuilding would be a massive operation, only possible if tackled as a grand-scale cooperative enterprise. Nehemiah made it happen; within days of his coming to Jerusalem, apparently, he had set everything in motion, and the wall was completed in just over seven weeks. It was a staggering achievement.

How, we ask, did Nehemiah do it? There is no secret here; Nehemiah's memoirs tell the whole story, and what they reveal is that, over and above faith and prayer, God-given leader-like wisdom marked his action at every stage. Specifically, he applied two principles that all pastoral leaders today and tomorrow must learn to apply if the churches or Christian groups committed to their care are to be truly built up. The first principle was that of partnership, whereby Nehemiah first motivated the Jerusalemites to snap out of their apathy and hopelessness and commit themselves to work with him wholeheartedly on the project, and then created a setup in which all the workers were able to feel personally important to the project as it went along.

The second principle was that of planning, whereby through harrowing ups and downs Nehemiah was able to sustain their confidence in ultimate success by being seen to have everything under control. Mobilizing, organizing, supervising, and encouraging, Nehemiah galvanized the deadbeats of Jerusalem into well-planned exertions that at once began to transform the entire scene and that did not cease till the whole task was accomplished.

A Passion for Faithfulness

FAITHFUL GOD, FAITHFUL WORD

The LORD . . . confirms the word of his servant
and fulfills the counsel of his messengers.

ISAIAH 44:24,26

How is it warrantable to treat the Bible as we actually have it as the Word of God, when we have no reason to think that any manuscript or version now existing is free from corruptions? It is sometimes suggested that in practice we are involved in an inescapable subjectivism by the necessity of relying on conjectural reconstructions of the text, and that we can have no confidence that any text we possess conveys to us the genuine meaning of the inspired Word.

It is, of course, true that textual corruptions are no part of the authentic Scriptures, and that no text is free from such slips. But faith in the consistency of God warrants an attitude of confidence that the text is sufficiently trustworthy not to lead us astray. If God gave the Scriptures for a practical purpose — to make men wise unto salvation through faith in Christ — it is a safe inference that he never permits them to become so corrupted that they can no longer fulfill it.

This attitude of faith in the adequacy of the text is confirmed, so far as it can be, by the unanimous verdict of textual scholars that the biblical text is excellently preserved, and no point of doctrine depends on any of the small number of cases in which the true reading remains doubtful. While the work of recovering the original text is not yet finished, and no doubt never will be finished in every minute particular, we should not hesitate to believe that the text as we have it is substantially correct, and may safely be trusted as conveying to us the Word of God with sufficient accuracy for all practical purposes. God's faithfulness to his own intentions is our guarantee of that.

"Fundamentalism" and the Word of God

FINDING HELP TOGETHER

We used to take sweet counsel together;
within God's house we walked in the throng.

PSALM 55:14

Ideally, the congregation to which we belong will be our primary field of fellowship, where our ideas of God's will for us are tested and, if sound, confirmed, and where from time to time indications of God's will for us are directly given.

It needs to be frankly acknowledged that the church in the West has been slow to appreciate the strength that comes from drawing on each other's wisdom and insight within the local congregation for personal direction on major decisions. It might well be that congregations in Africa, Asia, and Latin America could lead us into a more corporate (and biblical!) practice at this point than we have yet attained. Part of God's provision for guidance evidently is putting people of different age groups, social, cultural, and racial backgrounds in the same congregation. In their togetherness they then make up the body of Christ in its local mani-festation, with the diversity of the body parts on full display. The homo-geneous unit principle (like attracts like), on which the pioneer church growth leaders laid such stress, may be valid for beginning a church plant, but once a congregation has grown sufficiently in numbers to become self-supporting, adhering to that principle will quench the Spirit and arrest the congregation's qualitative growth into spiritual maturity. God does not want established congregations to consist of people who are all alike any more than he wants us as individuals to limit our close friendships to people just like ourselves. On the contrary, he wants each congregation to contain a wide variety of the human race, and he means us to find that the help we need in discerning his will comes to us through the minds and souls and voices of this wide cross section of Christian believers.

Guard Us, Guide Us

BORN AGAIN TO RUN

Let us run with endurance
the race that is set before us.
HEBREWS 12:1

The life of Christian endurance is like a long-distance race. The race
picture in the New Testament (1 Corinthians 9:24-27; Galatians 5:7;
Philippians 2:16; 2 Timothy 4:7; Hebrews 12:1-3) is telling us two things:
first, that perseverance is the only path to the prize of final glory, and
second, that what perseverance requires is a sustained exertion of concentrated effort day in and day out — a single-minded, wholehearted, self-
denying, flat-out commitment to praising and pleasing the Father through
the Son as long as life lasts.

As successful competitors in cross-country races, marathons, and
triathlons pace themselves into a winning rhythm, so it is meant to be
with Christians. As some athletes were, as we say, born to run, so all who
are born again are called to run, in the sense of putting all their energy
into steady godliness as their life strategy. Keeping up the winning
rhythm in the Christian life, as in the Boston Marathon, is constantly
demanding and sometimes agonizing. But the very meaning of perseverance and patient endurance is that you do it anyway, because you are
God's child running on what, in the profoundest sense, is for you the
home stretch.

This sustained inward effort, raised to the limit of what you can do
with the brains, gifts, and energy God has given you, is one central aspect
of Christian holiness, one without which a person's supposed holiness
would degenerate into self-indulgent softness. But true holiness is neither
self-indulgent nor soft. It is tough. It is virile. It has backbone and guts,
and a face set like flint. It is fueled by a heart of joy as the winning post
appears ahead. Real Jesus-likeness means this — nothing less — and real
holiness means real Jesus-likeness.

Rediscovering Holiness

ADORATION RATHER THAN CURIOSITY

I led them with cords of kindness, with the bands of love . . .
and I bent down to them and fed them.

HOSEA 11:4

It is a sign of love toward a child when we accommodate to his language and are willing to use baby talk in conversing with him. And so it is, said Calvin, when God in Scripture speaks to us in a simple, not very dignified way. It helps us to understand him, and the very fact that he does it assures us of his affection and goodwill. Following Origen and Augustine, Calvin developed the thought that in Scripture God scales himself down, condescending to our limited capacity in the manner described.

The insight that God adapts his speech to our limitations, though assuring us that Scripture mediates to us real knowledge of him, reminds us also that we do not and cannot know him as he is in himself. What frames and surrounds God's self-revelation is the mystery, utterly dark or overwhelmingly bright (Calvin says both from time to time), of that which in God remains unrevealed, namely his incomprehensible life, power, and activity, as those are known to himself. God constantly warns us to stay within the bounds of revelation, not to stray outside the circle of God-given light into the darkness that lies beyond, not to try to penetrate by guesswork into places where Scripture offers no thoughts for us to think.

Often Calvin reminds us, echoing 1 Timothy 6:16, that God "dwells in unapproachable light" where no man can see him, so that any speculative venture going beyond what he himself tells us in Scripture is a sort of Promethean presumption foredoomed to disaster. For Calvin, R. S. Wallace says, "Adoration rather than curiosity is the fitting attitude when searching out the secrets of revelation," and the humility of wisdom counsels us to keep most conscientiously within the bounds of what Scripture says.

Honouring the People of God

CROSS-CULTURAL KOINONIA

He made from one man every nation of mankind
to live on all the face of the earth.

ACTS 17:26

In cross-cultural Christian communication the right course will be neither to impose on folks of other cultures forms of Christian expression belonging to our own, nor to deny them access to our theological, liturgical, ethical, and devotional heritage, from which they will certainly have much to gain, but to encourage them once they have appreciated our tradition to seek by the light of Scripture to distinguish between it and the gospel it enshrines, and to detach the gospel from it, so the gospel may mesh with their own cultures directly. Thus the gospel may be set free to do its job, running and being glorified without hindrance.

If it is true (as I for one believe) that every culture and subculture without exception in this fallen world is a product not just of human sin but also of God's common grace, then respect for other cultures as such, and desire to see them not abolished but reanimated by gospel grace in their own terms, must undergird all particular criticisms of ways in which, missing the good life, they embrace the not-so-good life instead. This respect will set us all free for critical dialogue with all forms of human culture, Christian and non-Christian alike, while safeguarding us against both the appearance and the reality of cultural imperialism.

Active attempts to Christianize or re-Christianize all cultures is much to be desired. And if in the process Christians of other cultures criticize sub- and post-Christian elements in their own heritage, we must not mishear this as cultural imperialism in reverse. The *koinonia* which is the church's proper life is two-way traffic, taking as well as giving, and it requires us both to share what resources of Christian insight we have and to take gratefully any further insights that others offer us.

Serving the People of God

KEEP PRAYING, KEEP TRUSTING

When he drew near and saw the city,
he wept over it.
LUKE 19:41

We have it on firm scriptural authority that the Father's response to requests faithfully, humbly, hopefully, expectantly made by his own children, out of a pure heart and an honest desire for God's glory, is never going to be a flat no. One way or another God's response will be positive, though it may be, "I am adjusting the terms of your prayer to give you something better than you asked for." Or it may be, "I know this isn't the moment in which answering your prayer would bring you and others the most blessing, so I'm asking you to wait." Or, "I am answering your prayer, but it doesn't at the moment feel or look like an answer at all. Nonetheless, it is. Keep praying, keep trusting, and keep looking for what, down the road, I may be able in wisdom to let you see."

This is not to imply, however, that the pain of seemingly unanswered prayer — honest, earnest, pure-hearted, long-term petition — will ever be eliminated entirely from our lives as long as we are here on earth. Scripture seems clearly to indicate the contrary, particularly in connection with persons close to us.

Petitionary prayer makes a difference; in heaven we will find what difference our prayers made, and here on earth we are to go on praying for the physical and spiritual needs of others as love and compassion prompt us. But the pain of not seeing all the changes in people that we long to see is something we have to live with at present. The Lord Jesus himself knew this particular heartache, as his tears over Jerusalem showed (Matthew 23:37-38; Luke 19:41-42). We will find that Jesus our Master upholds us when our experience of disappointments after praying comes close to his.

Praying

CURE FOR DISILLUSIONMENT

We must pay much closer attention to what we have heard,
lest we drift away from it.

HEBREWS 2:1

Think of the casualties and dropouts of the modern evangelical movement, many of whom have now turned against it to denounce it as a
neurotic perversion of Christianity. They once saw themselves as evangelicals, but have become disillusioned and turned their back on it, feeling
that it let them down. Some leave for intellectual reasons, judging that
what was taught them was so simplistic as to stifle their minds and so
unrealistic and out of touch with facts as to be really if unintentionally
dishonest.

Modern evangelicalism has much to answer for in the number of
casualties of this sort that it has caused by its naivety of mind. Here again
the soberer, profound, wiser evangelicalism of the Puritan giants can
fulfill a corrective function, if only we will listen to its message. Puritan
authors regularly tell us of the *mystery* of God: that our God is too small,
that the real God cannot be put into a man-made conceptual box so as
to be fully understood, and that he was, is, and always will be bewilder-
ingly inscrutable in his dealing with those who trust and love him, so
that "losses and crosses" — bafflement and disappointment in relation to
particular hopes — must be accepted as a recurring element in one's life
of fellowship with him. They tell us also of the love of God: that it is a love
that redeems, converts, sanctifies, and ultimately glorifies sinners, and
that Calvary was the one place in human history where it was fully and
unambiguously revealed, and that in our own situation we may know for
certain that nothing can separate us from that love (Romans 8:38-39),
although no situation in this world will ever be free from flies in the oint-
ment and thorns in the bed.

A Quest for Godliness

THE TWIN PEAKS

I live by faith in the Son of God,
who loved me and gave himself for me.
GALATIANS 2:20

To know that nothing ever "will be able to separate us from the love of God in Christ Jesus our Lord" (Romans 8:39) is the height of Christian assurance. And "to know the love of Christ that surpasses knowledge" and to "be filled with all the fullness of God" (Ephesians 3:19) is the acme of Christian progress. These are the twin peaks of true Christian living in this world.

In all our knowledge of God's gracious giving, the "for me" in Galatians 2:20 is central. To know that from eternity my Maker, foreseeing my sin, foreloved me and resolved to save me, though at the cost of Cavalry; to know that the divine Son was appointed from eternity to be my Savior, and that in love he became man for me and died for me and now lives to intercede for me and will one day come in person to take me home; to know that the Lord "who loved me and gave himself for me" (Galatians 2:20) and who "came and preached peace" to me (Ephesians 2:17) has by his Spirit raised me from spiritual death to life-giving union and communion with himself, and has promised to hold me fast and never let me go — this is knowledge that brings overwhelming gratitude and joy.

"Thank God for this gift too wonderful for words!" (2 Corinthians 9:15, NLT). May all God's people come to appreciate it! In heaven we most certainly will, and it is a sad thing that any in this world should take up with a theology that in any measure deprives them of this cognitive foretaste of heaven here and now. I pray that our loving God will show the full glory of his love, in its particularity as well as its universality, to us all.

Celebrating the Saving Work of God

SCRIPTURE AND SPIRIT

> *All Scripture is breathed out by God.*
>
> 2 TIMOTHY 3:16

The wide range of the Spirit's ministry in connection with Scripture is not always appreciated, but we abuse our minds and miss the truth if we overlook it. The lordship of the Spirit was exercised in the whole process of producing the Bible and setting it before us, and that same lordship is exercised as the Spirit moves us to receive, revere, and study the Scriptures and to discern their divine message to us.

It is sometimes thought that when the Spirit interprets Scripture, guiding us into its "spiritual" meaning, the process may involve finding allegories and applications that could not be read out of the text by any normal means. But that is not so. The "spiritual" sense of Scripture is nothing other than the literal sense — that is, the sense the writer's words actually express — integrated with the rest of biblical teaching and applied to our individual lives.

Apart from the Spirit, there is no true learning of divine things from Scripture, and supposedly "spiritual" thoughts not founded on the Word are godless flights of fancy. (We should note that in the New Testament the word *spiritual* regularly relates to the new life in Christ that the Spirit gives and never means "intellectual, high-minded, or fastidious.") So those who would live under the authority of the Spirit must bow before the Word as the Spirit's textbook while those who would live under the authority of Scripture must seek the Spirit as its interpreter. Negligence and one-sidedness either way could be ruinous, and since a proper balance as this as in other matters comes naturally to none of us, we do well to be on our guard.

Keep in Step with the Spirit

REALISTIC WISDOM

The drippings of the honeycomb are sweet to your taste.
Know that wisdom is such to your soul.

PROVERBS 24:13-14

The wise are realists who adjust to the way things are. They develop skill at fitting in. As Cornelius Plantinga delightfully puts it, glancing at Proverbs and Ecclesiastes as he does so,

The wise eventually learn and then accommodate themselves to such truths as the following:

- The more you talk, the less people listen.
- If your word is no good, people will not trust you, and it is then useless to protest this fact.
- Trying to cure distress with the same thing that caused it only makes matters worse.
- If you refuse to work hard and take pains, you are unlikely to do much of any consequence.
- Boasting of your accomplishments does not make people admire them. Boasting is vain in both senses of the word.
- Envy of fat cats does not make them slimmer and in the end will rot your bones.
- If you scratch certain itches, they just itch more.
- Many valuable things, including happiness and deep sleep, come to us only if we do not try hard for them.[20]

Wise people know that accepting things that cannot be changed is the secret of contentment, and active goodwill toward others is the secret of sweetness. In all these ways they know how to live.

Such then is wisdom in general, as a personal quality and style of life under the version of God's covenant of grace that Israel knew.

The Way of Wisdom

LETTING THE BIBLE GUIDE US

For my thoughts are not your thoughts,
neither are your ways my ways, declares the LORD.
ISAIAH 55:8

The Bible is the sacred book of the Christian church as a whole, but evangelicals are self-consciously Bible-based in their believing and behaving in a way that other forms of Christianity characteristically are not.

Catholicism has historically venerated the Bible as authoritative, but has trusted tradition (the say-so of the ongoing church, voicing its historical consensus through its appointed officers) to interpret the Bible on all major matters. Protestant subjectivism refuses to categorize the Bible as God's own testimony to himself and teaching about himself; instead, it treats Holy Scripture as a flawed and often unhelpful, though sometimes stimulating and insight-triggering, resource for reconstructing and restating Christianity within the frame of current secular thought. But evangelicalism has historically affirmed the *infallibility* and *sufficiency* of the canonical Scriptures as a God-given guide in all matters of faith and life; their *necessity* as a control and corrective of human thought about God, which left to itself will always go astray; and the clarity or *perspicuity* of the entire collection as a body of intrinsically intelligible writings that demonstrably belong together and constantly illuminate each other. These three principles, taken together, yield a functional view of biblical authority that sets evangelicalism apart from all other forms of Christian faith.

Catholicism says that those who want to know the mind and will of God on Christian essentials should listen to the teaching church, and finally let tradition guide them; subjectivists say they should listen to expert theologians, and finally let their own thoughts guide them; but evangelicals say they should listen to Holy Scripture, and finally let its teaching guide them, however much reordering of their prior ideas and intentions this may involve, and however sharply it may set them at odds with the mindset of their peers and their times.

Honouring the Written Word of God

HATEFUL DESTROYER

*The god of this world has blinded the minds of the unbelievers,
to keep them from seeing the light of the gospel of the glory of Christ.*

2 Corinthians 4:4

We think of Satan as our spiritual enemy, and so he is, but we need to realize that the reason he hates humankind and seeks our ruin is that he hates God, his and our Creator. He is not a creator himself, only a destroyer; he is a fallen angel, the archetypal instance of good gone wrong; and now he seeks only to thwart God's plans, wreck his work, rob him of glory, and in that sense triumph over him.

When God initiates something for his praise, Satan is always there, trying to keep pace with him, planning ways of spoiling and frustrating the divine project. "Devil," his descriptive title, means "slanderer," one who thinks, speaks, and plans evil, first against God himself, secondarily against the human race. The bodiless intelligences that the Gospels call demons "have as king over them the angel of the bottomless pit. His name in Hebrew is Abaddon, and in Greek he is called Apollyon" (Revelation 9:11) — both names meaning "destroyer." For his fierce, sustained, pitiless hatred of humanity Satan is spoken of as a murderer, the Evil One, a roaring and devouring lion, and a great red dragon. For his habit of twisting truth as a means to his ends he is called a liar and a deceiver. He is malicious, mean, ugly, and cruel to the last degree.

The Satan of Scripture hates and seeks to fool all mankind, those who claim allegiance to him no less than others. Also, he is extremely cunning, much cleverer than we are, and is highly skilled at manipulating and using people to bring about his destructive goals. Altogether, the Devil is an enemy who has to be taken very seriously.

A Passion for Faithfulness

IT TAKES WORDS

And we have . . . the prophetic word,
to which you will do well to pay attention.

2 PETER 1:19

There is nothing of which the Bible is more sure than that God has from the first accompanied his redemptive acts with explanatory words — statements of fact about himself and his purposes, warnings, commands, predictions, promises — and that it is in responding specifically to these divine words that obedience consists. Moses, the prophets, Christ, the apostles, all spoke God's words to men; and what they said took the form of statement and inference, argument and deduction. God's word in their mouths was propositional in character. Christ and the apostles regularly appealed to Old Testament statements as providing a valid basis for inferences about God, and drew from them by the ordinary laws of grammar and logic conclusions which they put forward as truths revealed there — that the dead do not perish, that justification is by faith and not by works, that God is sovereign in saving mercy, and so forth. Plainly, they regarded the Old Testament as propounding a body of doctrinal affirmations.

We conclude therefore that if we are to follow Scripture's own account of itself, we are bound to say that whatever "is either expressly set down in Scripture, or by good and necessary consequence may be deduced from Scripture" (as the Westminster Confession puts it[21]), must be regarded as a revealed truth. The Bible confronts us with the conception that the Word of God which it embodies consists of a system of truths, conveying to men real information from God about himself.

"Fundamentalism" and the Word of God

IN STEP WITH JESUS

If you abide in my word,
you are truly my disciples.
John 8:31

Jesus himself taught, quite explicitly, that discipleship to him, across the board and in every respect, was to be conceived as modeling oneself on the Lord himself. This was his meaning when he said, "Take my yoke upon you, and learn from me" (Matthew 11:29). The picture is of two oxen pulling a cart or plow, one of them a veteran, the other a youngster in training. A wooden yoke fastened over both their necks links them side by side. The young ox, paired with the veteran, learns to pull by imitating the other; indeed its only choice for comfort in this twosome is to keep in step with the older partner. In the disciple's case, pairing with Jesus and learning from Jesus will be a lifelong business. The Savior's invitation to it is compassionate: "Come to me, all who labor and are heavy laden, and I will give you rest. Take my yoke upon you, and learn from me, for I am gentle and lowly in heart, and you will find rest for your souls. For my yoke is easy, and my burden is light" (11:28-30).

Modeling Christ, as part of the larger process of being modeled by Christ, is thus of the essence of the Christian life and of the divine-guidance process. Christians learn to live *in* Christ, to follow and fulfill the example that Christ has set us, and to recognize that this — only this — is the way of our maturation, namely, through imitation of him. It is by this means, in the first instance, that we are led in paths of righteousness, namely, by consciously keeping in step with our divine-human leader with whom we are inseparably yoked. The image is truly awesome, but very clarifying and very supportive.

Guard Us, Guide Us

THE LOOK THAT BRINGS CONFIDENCE

Looking to Jesus,
the founder and perfecter of our faith.
HEBREWS 12:2

The life of Christian endurance is lived by fixing our eyes on Jesus. The Greek wording in Hebrews 12:2 implies that we look away from everything else in order to concentrate on our object of attention. The secret of endurance, says the writer of Hebrews, is to concentrate on Jesus himself; "gaze steadily at him" is the thought being expressed.

The most vital truth for the life of holy endurance is that Jesus is our sustainer, our source of strength to action, our sovereign grace giver (Hebrews 2:18; 4:16), "the founder and perfecter of our faith" (12:2). Faith is a compound of knowing, trusting, hoping, and stubbornly persisting in trustful hope against all odds. Faith can do this because the one who has graciously brought us to faith, and whom we now trust, helps us to do it. "He has said, 'I will never leave you nor forsake you.' So we can confidently say, 'The Lord is my helper; I will not fear; what can man do to me?'" (13:5-6). "Let us then with confidence draw near to the throne of grace, that we may receive mercy and find grace to help in time of need" (4:16).

This confident, expectant approach is faith in action. It is precisely the glorified Lord Jesus who now helps us to stand steady as we gaze on him and cling to him by means of our focused, intentional, heartfelt prayer. It is often said that "Help!" is the best prayer anyone ever makes. When directed to the Lord Jesus, it is certainly the most effective. And that remains true for us now as ever it was for anyone, since, as the writer goes on to say, "Jesus Christ is the same yesterday and today and forever" (13:8).

Rediscovering Holiness

TEACHING US HUMILITY

For those whom he foreknew he also predestined
to be conformed to the image of his Son . . .
and those whom he predestined he also called.

ROMANS 8:29-30

The doctrine of predestination resolves three vital questions: First, how is it that I am a Christian today? Second, what confidence can I have of getting to heaven? Third, what have I to thank God for?

What the truth of predestination teaches me is this: First, I am a Christian today because God chose from eternity to make me one. He went the first mile when he sent his Son from heaven to die on the cross for my sins. He went the second mile when he called me by grace, working in my heart so that I responded to the gospel message in a way I would not have done had he not so worked. It is thanks to God's predestination that I am a Christian.

Second, I have every confidence of getting to heaven. The doctrine of predestination says that once you have believed, God promises to keep you believing. Once he has brought you to faith according to his predestinating purpose, he will complete that purpose. It is all his doing, and it is guaranteed by his sovereignty. So I am safe in his hands, and my hope is secure.

Third, I owe God thanks for my entire Christian life — for the fact that I have been converted no less than for the fact that there was a Savior for me to turn to.

The doctrine of predestination teaches us humility, the humility which acknowledges every spiritual benefit as God's gracious gift to me. Also, it reveals my security, telling me that God's purpose guarantees final glory for me. Finally, it prompts doxology, praise to God for the greatness of his grace to me. Those who embrace predestination praise God for more than others do, for they recognize more as God's gifts to them.

Honouring the People of God

THE STORY OF THE COSMOS RESTORED

> *The creation itself will be set free from its bondage to decay and obtain the freedom of the glory of the children of God.*
>
> ROMANS 8:21

From all eternity it has been God's gracious plan, purpose, and pleasure to restore the cosmos to perfection at the end of the day through the mediation of the "last Adam," the God-man Jesus Christ. All the decisive events in God's plan save the last have now been played out on the stage of world history. The key to understanding the plan, as it affects mankind, is to see that by God's appointment each man's destiny depends on how he stands related to the two representative men, Adam and Christ. What God planned was to exercise his kingship over his rebel world by bringing in his kingdom — that is, a state of bliss for sinners who, penitently returning to his obedience, should find under his sway salvation from sin's guilt, power, and evil effects. In this kingdom, Jesus Christ should be God's vice-regent, and trusting and obeying Christ should be the appointed way of returning from sin to God's service.

God, having achieved world redemption according to his plan through Christ's death, raised him to life and set him on the throne of the universe, where now he reigns, furthering his kingdom by sending the Spirit to draw men to himself and by strengthening them for faithful obedience in the face of mounting opposition till the day dawns for his return to judge all men and finally to renew all things.

In this story, the goal of God's action is to glorify himself by restoring and perfecting his disordered cosmos, and the gospel call is to abandon rebellion, acknowledge Christ's lordship, thankfully accept the free gift of forgiveness and new life in the kingdom, enlist on the victory side, be faithful in God's strength, and hope to the end for Christ's coming triumph.

Serving the People of God

PROPER COMPLAINING

Evening and morning and at noon
I utter my complaint and moan, and he hears my voice.

PSALM 55:17

Our culture has historically embraced the stiff-upper-lip ideal of human behavior, and habitually looks down on people who voice personal complaints. Western Christianity has followed suit.

The Bible indeed teaches self-control, but the Platonic ideal of calm stoical strength should not be thought definitive for the people of God. Scripture conceives the life of the human individual as a unity. The personal self (soul, spirit) is unitary in itself and uses the physical body, via which it lives, to express itself. Part of our legacy from Adam is that within the unitary human being, now subject to death and all that it means, the personal self has disintegrated to a degree, so that throughout history intellect and emotion have appeared as Plato saw them — that is, as two distinct energies constantly pulling against each other. But from the moment of our regeneration in Christ, through the implanting of a new, unifying, Godward energy, and through the indwelling of the Holy Spirit to sustain and channel this dual energy, God is at work reintegrating us: putting us back together, that is, as the thinking-and-feeling creatures, praising and praying, that we were always meant to be. Regenerate people feel through their minds and think through their feelings. They are self-aware in a God-conscious and God-centered way.

Complaints are integral to this new, regenerate life of communion and prayer and fellowship and worship and seeking God's honor and praise. The almost lurid intensity with which psalmists and others describe the sad situations out of which they pray is not just ancient Eastern imaginations going strong, though it is that, but essentially it is the God-centered feeling intellect and the God-centered thoughtful emotions of regenerate hearts contemplating the distance between God's best and the way things have now turned out.

Praying

HEALING FOR THE SICK

Be attentive to my words. . . . For they are life to those
who find them, and healing to all their flesh.

PROVERBS 4:20,22

The Puritans were physicians of the soul. Truth obeyed, they said, will *heal*. The word fits, because we are all spiritually sick — sick through sin, which is a wasting and killing disease of the heart. The unconverted are sick unto death; those who have come to know Christ and been born again continue sick, but they are gradually getting better as the work of grace goes on in their lives. The church, however, is a hospital in which nobody is completely well, and anyone can relapse at any time.

Pastors no less than others are weakened by pressure from the world, the flesh, and the Devil, with their lures of profit, pleasure, and pride, and pastors must acknowledge that they, the healers, remain sick and wounded and therefore need to apply the medicines of Scripture to themselves as well as to the sheep whom they tend in Christ's name. All Christians need Scripture truth as medicine for their souls at every stage, and the making and accepting of applications is the administering and swallowing of it. The ability to apply God's truth therapeutically implies the prior ability to diagnose spiritual ill-health, and diagnostic ability is learned as much by discovering and keeping track of one's own sins and weaknesses as by any other means.

The frequency with which Puritan pastors lament their own sinfulness should not be dismissed as a trivial cultural convention; it is in fact an assurance to us, as it was to their own first hearers and readers, that they know what they are talking about when they "rip up" our consciences (their phrase), diagnose our spiritual diseases, and prescribe a regimen of biblical directives for our cure.

A Quest for Godliness

SAFEGUARDS FOR INTERPRETING SCRIPTURE

Do your best to present yourself to God as one approved,
a worker who has no need to be ashamed,
rightly handling the word of truth.

2 TIMOTHY 2:15

To fall victim to secular philosophy and ideology has been a characteristic Protestant vice for three centuries, and it is one from which evangelicals are by no means free. To be an avowed Bible believer is no guarantee that one's interpretation of the Bible will always be right, or that secularist distortions will never invade one's mind to discolor one's thoughts.

How then may we avoid subjectivist eccentricity in our own biblical interpretation? The first necessity is precision in handling texts. To discover what each passage meant as a message about God written on his behalf to a particular envisaged readership must be our first step. But then, to determine what meaning God has for us in this historical material, we must go on to an *a posteriori* theological analysis and application according to the analogy of Scripture. By theological analysis, I mean seeing what truths about God and his world the passage teaches, or assumes, or illustrates. By theological application, I mean reflecting on how these truths impact our lives today.

When I say that this analysis and application must be *a posteriori,* I mean that nothing must be read into texts that cannot be read out of them. When I say that it must be faithful, I mean that nothing taught by any text may be disregarded or left unapplied. When I speak of the analogy of Scripture, I am referring to the traditional procedures of letting one part of Scripture throw light on another that deals with the same subject, and of maintaining internal theological coherence by interpreting ambiguous passages in harmony with unambiguous ones, and of allowing things that define themselves as primary and central to provide a frame of reference and a perspective for looking at those that are secondary and peripheral.

Celebrating the Saving Work of God

NEW COVENANT WISDOM

Christ the power of God
and the wisdom of God.
1 CORINTHIANS 1:24

What *New Covenant specifics* should we who live under that covenant add to the general portrayal of wisdom in the Old Testament?

An *epistemological* addition is needed first. We have said that wisdom is at every stage and in every aspect God's gift, received through his word by the agency of the Holy Spirit. It should now be said specifically that the word that brings wisdom is the apostolic message about Jesus Christ, which the canonical New Testament sets before us. This message consists of historical facts plus a detailed theological explanation of those facts that presents them as, among other things, fulfilling Old Testament predictions and promises. Where this history and theology are not center stage, there is no true wisdom.

Paul made that point when confronted by the Corinthian preference of the "wisdom" of flowery self-promoting rhetoric, whatever its religious content, over the plain, unvarnished, factual wisdom of the God-given cruciform gospel as he himself had preached it (see 1 Corinthians 1–3). This was "God's secret wisdom" (1 Corinthians 2:7, NIV), which turns all the world's wisdom into foolishness.

Modern scholars who dismiss the apostolic witness forfeit wisdom and embrace foolishness. Docility before God's revelation, which is what the apostolic witness is, is the only way.

TAKING THE WORD TO HEART

I will not leave you as orphans;
I will come to you.

JOHN 14:18

The Bible has a determinative role not only in evangelical belief but also in evangelical devotion. Hearing Scripture preached, reading it regularly, memorizing it (as those who were unable to read it for themselves have always had to do), internalizing it by meditation, and applying it to give content to one's personal worship, as well as to find direction for living one's life, are characteristic evangelical procedures for developing one's communion with the Father and the Son.

Central to conversion, as evangelicals understand it, is a living relationship with the living Lord, and the heart of evangelical testimony to the impact of the Bible on those who soak their souls in it is that the word of the Lord constantly brings home to them the presence and power of the Lord of the word. The transforming impact of the devotional commerce with the Bible, as evangelicals characteristically witness to it, is thus, in the most direct sense, the work of Christ. He walks, as it were, out of the pages of the Bible into our lives. He writes on our hearts the faith set forth by the Bible writers, so that again and again we find ourselves turning back to him in contrition, in excitement, in love, and in gratitude. We know inwardly that it is Christ himself who by his Spirit made this happen. Thus more and more we come to see how much we owe to him and how faithful he is in leading us.

Such inward experience is characteristic of lively, healthy evangelicals in every era, every culture, and every part of the world, and this universal, unitive experience is brought about through taking to heart the written Word of God, through which our heavenly Father and our gracious Savior communicate with us.

Honouring the Written Word of God

TRUE IN ALL IT TEACHES

Forever, O LORD, your word is firmly fixed
in the heavens.

PSALM 119:89

Evangelicals are accustomed to speak of the Word of God as *infallible* and *inerrant*. Infallible denotes the quality of never deceiving or misleading, and so means "wholly trustworthy and reliable." *Inerrant* means "wholly true." These terms express the conviction that all Scripture's teaching is the utterance of God "who never lies" (Titus 1:2), whose word, once spoken, "remains forever" (1 Peter 1:25), and that therefore it may be trusted implicitly.

This does not, however, guarantee the infallibility and inerrancy of any interpretation, or interpreter, of that teaching; nor does it in any way prejudge the issue as to what Scripture does, in fact, assert. This can be determined only by careful Bible study. We must allow Scripture itself to define for us the scope and limits of its teaching. The Bible is not an inspired "Inquire Within Upon Everything"; it does not profess to give information about all branches of human knowledge. It claims in the broadest terms to teach all things necessary to salvation (2 Timothy 3:15-17), but it nowhere claims to give instruction in (for instance) any of the natural sciences. Scripture provides instruction that is true and trustworthy, not on every conceivable subject, but simply on those subjects with which it claims to deal. We must allow Scripture itself to tell us what these are.

Approaching Scripture as being infallible and inerrant is far more likely to edify the church than any modern version of the thesis that the teaching of Scripture is only roughly right, and that, though we ought to believe what we suppose the Bible means, we cannot believe all that it actually says. Only highly sophisticated persons could stomach such an approach in any case, but in this case it is simply a wrong approach.

"Fundamentalism" and the Word of God

HOLY WORK

*I am doing
a great work.*

NEHEMIAH 6:3

Honest, faithful, honorable work of any sort, done as best one can and as helpfully to others as possible, glorifies God. So a believer may see his or her work as hallowed, whether that work involves handing fast food out of a window, cleaning offices late at night, bartering at the stock market, caring for children, plowing a field, balancing accounts, repairing a car, or (even) composing a manuscript. God gives his people all kinds of skills and interests and opportunities, and he receives their praise not only in verbal form, but in the form of all kinds of work well done in his name. What turns work, which might otherwise become drudgery, into a vocation is not the nature of the work itself, but the fact that it is done for the glory of the Lord.

Work means, precisely, useful, creative employment in the service of God and others — just that. Skills are involved in work, but salary may or may not accompany it. A lot of our work is unsalaried. Homemaking is a case in point, yet homemaking fulfills a crucially important calling from God at the most significant time of a child's life. Homemaking parents serve God and others in a profound way by caring for their children and by creating a home in which the entire family receives physical, emotional, and spiritual nurture. Homemaking as a call from God is sometimes overlooked, as are the para-homemaking aspects, as we may call them, of church life.

We need to get our minds off the equation that vocations and career equal profession and status and earnings. The reality of vocation extends far wider than that. All Christian voluntary work is vocational.

Guard Us, Guide Us

HUMBLE ENDURANCE

*For you have need
of endurance.*
HEBREWS 10:36

The resolute perseverance to which we are called is not the practice
of stoicism. The Stoic ideal was self-sufficiency and the stiff upper lip.
Stoicism saw it as beneath human dignity to give way to feelings of
sorrow, pain, grief, regret, or any kind of hurt; if you regularly act as if
you did not feel distress, you will progressively become the sort of person
who does not feel it.

Certainly there is a sort of heroism in this ideal. But it is the perverse
heroism of self-sufficient, self-glorifying pride, the sick heroism of
Milton's Satan in *Paradise Lost.* And it is at the opposite extreme from
the obedient, dependent heroism of Jesus, the perfect Man, who "offered
up prayers and supplications, with loud cries and tears, to him who was
able to save him from death, and he was heard because of his reverence"
(Hebrews 5:7). Yet he ended his prayer in Gethsemane facing the fact that
he was not to be *saved* from death, and accepting that fact as the good will
of his Father. Accordingly, strengthened through his prayer, Jesus walked
straight into the jaws of death, and "learned obedience" — that is, learned
both the practice and the cost of it — "through what he suffered" (5:8). He
was shamed, and scourged, and he died on the cross, in an agony that felt
like agony every moment until the ordeal was over.

Holy endurance of this Christlike sort is an expression not of pride,
but of humility; not of defiant self-reliance, but of ready obedience; not
of the tight-lipped fatalism in a bleak, uncaring universe, but of resolute,
though often pained and aching, submission to a loving Lord, of whom
it has been truly said, "Christ leads me through no darker rooms than he
went through before."[22]

Rediscovering Holiness

RIGHTLY APPROACHING PREDESTINATION

God chose you as the firstfruits to be saved,
through sanctification by the Spirit and belief in the truth.

2 THESSALONIANS 2:13

Come at predestination *biblically*, not speculatively. Do not be mesmerized by the doctrine of reprobation, about which the Bible says so little. "The secret things belong to the LORD our God, but the things that are revealed belong to us and to our children forever, that we may do all the words of [God's] law" (Deuteronomy 29:29). Approach predestination in that spirit, taking to heart Calvin's warning that we must not go an inch beyond what the Bible says, for if we do, we can expect to find our heads going dizzy, our balance being lost, and ourselves falling over the edge of an intellectual precipice into ruin. Stay within the limits of Bible teaching.

Second, come at predestination *pastorally*, as the New Testament always does. Paul wrote in Romans 8 about God's plan of election to encourage believers under pressure. In Ephesians 1, he celebrates election in order to evoke praise of God from his readers. In 1 Thessalonians 1:2,4 he presents it as a doctrine which brings Christians assurance: "We give thanks to God always for all of you. . . . For we know, brothers loved by God, that he has chosen you." The doctrine of election is a matter for worship, encouragement, and praise.

Finally, come at predestination *Christ-centeredly*. Meditate on John 6 and 10, where our Lord himself enunciates the truth of predestination (6:37-39,44-45; 10:14-16,27-29). A doctrine which the Lord Jesus himself expresses should not be taken lightly by us, especially when the very heart of it is that the Father through his plan of predestining grace is securing a people for the Son, thus furthering the glory of the Son, which is his final purpose. The glory of Jesus Christ as Savior is directly bound up with this doctrine of predestinating grace.

Honouring the People of God

THE STORY OF THE GRACE OF CHRIST

He died for all, that those who live might no longer live for themselves
but for him who for their sake died and was raised.

2 CORINTHIANS 5:15

In Jesus Christ, God has given the world a Savior whose great salvation more than matches man's great need, and whose great love (which should be gauged from the cross) will not be daunted or drained away by our great unloveliness.

Jesus is set forth as prophet, priest, and king; teacher and guide; mediator and intercessor; master and protector — and the focal point of his saving work is identified as his cross, concerning which each Christian can say that he "loved me and gave himself for me" (Galatians 2:20). Christ's death was an act of righteousness, for he endured it in obedience to his Father's will. As such, it wrought redemption, freeing us from the curse of God's law — that is, exposure to divine judgment — at the cost of Christ's own suffering. His death was redemptive because it achieved an act of propitiation, quenching God's wrath by dealing with the sin that evoked it. It propitiated God by being an act of substitutionary sin-bearing, in which the judgment which our sins deserved was diverted onto Christ's head — from the cross to the risen Christ's gift of a permanent new relationship with God, which Paul analyzes as justification (pardon plus a righteous man's status) and adoption (a place in the family with certainty of inheritance), and the writer to the Hebrews calls sanctification (acceptance by God, on the basis of consecration to him). With this new status is given new birth, the indwelling Spirit, progressive transformation into Christ's image, and glorification — in short, comprehensive subjective renewal. God's goal in all this is the perfect bliss of sinners, and the gospel call is an invitation to faith in Christ, through which all these gifts come to us, from the Savior's own hand, "for free."

Serving the People of God

TELLING IT LIKE IT IS

*Pour out your heart like water
before the presence of the Lord!*
LAMENTATIONS 2:19

In Lamentations, those who mourn the fall of Jerusalem are regenerate children of God (regeneration was an Old Testament fact, though its theology was not made known until Christ came) and their complaints are fundamentally prayers for deliverance from evil and for the fulfillment of God's promises of protection, provision, and relational enrichment. Their plea is that joyful fellowship with God may be restored and present pain become a thing of the past. As they feel with their minds and think with their feelings, their lament and complaints to God are acts of petition and promise-claiming, in a very strong form.

So complaining will be, or at least should be, a recurring element in the praying of the born again. The presence of complaint prayers in God's prayer book (the Psalms) shows that, so far from being irreverent, prayers of this kind, describing the distress of oneself and others in the freest and most forthright, forceful language imaginable, are entirely in order. Ignoring in our prayers situations that are not "just fine" would by contrast be barren unrealism.

Complaint prayers are among those that we were made and redeemed to offer. Telling it like it is and piling on the agony of our feelings about it is not merely *safe,* because of who God is (the hurting of the child engages the Father's helpfulness, not his hostility), nor is it merely a *solace,* because of who we are (for humans always find it a relief, a refreshment even, to tell their deepest troubles to someone who sympathizes), it honors God by *submitting* to his ordering of events thus far, however painful, and it is *sanctifying* in its Christlike honesty and adherence to God's ongoing purpose.

Praying

START WITH YOUR MIND

To give prudence to the simple, knowledge and discretion to the youth—
Let the wise hear and increase in learning,
and the one who understands obtain guidance.

PROVERBS 1:4-5

Much thought was given in the sixteenth and seventeenth centuries to educational theory, and the Puritan pastors as a body had a well-planned-out educational technique. The starting point was their certainty that the mind must be instructed and enlightened before faith and obedience become possible. "Ignorance is almost every error," wrote Richard Baxter, and one of his favorite maxims about preaching was "first light—then heat." Heat without light, pulpit passion without pedagogic precision, would be no use to anyone. Unwillingness on the part of church attenders to learn the faith and accept instruction from sermons was a sure sign of insincerity.

"If ever you would be converted, labor for true knowledge," Baxter told his working-class congregation, and when they did as a modern congregation would, and objected, "We are not learned, and therefore, God will not require much knowledge at our hands," he replied in part, "If you think . . . that you may be excused from knowledge, you may as well think that you may be excused from love and from all obedience; for there can be none of this without knowledge."

All the Puritans regarded religious feeling and pious emotion without knowledge as worse than useless. Only when the truth was being felt was emotion in any way desirable. When men felt and obeyed the truth they knew, it was the work of the Spirit of God, but when they were swayed by feeling without knowledge, it was a sure sign that the Devil was at work, for feeling divorced from knowledge and urgings to action in darkness of mind were both as ruinous to the soul as was knowledge without obedience. So the teaching of truth was the pastor's first task, as the learning of it was the layman's.

A Quest for Godliness

OUR CONSTANT CONCERN

Because of your hard and impenitent heart
you are storing up wrath for yourself on the day of wrath
when God's righteous judgment will be revealed.

ROMANS 2:5

Evangelicals have always seen the question of salvation as one of supreme importance, and their witness to the way of salvation as the most precious gift they bring to the rest of the church. This conviction rests not on the memory of the conversion of Paul or Augustine or Luther or Wesley or Whitefield or any other evangelical hero, but on the emphasis with which the Bible itself highlights salvation as its central theme. The Scriptures — or perhaps I should say, preachers like Christ, Peter, Paul, Isaiah, and Ezekiel, as recorded in the Scriptures — clearly regard ordinary human beings as lost, and accordingly call on them to repent, turn or return to God, come to Christ, put faith in him, and so find the pardon, peace, and newness of life that they need.

The main concepts that the New Testament uses to delineate this salvation are reconciliation, redemption, and propitiation, all won for us by the sacrificial death of Christ; forgiveness, remission of sins, justification, adoption; regeneration or renovation (new birth); the indwelling of the Holy Spirit as God's seal of ownership within us; sanctification; and glorification. By contrast the chief notions that are used to describe the condition of those who do not believe in Jesus Christ are spiritual deadness; darkness of mind; delusion with regard to God, gods, and supernatural powers generally; moral delinquency bringing guilt and shame; and a destiny of certain distress. Those who are not Christ's are perishing, and need to be saved. Historic evangelicalism — with some differences, I grant, of nuance in exposition and of evangelistic practice, but with great solidarity of substance — has constantly affirmed these things. Modern evangelicalism will stand revealed as a degenerate plan if it does not just as constantly do the same.

Celebrating the Saving Work of God

FINDING WISDOM IN CHRIST

Let the word of Christ dwell in you richly,
teaching and admonishing one another in all wisdom.

COLOSSIANS 3:16

For us who live under the realities of the New Covenant, a *Christological* addition is needed to the Old Testament's portrayal of wisdom.

The apostolic proclamation of God's wisdom *in Christ* is to be acknowledged in full. The following string of citations, culled almost at random, gives some idea of the ground that the wisdom of God in the person, place, and mediatorial ministry of Jesus Christ covers:

"We preach Christ crucified . . . Christ the power of God and the wisdom of God" (1 Corinthians 1:23-24; see also 1:18). "Christ Jesus, whom God made our wisdom and our righteousness and sanctification and redemption" (1 Corinthians 1:30). "In [Christ] are hidden all the treasures of wisdom and knowledge" (Colossians 2:3). "In Christ all the fullness of the Deity lives in bodily form, and you have been given fullness in Christ. . . . God made you alive with Christ. He forgave us all our sins, having canceled the written code, with its regulations, that was against us . . . he took it away, nailing it to the cross" (Colossians 2:9-10,13-14, NIV). "I have been crucified with Christ and I no longer live, but Christ lives in me. The life I live in the body, I live by faith in the Son of God, who loved me and gave himself for me" (Galatians 2:20, NIV). "He was delivered over to death for our sins and was raised to life for our justification" (Romans 4:25, NIV).

Where any of these truths — divine incarnation, penal substitutionary atonement, the gift of justification, union with Christ in his death and resurrection, and a new personal life through faith in him — have fallen by the wayside, the wisdom that acknowledges God's wisdom is thereby lacking.

The Way of Wisdom

THE SKILL OF APPLICATION

If you know these things,
blessed are you if you do them.
JOHN 13:17

All the biblical books were written to build up their readers in faith, obedience, and worship, and interpretation is neither complete nor correct without this threefold response. Just as it is possible to identify in all the books of Scripture universal and abiding truths about the will, work, and ways of God, it is equally possible to find in every one of them universal and abiding principles of loyalty and devotion to the holy, gracious Creator; and then to detach these from the particular situations to which the books apply them, and to reapply them to ourselves in the circumstances and conditions of our own lives today. Rational application of this kind, acknowledging but transcending cultural differences between the Bible worlds and ours, is the stock-in-trade of the evangelical pulpit and the recognized goal of the evangelical discipline of personal meditation on the written text.

The evangelical heritage enshrines within itself a clearer under-standing of the theory of application than can be learned from any other source, whatever may be thought of the often over-narrow application of Scripture that particular evangelicals sometimes make. Evangelicals do not find their models of interpretation in the "critical" commentaries of the past two centuries, which stop short at offering historical explanations of the text and have no applicatory angle at all; they find them, rather, in the from-faith-to-faith expository style of such older writers as Chrysostom, Luther, Calvin, many Puritans, Matthew Henry, J. A. Bengel, Thomas Scott, and J. C. Ryle, who concerned themselves with what Scripture means as God's word to their own readers as well as with what it meant as religious instruction for the readership originally addressed, and whose supreme skill lay in making appropriate applications of the material that they exegeted by grammatical-historical means.

Honouring the Written Word of God

TWO INTERPRETATION PRINCIPLES

*That you may learn by us not to go
beyond what is written.*

1 CORINTHIANS 4:6

Scripture yields two basic principles for its own interpretation. The first is that the proper, natural sense of each passage (i.e., the intended sense of the writer) is to be taken as fundamental; the meaning of texts in their own contexts, and for their original readers, is the necessary starting point for enquiry into their wider significance. In other words, Scripture statements must be interpreted in the light of the rules of grammar and discourse on the one hand, and of their own place in history on the other. This is what we should expect in the nature of the case, seeing that the biblical books originated as occasional documents addressed to contemporary audiences; and it is exemplified in the New Testament exposition of the Old. We must allow Scripture to tell us its own literary character, and be willing to receive it as what it claims to be.

The second basic principle of interpretation is that Scripture must interpret Scripture; the scope and significance of one passage is to be brought out by relating it to others. The Westminster Confession states it thus: "When there is a question about the true and full sense of any Scripture, it must be searched and known by other places that speak more clearly."[23] This, too, is in the nature of the case, since the various inspired books deal with complementary aspects of the same subject. This rule means we must give ourselves in Bible study to following out the unities, cross-references, and topical links which Scripture provides.

We must base our study of Scripture on the assumption that governed the New Testament men in their study of the Old — that God's revealed truth is a consistent unity, and any disharmony between part and part is only apparent, not real.

"Fundamentalism" and the Word of God

OUR PATH OF HOPE

> *Now faith is the assurance of things hoped for,*
> *the conviction of things not seen.*
> HEBREWS 11:1

The channel through which power to endure flows, subjectively speaking, is *hope*—faith's forward look.

We are to be upheld by our hope, the sure and certain hope of glory promised to us in the gospel—the glory to which a life of faithful endurance is guaranteed to lead us. "We have this hope as an anchor for the soul, firm and secure" (Hebrews 6:19, NIV). Anchored ships stay steady. Anchored Christians do the same. And the anchor that can and does hold us steady is the hope that is ours in Christ.

God made us hoping creatures, creatures who live very much in their own future, creatures whose nature it is to look forward, and to get excited about good things that we foresee, and to draw joy and strength to cope with the present from our expectations of future fulfillment and delight. In the absence of anything exciting to look forward to, existence itself becomes a burden and life no longer feels worth living. To be without hope is a tragic thing, the more so because it is needless. God never intended humankind to live without hope, and he has, in fact, given Christians the most magnificent hope that ever was.

The New Testament presents this hope in various ways, but the basic assertion is that which breaks surface when Paul identifies the "the riches of the glory of this mystery [his gospel message], which is Christ in you, the *hope of glory*" (Colossians 1:27, emphasis added). Jesus Christ himself, to whom we who believe are united even now, is the Christian's hope. Each of us is traveling along a path that he has appointed for us to an eternity of joy in which he will be the center, the focus, and the source of our endless delight.

Rediscovering Holiness

FEEDING FAITH

We also have believed in Christ Jesus,
in order to be justified by faith in Christ.
GALATIANS 2:16

Justification, said the Reformers, is by faith *only*, because Christ's vicarious righteousness is the *only* ground of justification, and it is *only* by faith that we lay hold of Christ for his righteousness to become ours. Faith is a conscious acknowledgment of our own unrighteousness and ungodliness, and on that basis a looking to Christ as our righteousness, a clasping of him as the ring clasps the jewel (so Luther), a receiving of him as an empty vessel receives treasure (so Calvin), and a reverent, resolute reliance on the biblical promise of life through him for all who believe. Faith is our act, but not our work; it is an instrument of reception without being a means of merit; it is the work in us of the Holy Spirit, who both evokes it and through it ingrafts us into Christ in such a sense that we know at once the personal relationship of sinner to Savior and disciple to Master, and with that the dynamic relationship of resurrection life, communicated through the Spirit's indwelling. So faith takes, and rejoices, and hopes, and loves, and triumphs.

One of the unhealthiest features of Protestant theology today is its preoccupation with faith — faith, that is, viewed man-centeredly as a state of existential commitment. Inevitably this preoccupation diverts thought away from faith's object. Though the Reformers said much about faith, even to the point of calling their message of justification "the doctrine of faith," their interest was not of the modern kind. The Reformers saw faith as a relationship not to oneself, but to the living Christ of the Bible, and they fed faith by concentrating on that Christ as the Savior and Lord by whom our whole life must be determined.

Honouring the People of God

CONSCIENCE EXPOSED

I always take pains to have a clear conscience
toward both God and man.

ACTS 24:16

The supreme concern in the minds and hearts of the people called Puritans was a concern about God — to know him truly and serve him rightly, and so to glorify him and enjoy him. Because this was so, they were very deeply concerned about conscience, for they held that conscience was the mental organ in men through which God brought his word to bear on them. Nothing in their estimation was more important for any man than that his conscience should be enlightened, instructed, purged, and kept clean. To them, there could be no real spiritual understanding, nor any genuine godliness, except as men exposed and enslaved their consciences to God's Word.

In saying this, the Puritans were doing no more than maintain an emphasis which went back to the first days of the Reformation. To the Reformers, conscience signified a man's knowledge of himself as standing in God's presence (*coram Deo*, in Luther's phrase), subject to God's Word and exposed to the judgment of God's law, and yet — if a believer — justified and accepted nonetheless through divine grace. Conscience was the court in which God's justifying sentence was spoken. Conscience was the soil in which alone true faith, hope, peace, and joy could grow. Conscience was a facet of the much-defaced image of God in which man was made; and vital Christianity was rooted directly in the apprehensions and exercises of conscience under the searching address of God's quick and powerful Word, and the enlightenment of his Holy Spirit.

Once, Christians were taught to commune with their consciences daily, in the regular discipline of self-examination under the Word of God; but how much of this remains today? Do we not constantly give evidence of our neglect of this secret discipline by unprincipled and rresponsible public conduct?

A Quest for Godliness

SAVED TO WALK IN WISDOM

I am the light of the world. Whoever follows me
will not walk in darkness, but will have the light of life.

JOHN 8:12

To a general description of wisdom from the Old Testament, we who live under the New Covenant need a *soteriological* addition and a *behavioral* addition.

Salvation, by common consent, is the theme of the entire New Testament — salvation, that is, in the sense of rescue from the guilt and power of sin, from the present and future wrath of God, from all the evil that marks and mars this present world order, from the dominion of the Devil, and from the condition of being without hope, without help, and without any positive relation to God. The Holy Scriptures, Paul reminds Timothy, "are able to make you *wise for salvation* through faith in Christ Jesus" (2 Timothy 3:15, emphasis added). It is the mark of wisdom to latch on to this and never lose sight of it.

Christians should also "walk" — live their lives, behave — in wisdom, "not as unwise but as wise" (Ephesians 5:15). This admonition is reinforced by a reminder that "the days are evil" (verse 16), after which Paul begins a detailed presentation of Spirit-filled living and family ethics, all irradiated by the knowledge of God in Jesus Christ. This shows that "wise" here is being used in a fully theological sense, so as to imply a responsible living out of Christian conviction and discernment. Wisdom in the New Testament sense is a matter of learning to imitate Christ in selfless love and humility; to make and keep peace in all relationships; to serve the needs of others; and to submit to pain, grief, and disgrace when circumstances inflict them. It is a mark of wisdom to aim at full Christlikeness in each of these respects.

Thus New Testament wisdom moves beyond its Old Testament counterpart, building on it and extending it in the light of Jesus Christ.

The Way of Wisdom

THE REALITY OF THE BIBLE'S HUMANNESS

Many have undertaken to compile a narrative
of the things that have been accomplished among us.

LUKE 1:1

Scripture, though divine, is fully human. The divine method of inspiration involved all the following items: accommodation to the personal qualities and cultural perspectives of the writers, including their literary styles; setting forth revelation in the form of the human story of how redemption was achieved and made known, and how the involved individuals fared through their faithfulness or lack of faithfulness to God; using a variety of witnesses and a pluriformity of presentation to exhibit redemption from the many angles from which the human witnesses perceived it; using the creativity of the authors who consulted sources, gave their books careful literary shape, and used poetical and rhetorical forms designed to evoke specific responses from readers; and incorporating all kinds of records (genealogies, liturgies, rubrics, census documents, and so forth) into the narrative.

The combination of immediate revelation, enhanced insight, and providential overruling that constitutes inspiration added something to the factors that constitute fully human writing but in no way subtracted from them. God used the literary creativity he had given these men; their humanity is part of the reality of the Bible, and it is to be celebrated and acknowledged. We don't honor God by minimizing the Bible's humanness any more than we honor him by minimizing its divinity.

An illuminating analogy exists between the inspiration of Scripture and the incarnation of the Son of God. In both cases, you have a mysterious union of divine and human. In both cases, you have perfection, as a result, in human form. This is a valid way of dispelling suspicion that the humanness of Scripture in some way requires fallibility and error on the human side. It was not so with Jesus; why should it be so with Scripture? Infallible Scripture is as fully human as is the infallible Savior.

Honouring the Written Word of God

FAITH FIRST, THEN UNDERSTANDING

"The word is near you, in your mouth and in your heart"
(that is, the word of faith that we proclaim).

ROMANS 10:8

God does not profess to answer in Scripture all the questions that we, in our boundless curiosity, would like to ask about Scripture. He tells us merely as much as he sees we need to know for our life of faith. And he leaves unsolved some of the problems raised by what he tells us, to teach us a humble trust in his veracity.

The question, therefore, that we must ask ourselves when faced with these puzzles is not, Is it reasonable to imagine that this is so? but, Is it reasonable to accept God's assurance that this is so? Is it reasonable to take God's word and believe that he has spoken the truth, though I cannot fully comprehend what he has said? The question carries its own answer. We should not abandon faith in anything God has taught us merely because we cannot solve all the problems which it raises. Our own intellectual competence is not the test and measure of divine truth. It is not for us to stop believing because we lack understanding, or to postpone believing till we can get understanding, but to believe in order that we may understand; as Augustine said, "Unless you believe, you will not understand." Faith first, sight afterward is God's order, not *vice versa;* the proof of the sincerity of our faith is our willingness to have it so.

Therefore, we should not hesitate to commit ourselves to faith in the Trinity, or to faith in the Incarnation, or to faith in Scripture as the infallible Word of the infallible God, even though we cannot solve all the puzzles, nor reconcile all the apparent contradictions. On all these articles of faith we have God's positive assurance, and that should be enough.

"Fundamentalism" and the Word of God

IMAGINARY CHRIST

Go into all the world and proclaim the gospel
to the whole creation.

MARK 16:15

How much is involved in declaring the gospel?

This question is rarely raised in evangelical circles; we assume — too readily — that we all know the answer. But it needs raising. One of the factors compelling us to raise it is a minimizing approach to the task of teaching Christians truth. The modern minister does not usually ask, How much ought I to teach? but rather, How little need I teach? What is the minimum of doctrine that will do? One reason for this, no doubt, is the reluctance of those in the pews to learn. When the modern minister finds that some aspect of biblical truth arouses no immediate interest or approval in his congregation, his instinct is to jettison it. And the tendency today is to encourage him to do so.

Thus, for instance, some will assure us that it is a waste of time preaching to modern hearers about the law and sin, for (it is said) such things mean nothing to them. Instead (it is suggested) we should just appeal to the needs which they feel already, and present Christ to them simply as one who gives peace, power, and purpose to the neurotic and frustrated — a super-psychiatrist, in fact.

Now, this suggestion excellently illustrates the danger of the minimizing approach. If we do not preach about sin and God's judgment on it, we cannot present Christ as Savior from sin and the wrath of God. And if we are silent about these things, and preach a Christ who saves only from self and the sorrows of this world, we are not preaching the Christ of the Bible. We are, in effect, bearing false witness and preaching a false Christ. An imaginary Christ will not bring a real salvation.

A Quest for Godliness

THE ROOT PROBLEM

I am going away, and you will seek me,
and you will die in your sin.
JOHN 8:21

No version of the gospel message goes deeper than that which declares man's root problem before God to be his sin, which evokes wrath, and God's basic provision for man to be propitiation, which out of wrath brings peace. Some versions of the gospel, indeed, are open to blame because they never get down to this level.

We have all heard the gospel presented as God's triumphant answer to human problems — problems of our relation with ourselves and our fellow humans and our environment. Well, there is no doubt that the gospel does bring us solutions to these problems, but it does so by first solving a deeper problem — the deepest of all human problems, the problem of man's relation with his Maker. And unless we make it plain that the solution of these former problems depends on the settling of this latter one, we are misrepresenting the message and becoming false witnesses of God — for a half-truth presented as if it were the whole truth becomes something of a falsehood by that very fact. No reader of the New Testament can miss the fact that it knows all about our human problems — fear, moral cowardice, illness of body and mind, loneliness, insecurity, hopelessness, despair, cruelty, abuse of power, and the rest — but equally no reader of the New Testament can miss the fact that it resolves all these problems, one way or another, into the fundamental problem of sin against God.

By sin, the New Testament means not social error or failure in the first instance, but rebellion against, defiance of, retreat from, and consequent guilt before God the Creator; and sin, says the New Testament, is the basic evil from which we need deliverance, and from which Christ died to save us.

In My Place Condemned He Stood

TRUE FREEDOM IN GOD'S TRUTH

The one who looks into the perfect law, the law of liberty,
and perseveres . . . he will be blessed in his doing.

JAMES 1:25

True freedom is only ever found under God's authority—and it is only ever found under the authority of Scripture, through which God's authority is mediated to men, and Christ by his Spirit rules his people's lives. Biblical authority is often expounded in opposition to lax views of truth. Not so often, however, is it presented as the liberating, integrating, invigorating principle that it really is. The common idea is that unqualified confidence in the Bible leads to narrow-minded inhibitions and crippling restraints on what you may think and do. The truth is that such confidence produces liberated living—living, that is, which is free from uncertainty, doubt, and despair—which otherwise is not found anywhere. The man who trusts his Bible knows what God did, does, and will do, what he commands, and what he promises. With the Colossians, the Bible believer understands "the grace of God in truth" (Colossians 1:6), for the Christ of Scripture has become his Savior, master, and friend. Since Scripture shines as a lamp to his feet and a light to his path (Psalm 119:105), he can pick his way through the pitfalls of our spiritually benighted world without stumbling and travel through life with what the title of a famous old tract called "safety, certainty, and enjoyment."

Such is the freedom (and the victory) found under the authority of the Bible. Such is the basic shape and style of the life in which the fullness of God's power comes to be known. And who can do without that? There are few aspects of the Christian message which the church and the world need so urgently to face as the truth—the precious, stabilizing, enriching truth—of the full trustworthiness and divine authority of the written Word of God.

Freedom and Authority

SALVATION BRINGS FREEDOM

For freedom Christ has set us free; stand firm therefore,
and do not submit again to a yoke of slavery.

GALATIANS 5:1

Christians have been set free from the law as a system of salvation. Being justified by faith in Christ, they are no longer under God's law, but under his grace. Their standing with God (the "peace" and "access" of Romans 5:1-2) rests wholly on the fact that they have been accepted and adopted in Christ. It does not, nor ever will it, depend on what they do; it will never be imperiled by what they fail to do. As long as they are in this world, they live not by being perfect, but by being forgiven.

The natural instinct of fallen man, as expressed in every form of religion that the world has ever devised, is to suppose that one gains and keeps a right relationship with ultimate reality (whether conceived as a personal God or in other terms) by disciplines of law observance, right ritual, and asceticism. This is how the world's faiths prescribe the establishing of one's own righteousness — the very thing Paul saw unbelieving Jews trying to do (Romans 10:3). Paul's experience had taught him that this is a hopeless enterprise. No human performance is ever good enough, for there are always wrong desires in the heart, along with a lack of right ones, regardless of how correct one's outward motions are, and it is at the heart that God looks first.

All the law can do is arouse, expose, and condemn the sin that permeates our moral makeup, and so make us aware of its reality, depth, and guilt. So the futility of treating the law as a covenant of works, and seeking righteousness by it, becomes plain, as does the misery of not knowing what else to do. This is the bondage to the law from which Christ sets us free.

Concise Theology

TWO-SIDED TESTING

I am afraid that as the serpent deceived Eve by his cunning,
your thoughts will be led astray from a sincere and pure devotion to Christ.

2 CORINTHIANS 11:3

Scripture speaks of both God and Satan trying people out to see what is in them, as students are tested in school examinations. The truth is that in every testing situation both Satan and God are involved. God tests us to bring forth excellence in discipleship, as Moses explained to the Israelites at the close of the wilderness wanderings:

> Remember the whole way that the LORD your God has led you these forty years in the wilderness, that he might humble you, *testing* you to know what was in your heart, whether you would keep his commandments or not.... Who fed you in the wilderness with manna ... that he might humble you and *test* you [to drill you in grateful, confident, disciplined, submissive reliance on himself], to do you good in the end. (Deuteronomy 8:2,16, emphasis added)

Satan, by contrast, tests us with a view to our ruin and destruction, as appears from Paul's reason for sending Timothy to encourage the harassed Thessalonian Christians: "I sent to learn about your faith, for fear that somehow the tempter had *tempted* you and our labor would be in vain" (1 Thessalonians 3:5, emphasis added); Satan might have persuaded them to give up their faith and so ruined their souls.

Satan was with the Israelites in the desert, laboring to ensnare them in unbelief and lawlessness, and often succeeding, in the short term at least; and God was with the Thessalonians in the furnace, disciplining them for their good, that they might share his holiness (Hebrews 12:10).

Temptation is always two-sided in this way; so whenever we are conscious of Satan seeking to pull us down, we should remind ourselves that God is present too to keep us steady and to build us up through the harrowing experience. That is something we must never forget.

A Passion for Faithfulness

OUR CAUSE FOR CERTAINTY

*You have exalted above all things
your name and your word.*

PSALM 138:2

The church has from the first professed to receive the Bible's testimony to its own divine origin, and believed that it was the Spirit who taught it to do so. The doctrine of the Spirit's witness to Scripture, thus understood, is and always was part of the catholic faith. This explains the certainty and confidence of evangelicals as to the divine truth and trustworthiness of the Bible.

Some have said that evangelicals cling to the idea of biblical infallibility as drowning men cling to a straw — not because it is worthy of their trust, but because they want something to cling to and there is nothing else within reach. We can see how perverse a misunderstanding this is.

The evangelical certainty of the trustworthiness and authority of Scripture is of exactly the same sort, and rests on exactly the same basis, as the church's certainty of the Trinity, or the Incarnation, or any other catholic doctrine. God has declared it; Scripture embodies it; the Spirit exhibits it to believers; and they humbly receive it, as they are bound to do. It is not optional for Christians to sit loose to what God has said, and treat questions which he has closed as if they were still open.

Why then should any Christian ever deviate from the Bible's view of itself? The same question arises in connection with unscriptural views of any doctrine. Christians fall into mental error, partly through mistaking or overlooking what Scripture teaches, partly through having their minds prepossessed with unbiblical notions so that they cannot take scriptural statements seriously. All heresy begins so. Unscriptural ideas in our theology are like germs in our system. They tend only to weaken and destroy life, and their effect is always damaging.

"Fundamentalism" and the Word of God

MEETING FAMILY RESPONSIBILITIES

*Now when shall I provide
for my own household also?*

GENESIS 30:30

The criteria for making vocational choices have to do with following God-given information, interests, and skills on the one hand, and God-given responsibilities on the other. When, for instance, you are responsible for the welfare of others in your family, you have to make sure that the work that you choose enables you to fulfill those responsibilities. Parents of young children are rightly giving highest consideration to their children's welfare when they opt, as they sometimes do, for a second- or third-choice vocation because they cannot pay for both family food and their own education at the same time. Or they may choose a job near grandparents or Good schools even though it means lower pay or less prestige. Or they may decide not to accept a promotion because it would mean interrupting their teenager's sports opportunities. Likewise, adult children will consider the well-being of their aging parents and, perhaps, reject a move to another state or refuse a job that allows no time for doctor's appointments and errands for their parent. Family members of people with special needs make lifelong career adjustments in order to provide for their children or siblings or parents in ways that few less-encumbered people could begin to understand.

Scripture ascribes real dignity to those kinds of sacrifices. "But if anyone does not provide for his relatives, and especially for members of his household, he has denied the faith and is worse than an unbeliever" (1 Timothy 5:8). Christians who have honored these family responsibilities will often be the first to testify of their joy in God's redeeming work, even though outsiders might see principled choices as vocational sacrifices.

Guard Us, Guide Us

OUR SHOCKING ILLUSIONS

People will be lovers of self, lovers of money, proud, arrogant,
abusive, disobedient to their parents, ungrateful, unholy.

2 TIMOTHY 3:2

Ours is not a good time for any sort of realism about God, Christianity, virtue, relationships, death and dying, or anything else except matters of technology. In our Western world fantastic technical skills are wedded to an extreme emotional childishness and immaturity, which bogs us all down deeper in sin's legacy of self-centeredness, self-absorption, and self-pity than any generation has ever sunk since Christianity entered the world.

Moreover, this is a post-Christian age intellectually, in which little sense of God's greatness and holiness remains. We think of him as everyone's heavenly grandfather, there to lavish gifts upon us and enjoy us the way we are. In the absence of any sense of our sinfulness, we expect VIP treatment from him all the time. It is our everyday habit to manipulate the idea of equality or fairness to ensure that we get as much of what we want as the next person does. Sacrifice for the good of others — parents for children, husbands and wives for each other, business managers for their employees and shareholders, political leaders for the community they claim to serve — is almost unheard of nowadays. Society has largely become a jungle in which we are all out hunting for pleasure, profit, and power, and are happy to shoot others if that is the way to get what we want.

Meantime, as compared with all Christians of up to about a generation ago, we have shockingly little sense of the reality, pervasiveness, shame, and guilt of sin. We cherish shockingly strong illusions about having a right to expect from God health, wealth, ease, excitement, and sexual gratification. We are shockingly unaware that suffering Christianly is an integral aspect of biblical holiness, and a regular part of business as usual for the believer.

Rediscovering Holiness

LETTING GO OF THE GOSPEL

Continue in the faith, stable and steadfast,
not shifting from the hope of the gospel.

COLOSSIANS 1:23

A theological challenge is issued to evangelicalism whenever the church loses, or threatens to lose, its grip on the gospel, or whenever Christians cease to walk according to the truth of the gospel.

Consider these two types of situation separately:

1. The church loses its grip on the gospel whenever it falls under the sway of an outlook that would swallow up the gospel by assimilating it into a larger, non-evangelical whole. For instance, Paul wrote to the Galatians because there the gospel was in effect being swallowed up by legalism. Or again: Paul wrote to the Colossians because there the gospel was in effect being swallowed up by polytheism. The most fundamental fault of both heresies was that they sought to add to the gospel of salvation by faith in Christ, thus treating it as no more than a part of a larger and more comprehensive whole. Paul answered both in the same way, by asserting the sufficiency of Christ as Savior and the completeness of the salvation that believers have in him.

2. Christians cease to walk according to the truth of the gospel either when they let their lives be governed by doctrinal error — as when the Galatians observed Jewish ceremonial law (Galatians 4:10) and the Colossians worshipped angels (Colossians 2:18) — or when they compromise the truth in practice under pressure from an influential body of non-evangelical opinion (as when Peter withdrew from table fellowship with Gentile Christians at Antioch under pressure from the Jerusalem party [Galatians 2:12]). Paul withstood such errors of practice no less vigorously than he opposed deviations from evangelical doctrine.

Evangelicals today face a situation in which all these tendencies appear in modern dress.

Honouring the People of God

THE STORY OF HUMANITY'S JOY

With joy you will draw water
from the wells of salvation.
ISAIAH 12:3

Humankind without Christ is in a pitiable state, whatever may or may not appear on the surface of life. We are guilty, lost, without hope as death approaches, short on self-mastery, pulled to and fro by conflicting allurements and distractions; there are skeletons of sensuality, callousness, arrogance, and other unlovely things in our cupboard; we regularly find frustration and discontent, partly because our reach exceeds our grasp, partly because we feel thwarted by circumstances, partly because we are so largely unclear what is worth our endeavor anyway.

The various things wrong with the folk to whom Jesus is seen ministering in the Gospels — hunger, chronic illness, fever, epilepsy, blindness, deafness, dumbness, lameness, leprosy, lunacy, organic deformity, and in three cases actual death — vividly picture these spiritual needs (and were undoubtedly included in the Gospels for that purpose). But Jesus Christ gives peace — with God, with oneself, with circumstances, and with other people — plus his own presence and friendship, plus a call to witness and service as the priority concerns of life in this world, plus a promise of enabling by the Holy Spirit, plus an assurance of final glory in the Savior's own company, and this brings integration, purpose, contentment, and joy such as one has not known before. And the promise is that as one travels the road of discipleship, so these things will increase.

In this story, God's goal is a purpose of compassion, namely to impart to us by this means the joy for which we were made; and the gospel call is a summons to enter through faith and obedience into the joy that Christ gives.

Serving the People of God

WHY IS PERSISTENCE NEEDED IN PRAYER?

Be gracious to me, O Lord,
for to you do I cry all the day.

PSALM 86:3

Jesus encouraged us "always to pray and not lose heart" (Luke 18:1). Persistent, insistent petitioning, according to our Lord Jesus, is most certainly appropriate when the pressure is on. But why is this, if God is truly our loving heavenly Father and wants to give us good gifts? Here is a question that is not always well answered. Why does Jesus teach us, and therefore clearly want us, to pray insistently and persistently about crucial needs? Four reasons, at least, may be given.

1. God the Father loves to be petitioned in a way that shows he is appreciated as the source of all that is good. This glorifies him.

2. The Father wants us to see that we are taking with absolute seriousness both our acuteness of need and his greatness as the one who can meet it. This takes us beyond superficiality in the way we think, feel, and live, and binds us closer to him because of the clarity with which we realize that he is really our only hope.

3. The Father knows that the more earnestly we have asked for a particular gift and the longer we have waited for it, the more we will value it when it is given, and the more wholeheartedly we will thank him for it. This will lead to increased joy.

4. The Father's larger plans for blessing us and others may require him to delay giving us what we ask for until the best time and circumstances for its bestowal are reached. To keep asking with patient persistence and waiting with expectation for the answer is thus sometimes necessary, and is always the reverent way to go. This strengthens the muscles of our faith, as constant walking strengthens the muscles of heart and legs.

Praying

THE COMPREHENSIVE GOSPEL

I did not shrink from declaring to you
the whole counsel of God.

ACTS 20:27

Note the comprehensiveness of the gospel as the Puritans understood it. Observe how much they took the word *gospel* to cover. It denoted to them the whole doctrine of the covenant of grace. Thus, to preach the gospel meant to them nothing less than declaring the entire economy of redemption, the saving work of all three persons of the Trinity.

The Puritan Thomas Manton spoke of "the sum of the gospel" as being "where you have all the Christian religion . . . in one short view and prospect."[24]

The importance of this is that it challenges our modern idea that preaching "gospel sermons" means just harping on a few great truths — guilt, and atonement, and forgiveness — set virtually in a theological vacuum. The Puritan view was that preaching "gospel sermons" meant teaching the whole Christian system — the character of God, the Trinity, the plan of salvation, the entire work of grace. To preach Christ, they held, involved preaching all this. Preach less, they would tell us, and what you do preach will not be properly grasped.

What the good news of a restored relationship with God through Christ means cannot be understood further than it is seen in this comprehensive context. Gospel preaching centers always upon the theme of man's relationship to God, but around that center it must range throughout the whole sphere of revealed truth, viewing the center from every angle of vision that the Bible provides. In this way, they would say, preaching the gospel involves preaching the whole counsel of God.

Nor should the preaching of the gospel be thought of as something confined to set evangelistic occasions. If one preaches the Bible biblically, one cannot help preaching the gospel all the time.

A Quest for Godliness

THE ALLURE OF UNIVERSALISM

If anyone's name was not found written in the book of life,
he was thrown into the lake of fire.

Revelation 20:15

Universalism is the belief that, as C. H. Dodd somewhere put it, "As every human being lies under God's judgment, so every human being is ultimately destined, in God's mercy, to eternal life." No evangelical, I think, need hesitate to admit that in his heart of hearts he would like universalism to be true. Who can take pleasure in the thought of people being eternally lost? But wishful thinking, based on a craving for comfort and a reluctance to believe that some of God's truth might be tragic, is no sure index of reality.

Yesterday's evangelicals felt the attraction of universalism, I am sure, just as poignantly as we do, but they denounced the doctrine as morally weakening and spiritually deadening. They equated it with the world's first falsehood, the Devil's declaration in Eden, "You will not surely die" (Genesis 3:4). And they preached and prayed as they believed — especially, it seems, prayed.

Universalism, like all other matters of doctrine, is ultimately a biblical question. Is there biblical warrant for universalist speculation? There does not appear to be. And there are Bible-based counterarguments. Does not universalism deny the sufficiency of Scripture? Does not universalism ignore something that Scripture stresses, namely the unqualified decisiveness of this life's decisions for our eternal destiny? Does not universalism imply that the preaching of Christ and the apostles, who warned people to flee from the judgment of hell-fire by repentance here and now, is either inept or immoral?

And is not universalism rejected by each Christian's own conscience? Surely there is no answer to the dictum of James Denney: "I dare not say to myself that if I forfeit the opportunity this life affords I shall ever have another, and therefore I dare not say so to another man."[25]

Celebrating the Saving Work of God

WAKE UP TO THE HOLY SPIRIT

*The Spirit is life
because of righteousness.*
ROMANS 8:10

Understanding the Holy Spirit is a crucial task for Christian theology at all times. For where the Spirit's ministry is studied, it will also be sought after, and where it is sought after, spiritual vitality will result. This has happened historically — those who have thought about and sought after the power of the Spirit in their own lives have regularly found what they were seeking, and in such cases our generous God does not suspend his blessing upon our getting details of theology all correct. Conversely, where the Spirit's ministry arouses no interest and other preoccupations rule our minds, the quest for life in the Spirit is likely to be neglected too. Then the church will lapse, as in many quarters it has lapsed already, into either the formal routines of Christian Pharisaism or the spiritual counterpart of sleeping sickness, or maybe a blend of both.

The Christian scene today in the Western world highlights the importance of attending to the doctrine of the Holy Spirit. The lack of divine energy and exuberance in most congregations, even some of the most notionally orthodox, is painful to see.

Have we ever yet grasped the supernatural reality of Holy Spirit life? It is as if God is constantly flashing before us on huge billboards the message REMEMBER THE HOLY SPIRIT! and our eyes are so lowered and trained on one another as we gossip about our current interests that we have not yet noticed what he is doing. We pay lip service to the Holy Spirit (everyone does these days), but we not yet take him seriously. In this we need to change. Christians, wake up! Churches, wake up! Theologians, wake up!

Keep in Step with the Spirit

UNDERSTANDING FROM ABOVE

Show yourself in all respects to be a model of good works,
and in your teaching show integrity, dignity,
and sound speech that cannot be condemned.

TITUS 2:7-8

The classic idea of *theologia* is that it is wisdom coming from within, divine illumination animating our discernments, devotions, and declarations; in other words, it is a function of spiritual life expressing itself in thought, speech, and decisions that are marked by divinely wrought understanding.

Such understanding assumes that one is anchored and drilled already in the standard of sound teaching that Paul told his deputies to enforce (1 Timothy 4:6,11-16; 2 Timothy 1:13; 2:1-2,23-25; 4:1-5; Titus 2:1-8,15); when teachers like Julian of Norwich, John Calvin, Ignatius Loyola, and John Owen insist that understanding is the root and fruit of devotion, they are not reducing the importance of clearheaded orthodoxy. Their point, and Paul's, is rather that true notions should lead to wisdom by becoming a source of insight and of life-change through the Holy Spirit.

When Paul prays that the Colossians might be filled with "the knowledge of [God's] will in all spiritual [i.e., Spirit-given] wisdom and understanding" (Colossians 1:9), he is asking God that *theologia,* as described, may increasingly become the mark of their lives. To be marked in this way demands more than becoming conscious of what action orthodox biblical beliefs would require, though that evidently is part of it (a part that pietists in the conservative evangelical tradition always did and still do assiduously maintain). But *theologia* should be conceived as the intellectual and moral dynamic animating the believer to work and worship, love and obedience, virtue and excellence, as he or she grips and obeys the revealed truth by which he or she has first been gripped.

The Way of Wisdom

271

DIFFERENCES BETWEEN SCIENCE AND SCRIPTURE

The heavens are yours; the earth also is yours;
the world and all that is in it, you have founded them.

PSALM 89:11

The sciences neither ask nor answer the questions about the world which the Bible answers.

Scripture, by contrast with the sciences, deals always with the first cause, God himself, and speaks to concerns beyond the scientists' reach. Science tells us how the cosmic order works; Scripture tells us who caused it to be, and why, and how its Maker is involved with it, and where he is taking it, and what significance any of it has for him. Scientific inquiry into how everything works fits easily into the biblical frame, but the sciences cannot approach the *who* and *why* questions the Bible answers.

The scientific method is to go and look, guess and check. It is an empirical study. The biblical method is to listen and learn, let God tell you. From science we learn how things happen; from Scripture we learn what they mean. The goals of scientific inquiry and of biblical study are thus different. Science studies the way each system works with a view to managing it and developing a technology. Scripture, by contrast, tells about the created cosmos in order to lead us to worship the God who made it, admire his workmanship, praise him for it, and manage everything for his glory.

These days, the scientist is so venerated in our society that he is allowed to pontificate as a scientist about religion, and people suppose that his science has taught him what he believes about God. It is a confusion, however, to suppose that it ever was or ever could be so.

Scripture's sustained focus on the Creator who is behind and beyond the cosmos, transcending it while working in and through it, puts biblical teaching on a different wavelength altogether from that to which the sciences are tuned.

Honouring the Written Word of God

LEADERS AS TARGETS

Put on the whole armor of God,
that you may be able to stand against the schemes of the devil.

EPHESIANS 6:11

In Satan's war on the saints and the church, in which temptation is his method and destruction his immediate goal, it is a rather grim law that the higher one's exposure and the greater one's influence as a leader, the more one's personal standards and wisdom will be put under attack. It is obvious that disgracing or distracting the leader is an excellent way of daunting, holding back, or otherwise sidelining the followers. People trust their leaders and follow in their steps; if leaders can be allured into bypaths and blind alleys, they will take many with them, and Satan will score heavily.

Also, leaders live in something of a goldfish bowl, so that when leadership scandals break, the damage and discouragement will be large scale and widespread. In the New Testament, Paul's letters to Timothy and Titus concentrate not on skills to learn but on the qualities of zeal, goodness, steadiness, and wisdom that the leader must maintain and model. This is because Paul is so conscious of the "snare of the devil" (1 Timothy 3:7; 2 Timothy 2:26) set for those who lead.

Satan through his agents, devilish and human, assaults all Christians, and leaders, it seems, most fiercely; all Christians therefore, and leaders supremely, must learn to pray with Nehemiah, "O God, strengthen my hands" (Nehemiah 6:9) — not only for constructive ministry, corresponding to the building of Jerusalem's wall, but also for mortal combat, corresponding to Nehemiah's defensive measures against Jerusalem's enemies (who purposed to "come among them and kill them and stop the work" [4:11]).

Those who seek God's strength will find it. The outcome will be salvation, not destruction: Satan will be thwarted and the church built up, and the God through whose help all the work is done will be glorified.

A Passion for Faithfulness

HOW TO THINK

Lead me in your truth
and teach me.
PSALM 25:5

The gospel does in truth proclaim the redemption of reason. All truth is God's truth; facts, as such, are sacred, and nothing is more un-Christian than to run away from them.

"Reason" means reasoning, as "faith" means believing and trusting. The Christian's intellectual vocation is to think about all things in such a way that his life of thought is part of his life of faith and homage to God. Whereas the non-Christian is led by faithless reason, the Christian should be guided by reasoning faith.

Broadly speaking, the proper function of reason in relation to faith is threefold. Its first task is to *receive* the teaching of God. Scripture pictures the believer as one called to take the attitude of a child, and who is looking to his divine Teacher for instruction (Psalm 25:4-5). God teaches the church through the Word, interpreted by the Spirit; accordingly, the Christian seeks the help of the Spirit to enable him to learn what Scripture teaches. His mind is necessarily active in this.

The second task of Christian reason is to *apply* the teaching of God to life: to bring it into constructive relationship with our other knowledge and interests, and to work out its bearing on the practical problems of daily life and action—moral, social, personal, political, aesthetic, or whatever they may be. This is really an extension of the first task, for the Bible is a book about life and itself instructs us, at any rate in principle, as to the practical bearings of its teaching.

The third task is to *communicate* God's truth to others. The duty of Christian witness involves reasoning. Faith is not created by reasoning, but neither is it created without it.

"Fundamentalism" and the Word of God

WRONG SHORTCUTS

For I have kept the ways of the LORD,
and have not wickedly departed from my God.

PSALM 18:21

Spiritual triumph through difficult times is the first part of David's story in Scripture, and twice in particular David refused point-blank to conclude that he should do what he could do, just because he kept in mind what he knew of God's revealed will. He knew that God had rejected King Saul and that he himself had been anointed to take Saul's place; and he knew that Saul was chasing him with an armed force, seeking his life; so he was living as a fugitive, trying to keep out of Saul's way.

One day, however, when David and his men were hiding in the recesses of a cave, Saul entered that cave alone. David's men said in effect, "This is God in action! He has given you the means of fulfilling his plan! Kill Saul now!" But David would not do it, because Saul was the Lord's anointed (1 Samuel 24). Shortcuts that are immoral in their own right are never the will of God.

Not long after, a virtual rerun of this incident took place (1 Samuel 26). David and Abishai found themselves standing over Saul's sleeping body, surrounded by Saul's army, also sleeping. Abishai whispered, "God has given your enemy into your hand this day" — let me kill him for you! But David again said no, for the same reason as before: "Who can put out his hand against the LORD's anointed and be guiltless?" (verses 8-9).

So far, so good; David escaped the temptation to do what was in his power to do, because he remembered the boundaries God had set. Circumstances may indeed give us obvious opportunities to break God's rules, but it is never God's will that we should do that. David practiced obedient restraint, and avoided self-deception, and in due course God honored him for it.

Guard Us, Guide Us

SUFFERING'S VALUE

He disciplines us for our good,
that we may share his holiness.

HEBREWS 12:10

Christian endurance means living lovingly, joyfully, peacefully, and patiently under conditions that we wish were different. There's an umbrella word we use to cover the countless variety of situations that have this character, namely the word *suffering*. Suffering is in the mind of the sufferer, and may conveniently be defined as getting what you do not want while wanting what you do not get. This definition covers all forms of loss, hurt, pain, grief, and weakness — all experiences of rejection, injustice, disappointment, discouragement, frustration, and being the butt of others' hatred, ridicule, cruelty, callousness, anger, and ill-treatment — plus all exposure to foul, sickening, and nightmarish things that make you want to scream, run, or even die. Suffering in some shape or form is everyone's lot from earliest days, though some know far more of it than others.

Suffering is specified in Scripture as part of every Christian's calling, and therefore of mine as much as of anyone else's. Suffering must be expected, and even valued, by all believers without exception. Suffering is to be expected, and we must prepare for it.

The world, of course, does not find value in suffering. It has no reason to. But Christians are in a different position, for the Bible assures us that God sanctifies our suffering to good ends. Our suffering produces character (Romans 5:3). Our suffering glorifies God (2 Corinthians 12:9-10). And our suffering fulfills the law of the harvest: Before there is blessing anywhere, there will first be suffering somewhere. Jesus first announced this law when he declared, "Truly, truly, I say to you, unless a grain of wheat falls into the earth and dies, it remains alone; but if it dies, it bears much fruit" (John 12:24).

Rediscovering Holiness

STRIPPED OF CULTURAL PRETENSIONS

For his sake I have suffered the loss of all things
and count them as rubbish, in order that I may gain Christ.
PHILIPPIANS 3:8

The key to persuasive Christian communication lies less in technique than in character. Paul was a great communicator, not because he was eloquent but because he knew his own mind and had a great capacity for identifying with the other person. He set no limit to what he would do, however unconventionally, to ensure that he did not by personal insensitiveness or cultural inertia set barriers and stumbling blocks in the way of men coming to Christ. His loving, imaginative adaptability in the service of truth and people is a shining example to all who engage in evangelistic communication, and cannot be pondered too often or taken too seriously.

Paul was a man who could, and did, share himself without stint. From his letters we know him well, and we can appreciate the trauma that lies behind the autobiographical passage of Philippians 3, where he tells us how Christ stripped him of cultural pretensions. F. W. Dillistone comments,

> Here was a man who possessed all the marks of privilege within a particular historical tradition. His pedigree, his tribal status, his religious dedication, his formal education, his personal commitment, had been such that by every standard of Jewish orthodoxy and by every sanction of national tradition he was justified in regarding himself as successful, superior, and secure. . . . Yet he had submitted every part of his historical inheritance to the judgment of the Cross. Nothing could be removed but everything could be re-interpreted. Those things which seemed positive gain could be judged as of no account in the service of Christ: those things which had seemed to be hindrances and handicaps might well prove positive assets in the new order of living. In any case there was henceforth to be no final confidence in the heritage from personal and past history.[26]

Serving the People of God

OUR SUPREME INCENTIVE TO PRAY

Whoever believes in the Son of God
has the testimony in himself.

1 JOHN 5:10

When we seek to express the persistence of our faith in the prayers we go on making as we face short-term disappointment and desolation, the fact to focus on for encouragement is that there is a covenanted family bond that unites us to God the Father, God the Son, and God the Holy Spirit, and unites the Three-in-One to us forever and ever. Paul writes, "The Spirit himself bears witness with our spirit that we are children of God, and if children, then heirs — heirs of God and fellow heirs with Christ" (Romans 8:16-17). Professed Christians who neither testify to this testimony nor rejoice in the identity it confirms are, to say the least, very much out of sorts. Being children of God is our supreme privilege and security — and is at all times the supreme incentive to us to pray.

The Christian's sonship to God the Father is both by adoption, which bestows the family status, and by regeneration, which is the work of the Holy Spirit renewing the heart and thereby bestowing in embryo the family likeness. Regeneration instills in us a God-centered, God-exalting cast of mind that is inexplicable in terms of anything that was there before, just as the source and destination of the wind are more than any observer can know (John 3:8). Regeneration is an outgoing of the same power that brought this world into being when previously there was nothing there at all — absolutely nothing in existence before God.

The twin blessings of adoption and regeneration, while not shielding us from any of life's grimmer experiences, do turn us into unique people with unique privileges and a unique destiny, and when the bad experiences come, it is vital that we do not forget who and what we are.

Praying

THE GOSPEL'S MAJOR POINTS

*Behold, I stand at the door
and knock.*
REVELATION 3:20

Note the emphases which characterized the Puritan preaching of the gospel, and indeed all preaching of it by evangelicals from Puritan times onward till about a century ago:

1. They diagnosed *the plight of man* as one not merely of guilt for sins, but also of pollution in sin and bondage to sin — the state of being wholly dominated by an inbred attitude of enmity to God. They sought to expose the sinfulness that underlies sins, and convince men of their own utter corruption and inability to improve themselves in God's sight. This, they held, was a vital part of the work of a gospel preacher; for the index of the soundness of a man's faith in Christ is the genuineness of the self-despair from which it springs.

2. They analyzed *the issue of sin* in terms of God's hostility in the present, as well as his condemnation in the future. Their constant aim was to make man feel that to be in a wrong relationship with God was intolerable here and now.

3. They stressed that *the goal of grace* is the glory and praise of God, and our salvation is a means to this end. God, they said, has chosen to redeem us, not for our sakes, but for his own name's sake.

4. They stressed *the sufficiency of Christ*. They did not teach men to trust a theory of the atonement, but a living Redeemer, the perfect adequacy of whose saving work they never tired of extolling.

5. They stressed *the condescension of Christ*. He was never to them less than the divine Son, and they measured his mercy by his majesty. They magnified the love of the cross by dwelling on the greatness of the glory which he left for it.

A Quest for Godliness

AFFIRMING THE TRINITY

Go therefore and make disciples of all nations, baptizing them in the name of the Father and of the Son and of the Holy Spirit.

Matthew 28:19

Whether one finds a doctrine of the Trinity in the New Testament depends on what one means by "doctrine." As Arthur Wainwright says, "In so far as a doctrine is an answer, however fragmentary, to a problem, there is a doctrine of the Trinity in the New Testament. In so far as it is a formal statement of a position, there is no doctrine of the Trinity in the New Testament."[27]

But if it is proper to give the name of "doctrine" to a position that is explicit and defined, it cannot be improper to give the same name to that which is basic and presuppositional to, and in that sense explicit in, positions that are explicit and defined; and since the Trinitarian way of thinking about God is in fact basic and presuppositional to all the New Testament's explicit soteriology — being the answer to the problem about the unity of God which the fact of Christ, the event of Pentecost, and the shape of subsequent Christian experience had raised — it is far more accurate, profound, and enlightening to affirm that the New Testament writers teach the doctrine of the Trinity than to do as is fashionable today and deny it. Though innocent of later Trinitarian formulations, these writers do in fact think of God in the tripersonal way that the later formulations were devised to safeguard and reject other conceptions as anti-Christian.

The true path is to affirm this and thereby negate all forms, old and new, of the idea that the Spirit is a creature of or a function of or a title for a unipersonal God. No version of this unitarian idea can express what the New Testament writers mean when they speak of the Spirit — or of Christ and the Father, for that matter.

WHOLE PERSON, WHOLE SOUL

I will give thanks to the LORD with my whole heart;
I will recount all of your wonderful deeds.

PSALM 9:1

Theologia — theology in the best sense — is really an aspect of the reality of sanctification; it is a pointer to, and a benchmark of, the way the Holy Spirit uses the Word of God to change people, making them more like Christ. In this process the Spirit operates intellectually, by imparting understanding of Christ and of all the Scriptures as witness to him; and motivationally, by engendering trust in Christ and sustaining within us a purpose of cleaving to revealed truth; and in addition behaviorally, by inducing the Christlike pattern of action that flows from this state of the soul.

When Augustine urged that theological *scientia* (cognitive acquaintance with the true and health-giving beliefs about God) has as its goal personal *sapientia* (wisdom in the sense of a practical understanding of truth, beauty, and the good life), he was indicating the process of *theologia* as we have characterized it. When the Puritan William Perkins defined theology as "the science of living blessedly for ever"[28] and when his disciple William Ames spoke of it as "the doctrine of living unto God,"[29] they were similarly charting the course from *scientia* to *sapientia*.

This is the whole-person, whole-soul track that we all need to get back on. A great deal of what is called theology today is specialist speculation and does not bear at all on the Christian's personal existence. But *theologia* needs, as we can now see, to be a matter of conscientious concern to every Christian who aims at a life that honors God.

The Way of Wisdom

TWO LIVES, NOT JUST ONE

I press on toward the goal for the prize
of the upward call of God in Christ Jesus.

PHILIPPIANS 3:14

Never underestimate the theological significance of eschatology, the study of the last things. Eschatology is first the key to understanding the unity of the Bible. Holy Scripture in its totality is a book of hope looking forward to a final consummation, and finding its unity in all its lines of thought and teaching about the divine action will bring in that final consummation toward which God is working.

Eschatology is, further, the clue to understanding the nature of the Christian life. That life is essentially a life of hope, a life in which nothing is perfect yet, but the hope of perfection is set before us, so that we may forget what is behind and reach out to what lies ahead and press toward the mark for the prize of the high calling of God in Christ Jesus. One of the things we modern Christians are very bad at, it seems to me, is remembering what the whole materialist culture around us encourages us to forget: that there are two worlds not just one, two lives not just one, and heaven really is more important than earth, for heaven's life is the goal for which this life is preparation.

Third, eschatology is the key to understanding the shape of world history. The church under the sovereign hand of God is the real center of what is going on and always will be. That is the Bible view.

Finally, eschatology is supremely relevant for teaching the gospel in these days. We face a great deal of pessimistic hopelessness on the part of people who feel they have seen through the false hopes of society and now have no hope at all. We need to speak loudly and clearly about the glory of the Christian hope.

Honouring the Written Word of God

KNOWING NOTHING

Deal with your servant according to your steadfast love,
and teach me your statutes.

Psalm 119:124

Biblical interpretation is an exacting mental discipline. But the Christian does not by his mental labor construct knowledge of God out of his own head, or contribute anything of his own to what God is teaching him; his labor is simply that of receiving and assimilating. He ascribes all the knowledge he gains not to his own keenness of wit, but to the effective instruction of the Holy Spirit. With Charles Simeon, he reminds himself when he approaches Scripture: "I know only one thing — that I know nothing." To say this and mean it is no doubt the hardest task in the world, but this is what he tries to do. He confesses himself blind, stupid, and ignorant through sin, and cries to God for enlightenment and instruction.

We have seen already that the biblical revelation terminates in mystery. The lamp of Scripture lights only a limited area of our darkness; beyond that area lie the secrets of God, into which men may not pry. Our knowledge of God, therefore, though true as far as it goes, is nowhere complete or exhaustive. The humble pupil of Scripture will recognize these limits and keep within them. He will not be so self-willed as, on the one hand, to build a speculative theological system which says more about God than God has said about himself, or, on the other, to ignore or tone down what Scripture does say because he finds it hard to fit in with the rest of what he knows. His aim is to learn all that God teaches, and give it all its due place. And he will never let himself suppose that now he has finished learning and knows everything; instead, he will keep listening to Scripture for further correction and instruction.

"Fundamentalism" and the Word of God

AN INWARD BATTLE

Lead me in the path of your commandments,
for I delight in it.
PSALM 119:35

When the Holy Spirit changes and renews the heart by instilling in us a recognition of Christ's reality and by uniting us to him in his risen life, our way of thinking is at once altered. Instead of active alienation from and defiance of God, what comes from our hearts is grateful love to God, and a desire to praise and please him. Yet the sinful dynamics of our fallen makeup still operate within us, and incessantly pull against the God-trusting, God-loving, God-serving disposition and motivation that the Spirit has implanted. Paul indicates the result: "The desires of the flesh are against the Spirit, and the desires of the Spirit are against the flesh, for these are opposed to each other, to keep you from doing the things you want to do" (Galatians 5:17).

Sometimes our knowledge of what we should do is overwhelmed by desire to do something else; and again and again we do the right thing in a sluggish, resentful, apathetic, self-pitying, self-absorbed, or self-seeking spirit with hearts having no deep concern about either the glory of God or the good of others. This happens, not because godly motivation was never there, but because the down-drag of sin in our system has, for the time being, swamped it. We constantly need, therefore, to be asking God to enable us to do the right things in the right way (with love and hope and zeal for God), and only the Holy Spirit who indwells us can bring that about.

When, however, all attention is centered on doing the things that Christian reason directs us to do, and the question of *how* we do it is ignored, as if performance is all that matters, then it can safely be said that reason is being overvalued.

Guard Us, Guide Us

LASTING COURAGE

Continue in the faith, stable and steadfast, not shifting from the hope of the gospel that you heard.

COLOSSIANS 1:23

Fortitude is a compound of courage and endurance. It lasts. Faith fosters fortitude by inducing purity of heart in those who are under pressure and suffering distress. As Kierkegaard declares in a book title, "purity of heart is to will one thing" — that one thing being the command and glory of God. This purity is advanced by the experience of suffering, as Christians grow in awareness that the life God is leading them into is the spiritual counterpart of Winston Churchill's "blood, toil, tears, and sweat." The world's allurements become much less alluring, and Christians know with great clarity of mind that a close walk with the Father and the Son, leaning hard on them and drawing strength from them through the Holy Spirit, is both what they need and what they want.

Three verses from Psalm 119 testify to this. "Before I was afflicted I went astray, but now I keep your word" (verse 67). Rough experiences challenge us to repent of past thoughtlessness and carelessness and to become more conscientious in doing our Father's will. "It is good for me that I was afflicted, that I might learn your statutes" (verse 71). As if to say: I did not see clearly what is really involved in the behavioral model spelled out for me in the Bible until trouble struck me. But I understand it better now. And finally: "I know, O LORD . . . that in faithfulness you have afflicted me" (verse 75). God's faithfulness consists in his unwillingness that his children should lose any of the depths of fellowship with himself that he has in store for them. So he afflicts us to make us lean harder on him, that his purpose of drawing us into closest fellowship with himself may be fulfilled.

Rediscovering Holiness

WHERE ALL PROBLEMS FIND SOLUTIONS

> *He who did not spare his own Son but gave him up for us all,*
> *how will he not also with him graciously give us all things?*
>
> ROMANS 8:32

The wisest thing ever said to me was the word of an old minister years and years ago. It was no more than a throwaway line in a conversation about something else. But it seems to me still the most pregnant sentence I have ever heard.

"Remember," he said, "God is sovereign in all things, and all problems find their solution at Calvary."

"All problems" in that statement was shorthand for all *spiritual* problems. But, mind you, most human problems are spiritual in the final analysis. They have in them a dimension that has to do with one's relationship with God, and you cannot get the human part of the problem right until the relationship with God has been put right as well. Paul was very clear on this.

Or take the pervasive modern problem of *forlornness*, or loneliness. But it is a little more than loneliness. It is the sense that in this great bustling world I am on my own and I am lost. I have no one to turn to, no one to help me, and I do not know where I am going. To this forlornness there is no answer save to know the love of God personally directed to me.

But how does a person come to know that love? Paul tells us: "God shows his love for us in that while we were still sinners, Christ died for us" (Romans 5:8). Take people to the foot of the cross and tell them of Jesus Christ crucified and what his death means, and at once a solution to forlornness begins to appear. Yes, God loves you and he did this for you. He cares for you. He wants you as his child. He adopts you into his family by virtue of what Christ has done for you. He will be with you and love you forever. Now you are no longer lost; you are found.

Serving the People of God

FAITHFUL PRAYER TO A FAITHFUL FATHER

If you then, who are evil, know how to give good gifts to your children,
how much more will your Father who is in heaven
give good things to those who ask him!

MATTHEW 7:11

The business of a father is to protect his children, as well as to nurture them in the way he wants them to go when they are grown. Within that frame, we see in Scripture his promises to answer prayer, promises that remain permanently valid, for God is always faithful to his own word. Feelings have their ups and downs, but whether the sun is shining or whether clouds are down and rain is falling, the promises of God still stand. In the Sermon on the Mount, Jesus says, "*Ask*, and it will be given to you; *seek*, and you will find; *knock*, and it will be opened to you" (Matthew 7:7, emphasis added). He is talking about persistent praying. All three verbs in the Greek are in the present tense and express continuous action. Jesus says, "Keep asking, keep seeking, keep knocking." Then he gives the reason why: "For everyone who asks receives, and the one who seeks finds, and to the one who knocks it will be opened" (verse 8). Amazing! But that is what Jesus says, and all his words are true.

So according to Jesus, there is no such thing as unanswered prayer when a faithful child of God brings requests to his or her heavenly Father. The prayer will be taken notice of. As we have seen, it may not be answered in the form in which we offer it. It may be answered by God making us aware that there are things in our life that have got to be changed before he can give us what we have asked for. Or we may not have asked for precisely the right thing in the first place. So God answers the prayer we *ought* to have made rather the prayer we *did* make.

Praying

PREPARING FOR WORSHIP

> *O LORD, in the morning you hear my voice;*
> *in the morning I prepare a sacrifice for you and watch.*
>
> PSALM 5:3

The Puritan ideals for worshippers included reverence, faith, boldness, eagerness, expectancy, delight, wholeheartedness, concentration, self-abasement, and above all a passion to meet and know God himself as a loving Father through the mediation of his Son. This ideal was common to them all.

How do we begin to get from where we are to where the Puritans show us that we ought to be in our own practice of worship? The Puritans would have met our question by asking us another: How do we *prepare* for worship? What do we do to rouse ourselves to seek God?

Here, perhaps, is our own chief weakness. The Puritans inculcated specific preparation for worship as a regular part of the Christian's inner discipline of prayer and communion with God. But we neglect to prepare our hearts; for, as the Puritans would have been the first to tell us, thirty seconds of private prayer upon taking our seat in the church building is not time enough in which to do it.

It is here that we need to take ourselves in hand. What we need is more preparatory "heart-work." An admonition from George Swinnock for Lord's Day preparation is, I think, for all its seeming quaintness, a word in season for very many of us:

> Prepare to meet thy God, O Christian! betake thyself to thy chamber on the Saturday night, confess and bewail thine unfaithfulness for, and unfruitfulness under, the ordinances of God; shame and condemn thyself for thy sins, entreat God to prepare thy heart . . . spend some time in consideration of the infinite majesty, holiness, jealousy, and goodness of that God, with whom thou art to have to do in sacred duties; ponder the weight and importance of his holy ordinances . . . and continue musing . . . till the fire burneth.[30]

A Quest for Godliness

ABOVE, BESIDE, WITHIN

The Spirit himself bears witness with our spirit
that we are children of God, and if children,
then heirs — heirs of God and fellow heirs with Christ.

Romans 8:16-17

The New Testament sense of God is uniformly Trinitarian; more particularly, it is Christ-centered and Spirit-generated to the core. It is true to say that the Christian awareness is of God above, beside, and within, but for the New Testament that is not enough; we need to be more precise. The authentic Christian awareness of God, as the New Testament writers exhibit it, is:

1. A sense that God in heaven, this world's maker and judge, is our Father, who sent his Son to redeem us; who adopted us into his family; who loves us, watches over us, listens to us, cares for us, showers gifts upon us; who preserves us for the inheritance of glory that he keeps in store for us; and to whom we have access through Christ, by the Spirit.

2. A sense that Jesus Christ, who is now personally in heaven, nonetheless makes himself present to us by the Spirit to stand by us, to love, lead, assure, quicken, uphold, and encourage us, and to use us in his work as in weakness we trust him.

3. A sense that the Holy Spirit indwells us (a) to sustain in us a personal understanding of gospel truth; (b) to maintain in consciousness our fellowship with the Father and the Son; (c) to reshape us in ethical correspondence to Christ; (d) to equip us with abilities for loving personal worship of God in praise and prayer and loving personal ministry to others; (e) to engender realization of our present moral weakness and inadequacy of achievement, and to make us long for the future life of bodily resurrection and renewal, the life of which the Spirit's present ministry to us is the firstfruits and the initial installment, guaranteeing the rest.

Celebrating the Saving Work of God

WISDOM'S SCOPE AND STRUCTURE

And he said to man, "Behold, the fear of the Lord, that is wisdom,
and to turn away from evil is understanding."

JOB 28:28

Wisdom begins with the worship of God for his goodness revealed in both the created and covenantal order, coupled with wonder at human folly — all the nuttiness of egoism, self-aggrandizement, idolatry, immorality, and mishandling of relationships (see Proverbs and Ecclesiastes). In this way, discerning doxology is the beginning not only of "the fear of the Lord" but of *theologia* too.

Wisdom goes on to ask what direction and style of life make sense in light of what is known of God's presence, preferences, and providential government. Within the reverential frame that "the fear of the Lord" has established, an across-the-board vision of humble, thoughtful, and God-centered living emerges. *Theologia* and "the fear of the Lord" thus raise the same questions and come up with similar answers.

Wisdom appears as a habit of contemplating life to see what, if anything, we should do about this or that in light of what in general terms Yahweh has already set forth. Here a sense of human limitation emerges, for wise people know that while God has told us much about what he is doing in his world, much is kept hidden from us, and we must not claim to know more of God's current actions than in fact we do (a point emphasized repeatedly in Ecclesiastes and on the grand scale in the book of Job). Even when in frantic pain, wise persons settle for not knowing, and not even trying to guess, God's unrevealed purposes in their lives. *Theologia* thinks similarly; it works out the application of divine truths to the ups and downs of life with full awareness of the limits of revelation and the greatness of the divine mystery.

The Way of Wisdom

READY TO GO, READY TO STAY

You yourselves are fully aware that the day of the Lord
will come like a thief in the night.

1 THESSALONIANS 5:2

"Be ready; the Lord may come at any time." That seems to be a motif
running through the New Testament. How are we to understand it?

It seems that the point of the imminent language in the New
Testament is twofold. First, since the coming is certain, we should hope
for it steadily. And since the date is unannounced, we need to be ready
for it every day, starting now. But Jesus in Matthew 24:48-50 hints at the
possibility of a longer wait than anyone bargained for. The parable speaks
of the servant who says, "My master is delayed," so he begins to become
slack and go wild. And recall how in 2 Peter 3 the apostle has to minister
to folk who are discouraged because the Lord hasn't returned already.
We must learn to live packed up and ready to go, and at the same time be
plugged soberly into the task of advancing Christ's kingdom and so be
ready to stay.

Whether we belong to the generation that will see him in the great
public Parousia, that unimaginably glorious "day of the Lord" that is
promised, we cannot say. But heart-stop and brain-stop day may come
to any of us at any time. That coming day should be understood as
an appointment already entered on the Lord Jesus' calendar. It is the
day when he will come for us personally to take us to be with himself.
One way or another, he is coming for each of us and should not find us
unprepared.

While our life continues, let us *work* and *pray* for the advancing of
the kingdom. Let us see that when he comes for us, whether it is soon or
late, those are the tasks in which he finds us engaged.

Honouring the Written Word of God

ANALYZING SCRIPTURE SCIENTIFICALLY

Is not my word like fire, declares the LORD,
and like a hammer that breaks the rock in pieces?
JEREMIAH 23:29

We have seen that Scripture is truth from God, profitable for doctrine and instruction; this is not a matter of inductive proof, but of divine testimony, received through the witness of the Spirit. Scientific criticism for the Christian, therefore, must mean the effort to understand and appreciate Scripture *as what it is* — God's truth in writing. Such criticism is an exercise of reasoning faith. But to subject Scripture to a scientific critical technique designed to help us tell true from false among fallible human records would be an act of unbelief that was both unscientific and uncritical; for it would be treating Scripture as something other than it is. "Scientific criticism" would be a complete misnomer for such a procedure.

To assume *a priori* that Scripture, like any merely human historical document, is doubtless partly true but also partly false would be a quite unscientific thing to do; for the method of science is to proceed *a posteriori* from the known to the unknown, and Christians know from Christ's teaching that all Scripture is truth from God. And to form conclusions as to which parts of Scripture are erroneous would be invalid and worthless as criticism, since it would be the result of evaluating Scripture by wholly inappropriate criteria.

For Christians to consent to study Scripture on the assumption that it is a fallible human book would not argue intellectual honesty so much as uncritical muddleheadedness. The only biblical criticism which they can consistently regard as valid is that which takes as its starting point the Bible's account of itself. Much modern criticism within the Christian church stands self-condemned as unscientific by its arbitrary refusal to take account of what God has told the church about the nature of Scripture.

"Fundamentalism" and the Word of God

WEDDED LOVE, ARDENT AND ROBUST

My beloved is mine,
and I am his.

SONG OF SOLOMON 2:16

The Puritans, in Edmund Morgan's words, "were neither prudes nor ascetics. They knew how to laugh, and they knew how to love."[31] The realism of their affirmations of matrimonial affection stemmed from the fact that they went to the Bible for their understanding of the marriage relationship — to Genesis for its institution, to Ephesians for its full meaning, to Leviticus for its hygiene, to Proverbs for its management, to several New Testament books for its ethic, and to Esther, Ruth, and the Song of Solomon for illustrations and exhibitions of the ideal.

The Puritans understood wedded love very thoroughly; that is clear from such passages as this, in which Daniel Rogers depicts what today would be called falling in love:

> Marriage love is ofttime a secret work of God, pitching the heart of one party upon another for no known cause; and therefore when this strong lodestone attracts each to the other, no further questions need to be made but such a man and such a woman's match were made in heaven, and God hath brought them together.[32]

Rogers recognizes that this "pitching" of the heart does not always happen, but stresses that steady affection on both sides is in every case a matter of divine command. Loving actions of all sorts, including physical mating, will ripen and deepen this affection, and lead to a warmth of conjugal love.

While insisting that love for the Lord must come first, the Puritans expected and indeed directed that wedded love should be ardent and robust. Though self-controlled, they were uninhibited people, and as they could be, and often were exuberant in expressing love for their God, so they believed that they should be with their spouses.

A Quest for Godliness

TWO WAYS TO READ SCRIPTURE

We must pay much closer attention to what we have heard,
lest we drift away from it.

HEBREWS 2:1

There are two different ways of reading Scripture which seem to me fundamental. One I call macroscopic or panoramic reading — reading straight through, over and over, start to finish. One needs this to keep oneself attuned to the overall perspective of Scripture. With that needs to go microscopic or detailed study of particular passages, where one takes a few verses, sets them in context, and digs into them.

In both ways, one needs to have some kind of scheme of questions to put to the text. People who read the Bible without any questions may get warm cheerful feelings, but they are not likely really to understand anything. The scheme that I have found helpful over years of study is constantly to be asking this sequence of questions:

1. *What does the passage show me about God?* The wise man will always start here.

2. *What does the passage show me about living?* This question opens one's eyes to notice the right ways of living, wrong ways of living, different sorts of situations in which people find themselves, the way of faith with all its difficulties and delights, the different emotional states and temptations that overtake people, and all the realities of human life that each passage presents.

3. *What does this mean for me in my own life here and now?* At this point one begins meditating and praying as one brings to the Scripture the particular tasks or pressures that lie ahead that day. Meditating is thinking it through in the presence of God. Prayer is talking to the Lord about it. Here is the proper conclusion of Scripture study. This personal discipline is quite distinct from any further digging for insights to relay in teaching and preaching. Application to oneself must come first.

Honouring the Written Word of God

STAYING INTERESTED IN GOD'S WORLD

Whatever is under the whole heaven
is mine.
JOB 41:11

God forbids Christians to lose interest in his world. He made man to rule the created order; man is set in it to have dominion over it and to use it for God's glory, and therefore he may, and must, study its contents and its problems. This belongs to his vocation both as a man and as a Christian.

The biblical revelation is given us not merely to show us how to gain heaven, but also to provide us with the principles for glorifying God by creative and imaginative living here and now. We are to use the minds he gave us to apply revealed truth to the whole of life.

We are certainly to be detached from the world in the sense that we do not regard it as our true home, nor look to it for our true reward, nor lose our heart to it. That is the point of the biblical warnings against "worldliness." Instead of this, we must cultivate the genuine, Christian "other-worldliness," that of the man who can always say, "To me to live is Christ, and to die is gain" (Philippians 1:21). But equally certainly we are not to be detached from the world in the sense that we turn our back on it and lose interest in it. God cares about it, and so must we.

When Christ enjoins us, as part of the first great commandment, "You shall love the Lord your God . . . *with all your mind*" (Matthew 22:37, emphasis added), he is telling us to use our minds not merely to learn biblical doctrine, but to apply that biblical doctrine to the facts of God's world as we know them, so we may interpret them correctly and make a right and reverent use of our knowledge.

"Fundamentalism" and the Word of God

FOR BETTER THINKING

Make every effort to supplement your faith with virtue,
and virtue with knowledge.

2 PETER 1:5

The Puritans were great *thinkers*. The Puritan movement was led mainly by ministers, and most of the leaders among the ministers were brilliant and articulate polymaths from the universities. The age was one of intellectual ferment in many areas, and Puritan teachers had to be abreast of many things — biblical exegesis, which was being practiced at a much higher level of competence than is usually recognized; the ins and outs of Reformed theology as it was debated at home and abroad and written about, usually in Latin, in the large volumes that continental divines produced so prolifically; the various controversies over contemporary heresies and sects; and, above all, the heritage of practical, pastoral, devotional theology that had begun to develop and was being constantly augmented throughout the Puritan era.

The leading Puritan theologians — Owen, Baxter, Sibbes, Preston, Perkins, Charnock, Howe — all achieve a massive, adoring simplicity when speaking of God that argues intense reflective study, deep and prayerful Christian experience, and a sharp sense of responsibility to the church corporately, to their hearers and readers individually, and to the truth itself. This quality gives Puritan theological writing a flavor — you could call it an unction — that one rarely finds elsewhere. Luther's dictum that the three things that make the theologian are prayer, thinking in God's presence, and conflict, outward and inward, seems to find verification in the great Puritans. As you read, you feel a power of thought and a spiritual authenticity in their writings that is matched by very few.

By comparison, a great deal of Christian communication in our own day is made to appear shallow, simplistic, and sloppy.

A Quest for Godliness

OUR CERTAINTY OF SALVATION

While we were still sinners, Christ died for us.
Since, therefore, we have now been justified by his blood,
much more shall we be saved by him from the wrath of God.

ROMANS 5:8-9

Should we not think of Christ's substitution for us on the cross as a definite, one-to-one relationship between him and each individual sinner? This seems scriptural, for Paul says, "[He] loved *me* and gave himself for *me*" (Galatians 2:20, emphasis added). If Christ specifically took and discharged my penal obligation as a sinner, does it not follow that the cross was decisive for my salvation not only as its sole meritorious ground, but also as guaranteeing that I should be brought to faith, and through faith to eternal life? For is not the faith that receives salvation part of God's gift of salvation, according to what is affirmed in Philippians 1:29 and John 6:44-45, and implied in what Paul says of *God calling* and John of *new birth*? And if Christ by his death on my behalf secured reconciliation and righteousness as gifts for me to receive (Romans 5:11,17), did not this make it certain that the faith that receives these gifts would also be given me, as a direct consequence of Christ's dying for me?

Paul and John insist, as do all the New Testament writers, that God in the gospel promises life and salvation to *everyone* who believes and calls on Christ (John 3:16; Romans 10:13); this, indeed, is to them the primary truth.

Thus, through the knowledge that God is resolved to evoke the response he commands, Christians are assured of being kept safe, and evangelists of not laboring in vain. It may be added: Is there any good reason for finding difficulty with the notion that the cross *both* justifies the "free offer" of Christ to all men *and also* guarantees the believing, the accepting, and the glorifying of those who respond, when this was precisely what Paul and John affirmed?

In My Place Condemned He Stood

GOOD WORDS, GOOD WORKS

Peace be with you. As the Father has sent me,
even so I am sending you.

John 20:21

Jesus, the church's Lord, has issued marching orders. Individually and corporately, all God's people are now in the world on the king's business. The appointed task is twofold.

First and fundamentally, it is the work of worldwide witness, disciple-making, and church planting (Matthew 24:14; 28:19-20; Mark 13:10; Luke 24:47-48). Jesus Christ is to be proclaimed everywhere as God incarnate, Lord, and Savior; and God's authoritative invitation to find life through turning to Christ in repentance and faith is to be delivered to all mankind. The ministry of church planter Paul, evangelist to the whole world (so far as strength and circumstances allowed), models this primary commitment.

Second, all Christians, and therefore every congregation of the church on earth, are called to practice deeds of mercy and compassion, a thoroughgoing neighbor-love that responds unstintingly to all forms of human need as they present themselves (Luke 10:25-27; Romans 12:20-21). Compassion was the inward aspect of the neighbor-love that led Jesus to heal the sick, feed the hungry, and teach the ignorant (Matthew 9:36; 15:32; 20:34; Mark 1:41; Luke 7:13), and those who are new creatures in Christ must be similarly compassionate. Thereby they keep the second great commandment and also give credibility to their proclamation of a Savior who makes sinners into lovers of God and of their fellow human beings. If the exponents of this message do not display its power in their own lives, credibility is destroyed. If they do, credibility is enhanced. This was Jesus' point when he envisaged the sight of the good works of his witnesses leading people to glorify the Father (Matthew 5:16; 1 Peter 2:11-12). Good works should be visible to back up good words.

Concise Theology

STILL SINNERS, STILL PROUD

Be not wise in your own eyes;
fear the LORD, and turn away from evil.
PROVERBS 3:7

It is not, perhaps, surprising to find Christians constantly, often unconsciously, lapsing into subjectivist assumptions. For when men become Christians they do not cease to be sinners. Sinners are no more ready to acknowledge God in their thinking, by allowing his utterances authority over their judgment, than they are to acknowledge God in their actions, by allowing his utterances authority over their behavior. Sin has its root in the mind, and this attitude of mind is its very essence. And when men become Christians, they are still prone in their pride to lapse into the assumption that there is no rationality or wisdom in merely taking their Creator's word; they are still apt to demand instead that their reason be permitted to make its own independent assessment of what he says and to have the last word in deciding whether or not it is credible.

This is as real and gross a moral lapse as any, though it is not always seen as such; and the temptation to it is strong and insidious. Once one succumbs, and relapses to any degree into this sinful habit of mind, one is instantly drawn to the conclusion that Christians who continue to base their thinking on an unquestioning belief of what God has said are fettering reason and stifling free thought. No doubt the serpent would have told Eve as much, had she asked him.

But it is not so. The true antithesis here, as we have seen, is not between faith and reason (as if believing and thinking were mutually exclusive), but between a faithful and a faithless use of reason.

"Fundamentalism" and the Word of God

THEIR TEAMWORK

> *The grace of the Lord Jesus Christ and the love of God*
> *and the fellowship of the Holy Spirit be with you all.*
>
> 2 CORINTHIANS 13:14

In our fellowship with God we must learn to do full justice to the part that each of the divine Three plays in the team job, as we may venture to call it, of saving us from sin, restoring our ruined humanness, and bringing us finally to glory.

Should we neglect the Father, losing our focus on the tasks he sets and the disciplines he imposes, we shall become soft, lazy, self-absorbed, unsteady, and erratic, with a dull and sleepy conscience — spoiled children, in the most literal sense, in God's family. God's spoiled children will reveal themselves as exploitative egoists who make heavy weather of any troubles and setbacks that come their way, thus failing spectacularly to live out the self-denying theocentricity to which they pay lip service.

Should we neglect the Son, whether through some doctrinaire revisionist Christology or simply by lapsing into natural religion with Islam, so that we lose our focus on the Son's mediation, blood atonement, risen life, royal glory, and heavenly intercession, we shall slip back into legalism, a version of the treadmill religion of works, probably linked in these days with a syncretist theology.

Should we neglect the Spirit, losing our focus on the fellowship with Christ that he creates, the renewing of nature that he effects, the assurance and joy that he evokes, and the enabling for service that he bestows, we shall slip back into formalism, a version of the religion of aspiration and perspiration that lacks both inspiration and transformation, a religion of mechanical observances, low expectations, deep ruts of routine, and grooves that quickly turn into graves.

True Trinitarianism in the head and the heart can take us beyond these pitfalls; but anything less virtually guarantees a spiritual development that is one way or another stunted and deformed.

Serving the People of God

LETTING GOD SHAPE US

For you have need of endurance,
so that when you have done the will of God
you may receive what is promised.

HEBREWS 10:36

Why does God regularly make it necessary for us to be patient, persistent, and persevering as we ask for specific blessings and then wait on him for the answers? As the two questions overlap, so may our responses to them.

First, by compelling us to wait patiently for him to act, *God purges our motives.* Often our first formulation of a request is more self-centered and self-serving than it ought to be, just because of the many layers of egocentricity that encase our sinful selves, like the successive skins that encase the heart of an onion. As we wait on God, repeatedly renewing our requests, he leads us to see that the initial motivations of our asking, heartfelt as it doubtless was, were more concerned with comfort, convenience, and glory for ourselves, and less with his honor, praise, and glory than was right. Thus, by showing us how he sees our praying, our heavenly Father peels off us some of those layers of self-absorption, so that we reshape our requests, and our motives become pure in his sight. These repeated and repeatedly revised petitions are not the "vain repetitions" Jesus warns his disciples against (Matthew 6:7, KJV) but are our progressively distilled longings that God will glorify himself by the way he enriches us his servants. Through the waiting process God is attuning us more directly to himself.

Second, by compelling us to wait for him, *God shapes his giving in a natural way.* Though quick and spectacular answers to prayer are sometimes given, it is not God's way to multiply miracles indiscriminately. Miracles are always the exception, never the rule, and God's evident will for most of his servants a great deal of the time is that they live wisely, obediently, and reverently within the ordinary processes of ordinary life.

Praying

FOR BETTER WORSHIP

Ascribe to the LORD the glory due his name;
worship the LORD in the splendor of holiness.

PSALM 29:2

The Puritans were also great *worshippers.* They served a great God, the God of the Bible, unshrunk by any of the diminishing and demeaning lines of thought about him that press upon us today. Scripture had given them a vision of the transcendent Creator who rules and speaks, the holy God who hates sin and judges it, and yet out of incomprehensible love has sent his Son to bear sin's curse on the cross so that guilty sinners might be justly justified and saved.

Also, Scripture had shown them Christ the Mediator now glorified and reigning, and effectually calling blind, deaf, impotent, spiritually dead souls to himself by his Spirit's secret agency as God's human messengers — pastors and parents, friends and neighbors — labored to instill into them the message of law and gospel.

Finally, Scripture had told them of God's everlasting covenant relationship with believers — that total commitment on his part which guarantees blessing for eternity and entitles Christians to call on their Creator as "my God, my Father," just as each of them calls on Jesus as "*my* Savior, *my* Lord, and *my* God."

All this thrilled their hearts, and produced in them an ardent, overflowing spirit of worship that on fast days at least, when time did not press, led pastors to pray extempore in their services for up to an hour at a time. It is a fact of Christian history that those who are consciously worshipping a great God do not find that worship services lasting two or three hours are a bore; on the contrary, they are experienced as a joy. By comparison, the modern Western passion for services lasting not more than sixty minutes raises the suspicion that both our God and our own spiritual statures are rather small.

A Quest for Godliness

SOURCE OF ALL OUR GOOD

We ourselves, who have the firstfruits of the Spirit . . . wait eagerly
for adoption as sons, the redemption of our bodies.

ROMANS 8:23

When Paul speaks of the God-sent Holy Spirit, his perspective is always eschatological, looking forward to the end of which our present experience of redemption and life in the Spirit is the beginning. The Spirit is the gift of the new age, guaranteeing what is to come (Romans 8:23; Ephesians 1:13-14).

In relation to the individual Christian, the Spirit's ministry is fourfold. He *enlightens,* giving understanding of the gospel so that the "spiritual person" has "the mind of Christ" (1 Corinthians 2:15-16). He *indwells* as the seal and guarantee that henceforth the Christian belongs to God (Romans 8:9-11; 1 Corinthians 3:16-17; 6:19). He *transforms*, producing in us the ethical fruit of Christlikeness: love, joy, peace, patience, kindness, goodness, faithfulness, gentleness, self-control (2 Corinthians 3:18; Galatians 5:22-24), plus prayerfulness and hope (Romans 8:26-27; 15:13). And he *assures*, witnessing to our adoption by God, our eternal acceptance, and our future inheritance (Romans 8:15-25,31-39, which is a transcript of the Spirit's witness; Galatians 4:6).

In short, as the Christian's whole life is life in Christ in terms of its meaning, center, and direction, so the Christian's whole life is life in the Spirit from the standpoint of his knowledge, disposition, and ability to love and serve. Putting off the old man and putting on the new man, which God renews (Ephesians 4:20-24; Colossians 3:9-10), and being newly created in Christ (2 Corinthians 5:17), corresponds in Paul's writings to new birth in John's, and though Paul nowhere says this explicitly, it is plain that the initial inward renewal is the Spirit's work, as the living that expresses it. All that we ever contribute to our own Christian lives, according to Paul, is folly, inability, and need. Everything that is good, right, positive, and valuable comes from Christ through the Spirit.

Celebrating the Saving Work of God

LOVE'S STEADY FLOW

> *Hope does not put us to shame, because God's love*
> *has been poured into our hearts through the Holy Spirit.*
>
> ROMANS 5:5

In Romans 5:5, "God's love" means "knowledge of God's love": Paul is speaking about the Spirit's witness. In the previous four verses he celebrated the peace and joy and hope that flow from knowing one has been justified by faith; now he grounds all three, along with the blessing of justification itself, in the love of God, of which the Spirit assures us. It is by assuring us of our acceptance and status and future happiness in Christ, says Paul, that God has poured his love into our hearts.

That verb *poured* means what it sounds like it means. It speaks of abundance. If I wanted to illustrate such pouring, I would go and get a bucket, fill it with water, and then steadily tip it over. Pouring gives you not just a drop or a trickle, but an abundant steady flow. So the thought is of an abundant witness to the saving love of God, given in all believers' hearts by the Holy Spirit.

So you can see that assurance, assurance of being Christ's, assurance of being an heir of glory, assurance of being beyond the stage in which one had to fear judgment for sin, assurance of being accepted, and assurance of being eternally an object of God's favor and generosity — that ought to be strong in all Christian hearts, being poured in by the Holy Spirit. When Paul says "our hearts," he means the hearts of believers. And that, when it's reality, really is heaven on earth. Heaven's awareness of our glorious God, heaven's consciousness of divine things, heaven's realization of our relationship to the Savior who loves us — it begins here and now through the witness of the Spirit.

Keep in Step with the Spirit

FEELING NEEDY ENOUGH

I am poor and needy; hasten to me, O God!
You are my help and my deliverer; O LORD, do not delay!
PSALM 70:5

I find it most helpful to remind myself, at the beginning of my devotional period, who God is and what I am. That is to say, I remind myself that God is great, transcendent, that he loves me and wants to speak to me right now. And I recall that I am the original sinner, the perverse and stupid oaf who misses God's way constantly. I have made any number of mistakes in my life up to this point and will make a lot more today if I don't keep in touch with God, and with Christ, my Lord and Savior, as I should.

There is nothing like a sense of hunger to give one an appetite for a meal, and there is nothing like a sense of spiritual emptiness and need to give me an appetite for the Word of God. Let that be the theme of our first minute or two of prayer as we come to our devotional times, and then we will be tuned in right. God says, "Open your mouth wide, and I will fill it" (Psalm 81:10).

The quantity of theological notions in one's mind, even correct notions, doesn't say anything about one's relationship with God. The fact that one knows a lot of theology doesn't mean that one's relationship with God is right or is going to be right. The two things are quite distinct. As a professional theologian I find it both helpful and needful to focus this truth to myself by saying to myself over and over again, "What a difference there is between knowing notions, even true notions, and knowing God." My times with the Bible, like those of all Christians, are meant to be times for knowing God.

Honouring the Written Word of God

EVERYTHING EXPOSED

Then he will say to those on his left, "Depart from me, you cursed,
into the eternal fire prepared for the devil and his angels."

MATTHEW 25:41

The certainty of final judgment forms the frame within which the New Testament message of saving grace is set.

This judgment will demonstrate, and so finally vindicate, the perfect justice of God. In a world of sinners, in which God has "allowed all the nations to walk in their own ways" (Acts 14:16), it is no wonder that evil is rampant and that doubts arise as to whether God, if sovereign, can be just, or, if just, can be sovereign. But for God to judge justly is his glory, and the Last Judgment will be his final self-vindication against the suspicion that he has ceased to care about righteousness.

In the case of those who profess to be Christ's, review of their actual words and works will have the special point of uncovering the evidence that shows whether their profession is the fruit of an honest regenerate heart (Matthew 12:33-35) or merely the parrot cry of a hypocritical religiosity (Matthew 7:21-23). Everything about everybody will be exposed on Judgment Day (1 Corinthians 4:5), and each will receive from God according to what he or she really is. Those whose professed faith did not express itself in a new lifestyle, marked by hatred of sin and works of loving service to God and others, will be lost (Matthew 18:23-35; 25:34-46; James 2:14-26).

Fallen angels (demons) will be judged on the last day (Matthew 8:29; Jude 6), and the saints will be involved in the process (1 Corinthians 6:3), though Scripture does not reveal their precise role.

Knowledge of future judgment is always a summons to present repentance. Only the penitent will be prepared for judgment when it comes.

Concise Theology

OLD GOSPEL, NEW GOSPEL

If you accept a different gospel from the one you accepted,
you put up with it readily enough.

2 CORINTHIANS 11:4

Evangelicalism today is in a state of perplexity and unsettlement. There is evidence of widespread dissatisfaction with things as they are and of uncertainty as to the road ahead. This is a complex phenomenon, but if we go to the root of the matter, we shall find that these perplexities are all ultimately due to our having lost our grip on the biblical gospel. Without realizing it, we have during the past century bartered that gospel for a substitute product which, though similar enough in points of detail, is as a whole a decidedly different thing. Hence our troubles, for the substitute does not answer the ends for which the authentic gospel once proved itself so mighty. Why?

The reason lies in its own character and content. It fails to make men God-centered in their thoughts and God-fearing in their hearts because this is not primarily what it tries to do. It is too exclusively concerned to be "helpful" to man — to bring peace, comfort, happiness, satisfaction — and too little concerned to glorify God. The old gospel was "helpful," too — more so, indeed, than is the new — but (so to speak) incidentally, for its first concern was always to give glory to God. It was always and essentially a proclamation of divine sovereignty in mercy and judgment, a summons to bow down and worship the mighty Lord on whom man depends for all good, both in nature and in grace.

Whereas the chief aim of the old was to teach men to worship God, the concern of the new seems limited to making them feel better. The subject of the old gospel was God and his ways with men; the subject of the new is man and the help God gives him. There is a world of difference.

In My Place Condemned He Stood

SEEING GOD IN THE DARK

The LORD who delivered me from the paw of the lion
and from the paw of the bear
will deliver me from the hand of this Philistine.

1 SAMUEL 17:37

How do we find strength in God when our world is in ruins?

In 1 Samuel 30, David and his men came to Ziklag to find their camp destroyed and their families taken captive. David's resulting distress might well have destroyed him; his grief—an entirely natural reaction—might have slid into depression and desperation, ending his career as a leader and probably his life ("for the people spoke of stoning him"). But as he fought the paralysis of grief, we see in David the spiritual reaction of faith: "David strengthened himself in the LORD his God" (verse 6).

How did he do it? I believe David ran five thoughts through his mind:

1. *My God reigns.* He reminded himself that God is in total control of all that happens, and that having brought him into this extremity, God was certainly able to bring him out of it.

2. *My God forgives.* David thought of God's pardoning mercy. He recalled that "with you there is forgiveness, that you may be feared" (Psalm 130:4). Right-minded reverence is rooted in a knowledge of God's mercy in the remitting of one's sins.

3. *My God cares.* David thought, too, of God's covenanted protection. "The LORD is my shepherd" (Psalm 23:1). Himself a shepherd, David knew that the shepherd's job is precisely to look after the sheep. So he must not suppose that God had abandoned him. Even in ruined Ziklag, God was with him to love and bless him.

4. *My God is consistent.* David thought of his previous experiences of God's goodness. God does not lose interest in those he has once begun to love and bless.

5. *My God is faithful.* David, we may confidently say, found strength in trusting the fidelity of his promise-keeping God.

Serving the People of God

FOR GREATER HOPE

> *"The LORD is my portion," says my soul,*
> *"therefore I will hope in him."*
> Lamentations 3:24

The Puritans were great *hopers*. One notable strength of the Puritans, setting them far apart from Western Christians today, was the firmness of their grip on the biblical teaching about the hope of heaven. Basic to their pastoral care was their understanding of the Christian's present life as a journey home, and they made much of encouraging God's people to look ahead and feast their hearts on what is to come.

The classic works here are Richard Baxter's massive *The Saints' Everlasting Rest*, written to show how the hope of glory, analyzed by biblical study and internalized by meditation, should give believers energy and direction for present living, and Bunyan's *Pilgrim's Progress*, both parts of which reach their climax with triumphant passages through Jordan to the celestial city. The vividness of the vision of heaven in both Baxter and Bunyan is remarkable by any standards; sanctified imagination gives concreteness and color to theological perception, resulting in extraordinary power to convey the flow of glory to the Christian heart.

The Puritan point, which was first, of course, a New Testament point, was that Christians should know what their hope is and draw from it power to resist whatever discouragements and distractions present circumstances may produce. The unreadiness for pain and death that Western Christians too often reveal today contrasts unhappily with the realism and joyful hope that the Puritan masters inculcated in order to prepare the saints to leave this world in peace when their time came.

A Quest for Godliness

SPIRIT AND WORD

Do not quench the Spirit. Do not despise prophecies, but test everything;
hold fast what is good. Abstain from every form of evil.

1 THESSALONIANS 5:19-22

Just as the Word is insufficient without the Spirit, so the Spirit is insufficient without the Word. Well may Charismatics and others censure those who seem in practice to embrace the idea that biblical orthodoxy is all that matters and biblical teaching alone produces a healthy church. The critics are right to point out that idolizing orthodoxy is not the same as worshipping God and that complacent "orthodoxism," by inflating pride, actually quenches the Spirit.

But pneumatic preoccupation can slow down maturity, too. Many Charismatics appear anti-intellectual in basic attitude, impatient with biblical and theological study, insistent that their movement is about experience rather than truth, content with a tiny handful of biblical teachings, and positively zany in their unwillingness to reason out guidance for life from the Scriptures. Endless possibilities of self-deception and satanic befoolment open up the moment we lay aside the Word to follow supposedly direct instruction from the Spirit in vision, dream, prophecy, or inward impression.

The history of fanaticism is gruesome; I do not want to see it return among my Charismatic friends. But this is always a danger when the formation of the mind by the Word is in any way neglected. What is needed across the board is constant instruction in biblical truth with constant prayer that the Spirit will make it take fire in human hearts, regenerating, redirecting, and transforming into Christ's likeness at character level. Whatever agenda others have, the fulfilling of Christ's prayer that his people would be sanctified by the Spirit through God's Word of truth should be the inerrantist's first concern.

Celebrating the Saving Work of God

WHO IS THE "WRETCHED MAN"?

So then, I myself serve the law of God with my mind,
but with my flesh I serve the law of sin.

ROMANS 7:25

Who is the "I" in Romans 7:14-25 — the passage which leads to the
cry "Wretched man that I am! Who will deliver me from this body of
death?" (verse 24)? This is a problem which has divided expositors since
Augustine's day, and on which differences of view still remain wide. What
seems to me the more satisfactory view is as follows.

The passage is in the present tense because it describes a present state.
It reproduces Paul's theological self-knowledge as a Christian: not all of it,
but just that part which is germane to the subject in hand — namely, the
function of the law in giving knowledge of sin. (The other side of Paul's
self-knowledge, that given him by the gospel, is set out in Romans 8.)

The thesis of this paragraph, "I am of the flesh, sold under sin" (verse
14), is stated categorically and without qualification — not because this
is the whole truth about Paul the Christian, but because it is the only
truth about himself that the law can tell him. What the law does for the
Christian is to give him knowledge of the sin that still remains in him.
When he reviews his life in light of the law, he always "finds" and "sees"
that sin is still there, and he is still to a degree being taken captive by it
(verses 21-23). The wretchedness of the "wretched man" thus springs from
the discovery of his continuing sinfulness, and the knowledge that he
cannot hope to be rid of indwelling sin, his troublesome inmate, while
he remains in the body. He is painfully conscious that for the present his
reach exceeds his grasp; he therefore longs for the eschatological deliverance through which the tension between will and achievement, purpose
and performance, plan and action, will be abolished.

Keep in Step with the Spirit

PREACHING IS INCARNATIONAL

Christ is proclaimed, and in that I rejoice.
Yes, and I will rejoice.

PHILIPPIANS 1:18

Preaching is God's revealed way of making himself and his saving covenant known to us. The Bible shows God the Creator to be a communicator, and the theme and substance of his communication since Eden to be a gracious, life-giving relationship with believing sinners. All the factual information and ethical direction that he currently communicates through his written Word feeds into this relationship, first to establish it through repentance and commitment to Jesus Christ, and then to deepen it through increasing knowledge of God and maturing worship. This is the covenant life of God's people, which is both initiated and sustained through God's personal communion with them.

The Bible makes it appear that God's standard way of securing and maintaining his person-to-person communication with us, his human creatures, is through the agency of persons whom he sends to us as his messengers. By being made God's spokesmen and mouthpieces for his message, the messengers become emblems, models, and embodiments of God's personal address to each of their hearers, and by their own commitment to the message they bring, they become models also of personal response to that address. Such were the prophets and apostles, and such supremely was Jesus Christ, the incarnate Son, who has been well described as being both God for man and man for God. That is the succession in which preachers today are called to stand.

Why does the New Testament stress the need for preaching? Not just because the only way to spread the good news in the ancient world was by oral announcement. But it is also, surely, because of the power of "incarnational" communication, in which the speaker illuminates that which he proclaims by being transparently committed to it in a wholehearted and thoroughgoing way.

Honouring the Written Word of God

ETHICS FROM GOD'S AWESOMENESS

*Let your light shine before others, so that they may see your good works
and give glory to your Father who is in heaven.*

MATTHEW 5:16

Christian morality is an expression, function, and corollary of Christian
theology.

Our ethics are to be drawn from our dogmatics, and our view of
both will be deficient if we fail to see this. Christian morality is not to be
equated with secular morality, or the morality of a national cultural heritage; Christian duty is determined by Christian doctrine; orthopraxy, as
we may call it, follows from, and is controlled and shaped by, orthodoxy.
Nor should any statement of Christian orthodoxy be thought complete till
it includes a declaration of God's will for human behavior, which is what
Christian morality is about. Christian morality is precisely the doctrine of
God's commands to mankind, set within the frame of the doctrines of his
works for humankind and his ways with humankind.

God the Creator, the God of the Bible, wants his human creatures to
serve, please, and glorify him by specific types and courses of action that
he likes to see, and he directs us accordingly, with sanctions encouraging
us to do right and discouraging us from doing wrong. Christian morality,
according to Scripture, is a blueprint for living under the authority of this
awesomely and intrusively personal Lord, by whose grace we have been
saved to serve, and to whom we must one day give account.

So Christian morality is a morality of divine command, based on the
reality of a divine gift, and both the gift and the command are elements in
the doctrine of God as such. Ethics, therefore, must never be thought of
as independent of dogmatics, and study in either of these fields should be
understood as obligating study in the other one as well. Otherwise, ultimate inadequacy in our chosen field, whichever of the two it is, becomes a
forgone conclusion.

Serving the People of God

WHY SO HARD?

The gate is narrow and the way is hard
that leads to life.
MATTHEW 7:14

Why is persistent praying so difficult? It is because the *world*, the *flesh*, and the *Devil* combine to oppose all forms of the life of prayer and to resist all our efforts to live it.

The *world*, meaning community life organized without and against God, will seek to distract and derail us from our praying by implying that this is a weird and pointless way to behave. The broad way of the world, namely, living without regard for God, is a way that it has always been tempting to lapse into.

The *flesh*, meaning the inner dynamics of our human hearts as twisted by still-present indwelling sin and not yet fully reordered by grace, is weak, as we can see from what took place in Gethsemane. When the disciples ought to have been praying with and for Jesus, he found them asleep. Again and again, when we have something spiritually significant to do (and that includes prayer, every time), desire, motivation, strength of heart (that is, of mind and will), zeal, and single-minded concern for God's service and glory will be lacking, and we will need to ask our Lord to reenergize us through the Holy Spirit to keep us from total collapse. When Jesus said, "Watch and pray that you may not enter into temptation" (Mark 14:38), this was undoubtedly what he had in mind.

And then, of course, there is the *Devil*, "your adversary," as Peter calls him, who "prowls around like a roaring lion, seeking someone to devour" (1 Peter 5:8). Active faith that calls on the Father, the Son, and the Spirit for strength to stand firm against all distortions of revealed truth, all discouragements from faithfulness to it, and all temptations to despair will make you invulnerable to Satan's frontal attacks. Nothing changes that.

Praying

ACTS OF WAR

No soldier gets entangled in civilian pursuits,
since his aim is to please the one who enlisted him.

2 TIMOTHY 2:4

Faith will keep us going in obedience; pray always. Faith will keep us in expectation; hope always. Faith will keep us hanging on to God in prayer despite all the discouragements we feel; grip God's promises always.

If you find that your thoughts wander when you are praying silently, pray aloud. If you find that once the day gets going, you can never find time to pray, get up earlier and pray before you do anything else. If you find that your thoughts and words simply won't come together, write out the petition that you are seeking to get into focus and use your own written prayer to present the matter to God. Take note of whatever distracts you from prayer and try to avoid it. These are just commonsense tools of help. They will not make hanging on in prayer easy, but they may help to make it possible.

Get real then in prayer. Get serious and keep going.

It may bring clarity and realism here to declare explicitly that petitioning, praising, meditating, and maintaining each of these under pressure are acts of war — defensive and counterattacking warfare against the supernatural being who is God's sworn enemy and ours too. In all our communion with God, Satan and his hosts are opposing us every step of the way, constantly seeking to weaken us and drain our strength by indirect means in addition to the direct attacks that they periodically mount against us.

It is always in the place of persistent prayer, as we call out to our heavenly Father and Christ the risen Lord to help us, that each victory in this war begins to be won. So, God help us to persist in our praying; God help us, then, to be found hanging on.

Praying

FOR BRAVER WARFARE

The LORD goes out like a mighty man,
like a man of war he stirs up his zeal; he cries out,
he shouts aloud, he shows himself mighty against his foes.

ISAIAH 42:13

The Puritans were also great *warriors.* They saw the Christian calling as, from one standpoint, an unending fight against the world, the flesh, and the Devil, and programmed themselves accordingly. As John Geree described the Puritan, "His own life he accounted a warfare, wherein Christ was his captain, his arms, prayers, and tears."[33]

One all-time classic of Puritan literature is William Gurnall's *The Christian in Complete Armour,* described as "a treatise of the saints' war against the devil," exposing "that grand enemy of God and his people, in his policies, power, seat of his empire, wickedness, and chief design he hath against the saints"; from this book "the Christian is furnished with spiritual arms for the battle, helped on with his armor, and taught the use of his weapon." This work of more than 800,000 words was described by C. H. Spurgeon as "peerless and priceless," and John Newton said he would choose it if he could read only one book beside the Bible.

Bunyan's *Pilgrim's Progress* is a story of almost constant fighting, both verbal and physical, and the ideal Puritan pastor, Mr. Great-heart, who acts as guide, instructor, and protector to Christian's party, is cast for the role of giant-killer as well, fighting and destroying giants Grim, Maul, Slay-good, and Despair as he goes along.

The Puritans fought for truth against error, for personal holiness against temptations to sin, for ordered wisdom against chaotic folly, for church purity and national righteousness against corruption and hostility in both areas. One facet of their greatness was their principled hostility to all evils that stood in the way of godliness and true faith, and their willingness, much as they loved peace, to go out and fight those things, and to keep fighting as long as the evils were there.

A Quest for Godliness

OUR LIVES ARE IN THE BIBLE

He commanded us to preach to the people
and to testify that he is the one appointed by God
to be judge of the living and the dead.

ACTS 10:42

The activity of preaching the Bible (of which I take the public reading of Scripture to be part) unlocks the Bible to both mind and heart, and the activity of hearing Scripture preached, receiving what is said, meditating on the text as preaching has opened it up, and letting it apply itself to one's own thoughts and ways actually leads us into the Bible in terms of enabling us to comprehend and lay hold of what it, or better, God in and through it, is saying to us at this moment. Where such a personal relation to the Bible has not become part of one's life, though one may know much about its language, background, origins, and the historical significance of its contents, it remains in the deepest sense a closed book. And those who in this sense do not yet know what to make of the Bible will not know what to make of their own lives either.

One way to express this is to say that our lives are in the Bible, and we do not understand them until we find them there. But the quickest and most vivid way in which such understanding comes about is through being addressed by the Bible via someone for whom the Bible is alive and who knows and can articulate something of its life-changing power. This is a further reason why preaching is always needed in the church: Whenever preaching fails, understanding of Scripture in its relation to life will inevitably fail also.

No congregation can be healthy without a diet of biblical preaching, and no pastor can justify himself in demoting preaching from the place of top priority among the tasks of his calling.

Honouring the Written Word of God

NEW BIRTH EXPLAINED

God is faithful, by whom you were called into the fellowship
of his Son, Jesus Christ our Lord.

1 CORINTHIANS 1:9

"Effectual calling," as the *Westminster Shorter Catechism* explains, "is
the work of God's Spirit, whereby convincing us of our sin and misery,
enlightening our minds in the knowledge of Christ, and renewing our
wills, he doth persuade and enable us to embrace Jesus Christ, freely
offered to us in the gospel."[34]

This effectual calling is first of all *a work of divine grace*. It is not
something a man can do for himself or for another. It is the first stage in
the application of redemption to those for whom redemption was won; it
is the event whereby, on the grounds of the eternal, federal, representative
relation to Christ that election and redemption have established, the elect
sinner is brought by the Holy Spirit into a real, vital, personal union with
his covenant Head and Redeemer.

Second, it is *a work of divine power*. It is effected by the Spirit, who
acts both *mediately by the word, in the mind, giving understanding and
conviction, and also immediately,* with the word, in the hidden depths
of the heart, implanting new life and power, effectively dethroning sin
and making the sinner both able and willing to respond to the gospel
invitation.

Third, effectual calling is *a work of divine freedom*. Only God can
effect it, and he does so at his own pleasure. "It depends not on human
will or exertion, but on God, who has mercy" (Romans 9:16).

The work of effectual calling will proceed as fast as God wills, but no
faster, and the counselor's role is accordingly that of the midwife, whose
task it is to see what is happening and give appropriate help at each stage,
but who cannot foretell, let alone prearrange, how rapid the birth process
will be.

A Quest for Godliness

PREACHING WITH AUTHORITY

They were astonished at his teaching,
for his word possessed authority.

LUKE 4:32

What does it mean for preaching to be marked by authority?

The answer I propose is that authority in preaching is a reality in every situation in which the following things are true.

1. There is no doubt about the *nature* of what is happening: *The Bible is doing the talking.* The preacher is treating himself as a mouthpiece for the biblical Word of God, and that Word is coming through. He is making it his business to focus everyone's attention on the text, to stand behind it rather than in front of it, to become its servant, and to let it deliver its message through him.

2. There is no doubt about the *purpose* of what is happening: *Response to God is being called for.* The preacher is seeking not only to inform and persuade, but to evoke an appropriate answer to what God through the text is saying and showing.

3. There is no doubt about the *perspective* of what is happening: *The preaching is practical.* (This point is an extension of the last.) The more explicit the practical perspective, and the more overtly it involves the listeners, the more the divine authority of the preaching will be felt.

4. There is no doubt about the *impact* of what is happening: *The presence and power of God are being experienced.* The preaching mediates an encounter not merely with truth, but with God himself.

Preaching is marked by authority when the message is a relaying of what is taught by the text, when active response to it is actively sought, when it is angled in a practical, applicatory way that involves the listeners' lives, and when God himself is encountered through it.

Honouring the Written Word of God

CAN YOU WAIT?

O LORD, be gracious to us;
we wait for you.
ISAIAH 33:2

Another reason persistent prayer is necessary is that God's nurturing strategy sometimes rules out immediate answers. Children say to parents, "I can't wait." And all of us who are parents have from time to time said to our children, "You've got to learn to wait." The ability to wait is one of the differences between childishness and maturity. Mature people are, among other things, persons who have learned to wait. God is in the business of maturing us in Christ, and this lesson is integral to adult Christianity.

This is what the writer of Hebrews describes as the path to spiritual maturity: "It is for discipline that you have to endure" (12:7). Sometimes God uses delayed responses to prayer to discipline and train our spiritual muscles. We hang on in prayer, and our faith muscles grow stronger. We learn to curb our impulse to doubt, to blow up in anger, to grab whatever we can get. We learn to trust God — and to keep on praying.

Discipline means training. But training for what? Paul makes the absurd-sounding claim that we who are justified by faith and know peace with God can "rejoice in our sufferings" (Romans 5:3). Did Nehemiah and Hannah and Job and Paul suffer while waiting for God as they prayed over and over their troubles? If we define suffering to cover all forms of "not getting what you like while not liking what you get," the answer is, of course they did. We suffer similarly when our prayers seem to be achieving nothing. In the meantime, besides keeping on praying, we can allow this suffering and waiting to move us along the process that Paul so vividly describes: "Suffering produces endurance, and endurance produces character, and character produces hope" (verses 3-4).

Praying

SOURCES

Celebrating the Saving Work of God (Regent College Publishing, 2008)

Concise Theology: A Guide to Historic Christian Beliefs (Tyndale, 1993, 2001)

Evangelism and the Sovereignty of God (InterVarsity, 1967, 2008)

Freedom and Authority (Regent College Publishing, 1994, 2003)

"Fundamentalism" and the Word of God (Eerdmans, 1958, 1985)

Guard Us, Guide Us: Divine Leading in Life's Decisions (Baker, 2008), by J. I. Packer and Carolyn Nystrom

Honouring the People of God (Regent College Publishing, 2008)

Honouring the Written Word of God (Regent College Publishing, 2008)

In My Place Condemned He Stood: Celebrating the Glory of the Atonement (Crossway, 2007), by J. I. Packer and Mark Dever

Keep in Step with the Spirit: Finding Fullness in Our Walk with God (Baker, 2005)

Keeping the Ten Commandments (Crossway, 1994, 2007)

Never Beyond Hope: How God Touches and Uses Imperfect People (InterVarsity, 2000, 2005), by J. I. Packer and Carolyn Nystrom

A Passion for Faithfulness: Wisdom from the Book of Nehemiah (Crossway, 1995, 2001)

Praying the Lord's Prayer (Crossway, 2007)

Praying: Finding Our Way Through Duty to Delight (InterVarsity, 2006), by J. I. Packer and Carolyn Nystrom

A Quest for Godliness: The Puritan Vision of the Christian Life (Crossway, 1990, 1994)

Rediscovering Holiness: Know the Fullness of Life with God (Regal, 2009)

Serving the People of God (Regent College Publishing, 2008)

The Way of Wisdom (Zondervan, 2000), edited by J. I. Packer and Sven K. Soderlund

NOTES

1. John Newton, "Let Us Love and Sing and Wonder," 1774.
2. The Westminster Confession of Faith, I, x (1646).
3. The Westminster Shorter Catechism, Answer 1 (1674).
4. Anne R. Cousin, "The Sands of Time Are Sinking," 1857, based on Samuel Rutherford's letters.
5. J. Gresham Machen, *What Is Faith?* (New York: Macmillan, 1925), 17f.
6. C. S. Lewis, *Reflections on the Psalms* (Orlando: Harvest Books, 1958), 93.
7. Dietrich Bonhoeffer, *Letters and Papers from Prison*, ed. Eberhard Bethge, enlarged edition (London: SCM Press, 1971), 279.
8. John Calvin, *Institutes of the Christian Religion*, III, iii, 5 (1599).
9. George Dana Boardman.
10. St. Augustine.
11. Martin Luther, quoted in Stephen J. Nichols, *Martin Luther: A Guided Tour of His Life and Thought* (Phillipsburg, NJ: P&R, 2002), 63.
12. J. R. W. Stott, *God's New Society: The Message of Ephesians* (Downers Grove, IL: InterVarsity, 1979), 123.
13. John Owen.
14. Cited from *Tyndale Bulletin* 25 (1974): 42–43.
15. Tom Smail, *The Giving Gift* (London: Hodder & Stoughton, 1988), 35.
16. Edward Farley, *Theologia* (Philadelphia: Fortress, 1983), 35.
17. Ludwig Köhler, *Old Testament Theology* (Philadelphia: Westminster, 1957), 106–107.
18. John Calvin, *Institutes of the Christian Religion*, II, xvii, 1–2 (1599).
19. John Murray, *The Epistle to the Romans* (Grand Rapids, MI: Eerdmans, 1959), 35–36.
20. Cornelius Plantinga, *Not the Way It's Supposed to Be* (Grand Rapids, MI: Eerdmans, 1995), 118.
21. The Westminster Confession of Faith, I, vi (1646).
22. Richard Baxter.
23. The Westminster Confession of Faith, I, ix (1646).
24. Thomas Manton, *Works*, II (James Nisbet: London, 1871), 102f.
25. James Denney, *Studies in Theology* (London: Hodder & Stoughton, 1902), 244.

26. F. W. Dillistone, *Christianity and Communication* (New York: Scribner, 1956), 106f.

27. Arthur Wainwright, *The Trinity in the New Testament* (London: SPCK, 1962), 4.

28. William Perkins, *A Golden Chain*, quoted in Ian Breward, ed., *The Work of William Perkins* (Abingdon, UK: Sutton Courtenay, 1970), 177.

29. William Ames, *The Marrow of Theology*, trans. J. D. Eusden (Grand Rapids, MI: Baker, 1997), 77.

30. George Swinnock, *The Works of George Swinnock*, I (Edinburgh: James Nichol, 1868), 229–230.

31. Edmund Morgan, 15.

32. Daniel Rogers, *Matrimonial Honour* (London: Thomas Harper for Philip Nevil, 1642).

33. John Geree, "The Character of an Old English Puritan, or Non-Conformist" (London: 1946). Printed by W. Wilson for Christopher Meredith at the Crane in Paul's Church-yard, http://www.reformedreader.org/character_of_an_old_english_puri.htm.

34. The Westminster Shorter Catechism, Answer 31 (1674).

SCRIPTURE INDEX

TOPICAL INDEX

means of, 231
meditation, 73, 94, 178, 213, 249, 294
meekness, 186
mercy, 36, 37, 44, 60, 66, 308
deeds of, 298
Jesus as, 121
Meyer, F. B., 152
mind, 246, 274, 295, 310. *See also* intellect
of Christ, 303
sin rooted in, 299
mindset, 60, 192
ministry, 40, 99, 155, 157
Christ's heavenly, 183
of Holy Spirit, 175, 209, 226, 252, 289, 303
leading to, 87
miracles, 301
mistrust, 79
morality, 133, 313. *See also* law
Morgan, Edward, 293
motivation, 177, 184, 301
mystery, 122, 206, 221, 224, 283

natural order, 95
nature, 54, 59, 216
need, 87, 232
spiritual, 266, 305
Nehemiah, 34, 42, 56, 87, 99, 184
defenses and, 273
work of, 217
new birth, 48, 53, 54, 106, 247
effectual calling in, 318
salvation and, 121
New Covenant, 238, 248, 254
New Testament, 46, 50, 117, 137, 179. *See also* Scripture
exposition of Old Testament

in, 250
hope in, 251
salvation as theme of, 254
Trinitarian theme of, 289
word of God in, 194
Newton, John, 316

obedience, 19, 69, 73, 111
to God's Word, 230
to law, 140
learned, 242
possibility of, 209
restraint and, 275
Scriptural interpretation and, 249
Old Testament, 153, 162, 211, 230. *See also* Scripture
omnipotence, 41, 160
omnipresence, 183
omniscience, 160
openness to God, 180
optimism, 16
order, 95, 140
Orr, Edwin, 94
orthodoxy, 313
orthopraxy, 313
Owen, John, 28, 83

Paraclete, 24
partnership, 217
passion, 191, 288
pastors, 236
patience, 66, 131, 201, 207, 301
Paul, 215, 277
peace, 91, 131, 266, 309
penance, 120
penitence, 105. *See also* repentance
Pentecost, 138
people, 37, 64. *See also* humanity

of church, 22
of God, 280
of individual's life, 235
of Scripture, 250, 282
universalism, 269

victory, 259, 315
vocation, 241

Wainwright, Arthur, 280
waiting, 21, 301, 320
Wallace, R. S., 221
warfare, spiritual, 165
Watts, Isaac, 12
weakness, 70, 198, 288
Wesley, John, 83
Western civilization, 16, 26, 49
Westminster Confession, 76, 230, 250
Westminster Shorter Catechism, 318
Whitefield, George, 121, 124
will, 47, 285
    free, 164
    of God, 25, 58, 158, 219, 301, 313
    of Holy Spirit, 174
wisdom, 12, 43, 130, 181
    acts of, 210
    of Bible, 77, 248, 254
    checking up on, 135
    to discern God's will, 25, 58
    goal-setting and, 154, 210
    of God, 26, 81, 158, 163, 204, 210, 248
    human, 204
    humility and, 221
    living in, 111
    meekness and, 186

New Covenant, 238, 254
New Testament, 248
Old Testament, 254
practical, 56, 130, 281
realistic, 227
rediscovering old, 10
for salvation, 254
sources of, 238, 271
strategies and, 173
truth as, 79
worship and, 290
witness, 94, 161, 298
    apostolic, 238
    false, 258
    of Holy Spirit, 9, 129, 175, 176, 188, 262, 303, 304
Word of God, 93, 110, 281, 310. *See also* Scripture
words, 109, 212, 230
work, 141, 171, 241
    God's, 46
    good works, 171, 298
    justification by, 42, 260
    purposeful, 128
    quality of, 184
world, 295, 298, 314
worship, 94, 106, 179, 209, 288
    eucharistic, 52
    focus of, 50
    public, 28
    Puritan, 288, 302
    Scriptural interpretation and, 249
    time for, 302
    wisdom and, 290
wrath, 214, 258

zeal, 34, 94, 145, 213, 314

ABOUT THE AUTHOR

J. I. PACKER currently serves as the Board of Governors' Professor of Theology at Regent College in Vancouver, British Columbia. An ordained Anglican minister, he holds a Doctorate in Philosophy from Oxford University. His many published works include *Rediscovering Holiness, Evangelism and the Sovereignty of God,* and the best-selling *Knowing God.*